TASTING CHART

DATE: *October 24*

NAME: *Ch. Guiraud (A.C.)*   REGION: *Sauternes*   CLASS: *2*

YEAR: *1966*   MERCHANT: *Château-Bottled (C.B.)*

SUPPLIER: _____   PRICE: _____

Cloudy	Dull	Clear, Lively	APPEARANCE

x (between Dull and Clear, Lively)

Unpleasant	Nondescript	Clear	Pleasant	Extremely Pleasant	AROMA

x (at Pleasant)

Very Sweet	Sweet	Medium Dry	Dry	Very Dry

x (at Very Sweet)

Extremely Light	Light	Medium	Full	Heavy	BODY

x (at Full)

Soft	Firm	Harsh

x (at Firm)

Acid	Balanced	Flabby

x (at Balanced)

Unpleasant	Flavorless	Light	Moderate	Full-Flavored

x (at Full-Flavored)

Rough Finish	Mild Finish	Smooth Finish

x (at Smooth Finish)

Fades Quickly	Gone within 5 secs.	Lingers up to 1 min.	Lingers 1–60 min.	Lingers + 1 hour

x (at Lingers up to 1 min.)

NOTABLE CHARACTERISTICS: *Intense aroma and full flavor.*

FOOD/OCCASIONS: *Sipping, sponge desserts, or nonacidic fruit.*

GENERAL COMMENTS: *Good example from a fine château.*

TASTING CHART

DATE: *October 24*

NAME: *Beaujolais A.C.*   REGION: *Bj.*   CLASS: _____

YEAR: *1969*   MERCHANT: *Piat*

SUPPLIER: _____   PRICE: _____

Cloudy		Dull		Clear, Lively
				x

APPEARANCE

Unpleasant	Nondescript	Clear	Pleasant	Extremely Pleasant
				x

AROMA

Very Sweet	Sweet	Medium Dry	Dry	Very Dry
		x		

Extremely Light	Light	Medium	Full	Heavy
	x			

BODY

Soft		Firm		Harsh
	x			

Acid		Balanced		Flabby
		x		

Unpleasant	Flavorless	Light	Moderate	Full-Flavored
			x	

Rough Finish		Mild Finish		Smooth Finish
			x	

Fades Quickly	Gone within 5 secs.	Lingers up to 1 min.	Lingers 1–60 min.	Lingers + 1 hour
		x		

NOTABLE CHARACTERISTICS: *Strawberry aroma, fresh fruity flavor.*

FOOD/OCCASIONS: *Alone, or luncheon wine or cheese.*

GENERAL COMMENTS: *One of the best examples of Beaujolais.*

WINES
AND THE
ART OF TASTING

WINES

AND THE

ART OF TASTING

❦

Jack Durac

A SUNRISE BOOK

E. P. DUTTON & CO., INC. NEW YORK 1974

FIRST EDITION

10 9 8 7 6 5 4 3 2 1

Published simultaneously in Canada by Clarke, Irwin & Company
Limited, Toronto and Vancouver
ISBN: 0-87690-113-5 (cloth)
ISBN: 0-87690-122-4 (paper)

Library of Congress Cataloging in Publication Data

Durac, Jack.
  Wines and the art of tasting.
  (A Sunrise book)
  1. Wine and wine making. I. Title.
TP548.D85 1974   641.2'2   73–18284

Dutton-Sunrise Inc.,
a subsidiary of E. P. Dutton & Co., Inc.

DESIGN AND TYPOGRAPHY: JEANETTE YOUNG

To Hélène-Claire

Contents

Introduction

If you are the sort of person who enjoys wine, I hope this book will entertain you; if you are the sort of person who also suffers needless embarrassment at the hands of wine waiters or when purchasing wine, I hope it will inform as well as entertain you.

In fairness, you should be warned that I am an enthusiast. I enjoy the appearance, aroma, and taste; the labels and shapes of the bottles, the process of aging wines and their annual variations, the history and geography. Most writers on the subject of wine start by assuring us that the cardinal rule is to "drink what you enjoy." They then spend the rest of their time telling us what we *should* enjoy.

This book is no exception—partly because my pleasure in Bordeaux wines will have its head. For the rest, my aim is to encourage a challenging attitude. In as many cases as possible I have followed my principal recommendations with a Tasting Practice. This allows you to check my views, and indeed those of other writers on the subject of wine, by putting them to the test of direct experience.

Since this book is intended to be both an introduction to wines and a practical course of self-instruction, throughout I have attempted to illustrate major points by reference to actual tasting experiences. Although it is to be hoped that some readers will attempt all or most of the proposed Tasting Practices, they should be used flexibly. It is better to develop an attitude of expectant curiosity toward wine rather than passively to accept the judgment of experts. Even though you will find that they are rarely to be faulted, remember that many of the dicta of the wine trade and of connoisseurs have not been scrutinized. So there is no need to feel puzzled or perturbed if your assessments and opinions differ from prediction. Whether you confirm their judgment or develop your own, you will be widening the range of your experience and increasing your appreciation of wine—as well as enjoying yourself.

TASTING PRACTICES   The Tasting Practices have been designed for a group of four to eight people, but they can easily be carried out alone. In solitary contemplation you do, however, lose the joys of conversation and the exchange of opinions—and naturally you will be limited to tasting a narrower range of wines. Ideally, in a Tasting Practice, two to four wines accompanied by an appropriate snack are shared by four to eight people. If your group numbers four or less, buy *half-bottles* and calculate your needs on the basis of one half-bottle per person. Remember that some of the wines will keep for a day or two if properly corked and stored in a cold place.

Since some readers who live outside the larger cities may have difficulty in obtaining specific wines, I frequently suggest generic alternatives, e.g., "use a young Moselle or a young Rhine wine."

WINE CATALOGUES   Keep the catalogues of several wine merchants at hand so you can select in advance the wines for each Tasting Practice. Some of the catalogues provide pleasant browsing and dreaming, but in addition they give you an idea of the range of wines available. Most catalogues also classify the wines into different regions and/or types, and this too is helpful. Some of the more ambitious wine catalogues provide useful information not only about the particular wines listed for sale but about harvest prospects, the progress of interesting vintages, and the like.

VINTAGE WINES   As with most skills, the appreciation of wine is acquired by practice, gradually. Your sensitivity and pleasure will increase with experience and you will steadily progress toward keener discrimination. Some wines have an immediate and more obvious appeal (e.g., rosé and sparkling wines) than some of the complex wines, such as claret. It is difficult for new wine drinkers to enjoy these complex wines on first acquaintance. A "basic training" spent on everyday wine serves as a useful preparation. If you go directly to subtle vintage wines, you may be perplexed, disappointed, and, worst of all, disinclined to try again.

The significance of vintages can be grossly exaggerated. In the great bulk of the wine we drink, the year of the harvest (vintage) is of no importance whatever. In the case of the world's greatest wines—those from Bordeaux, Burgundy, Mosel, or Rheingau—the vintage is of consequence. However, this has given rise to the false impression that vintages are of vital significance and apply equally to all wines. Except in the most unusual (rare) climatic conditions, vintages are of little significance in the Loire, the Rhone, Beaujolais, Provence, Piedmont, Tuscany, Spain, Portugal, and California.

The slavish adherence to "good years" and the concomitant avoidance of "bad years" is as undesirable as it is unnecessary. It may, however, produce one useful outcome. The excessive prices asked and received for wines of the well-known "good years" leave the prices of wines produced in unsensational years at reasonable price levels. It is worth bearing in mind that the differences in price for wines of particularly fine years and those from average years *do not reflect* the actual differences in quality. It pays to be adventurous and not too fashionable.

The differences between *harvests* are rarely extreme. The differences between the *wines* produced in different harvests are rarely of *major* importance. Wines from "poor years" are generally entirely palatable but fail to reach the heights; they may simply be light in quality and not, as some people seem to believe, distasteful or undrinkable. Or they may have an excellent flavor but contain excessive tannin—not a capital offense.

It is by no means true that older wines are always superior to young ones. Most white wines are at their best within one to six years of production—and closer to one than to six in the majority of these wines. A small minority of white wines (mostly of the sweet type) will survive for more than six years and make a satisfactory drink. Hence, older white wines need not be sought after. Among the reds, only a few types show great improvement with age and even these will not continue to improve indefinitely. Again, an older red wine may not be superior to a youngster. It may in practice be considerably inferior. An excessive reliance on vintage charts is undesirable because they are intended as *general* guides, at best. The quality of a particular harvest is seldom as uniform as a list suggests, hence the warnings generally appended to vintage charts. There are many attractive wines made even in poor years and regrettably numerous disappointing wines in fine years. Vintages are of no significance in selecting sherry or brandy as their development is completed before bottling. Old brandy (or sherry) has no advantage over recently produced bottles and the younger may well be more reliable.

For historical reasons which need not be gone into here, the drinking of wine in English-speaking countries has acquired unpleasant overtones of snobbery. The silly idea that vintage wines were the only ones worth drinking spread and, as a result, anything less than château-bottled perfection was described by that disagreeable word "plonk." The implication that everyday wine is trashy and that to take pleasure in drinking it is to reveal an "uneducated palate" does not prevent vast numbers of people from drinking these wines with regularity. The most rewarding attitude stresses enjoyment of a wine's pleasant qualities rather than an eager search for its weaknesses.

Only a minority of wines benefits from aging. The great majority are best drunk young and fresh. Leaving them to gather dust while acquiring bottle age results in a loss of their most attractive quality—freshness. This is not to deny the great interest which attaches to the process of aging in those wines that *do* improve in the bottle. Some of the Tasting Practices are concerned with this very process.

Quite apart from the Tasting Practices suggested in this book, you should consider purchasing a small selection of everyday wines to keep on hand. If you are a beginning wine drinker, you may well find that cool rosé wines are particularly easy to enjoy as they are light, refreshing, and rarely have nasty qualities. You might then try moving on to a light red table wine such as Beaujolais. Then try extending your small stocks to include one or two sweet wines for desserts and fruit and a dry white wine for fish dishes. As you find yourself becoming increasingly comfortable with the wines, and depending on your progress up the scale of Tasting Practices, you might wish to try a special wine for a particular occasion. Sooner or later you will strike one that transforms your view of what wine is and can be. There are some quite exceptional great wines and it is said, I am sure correctly, that most people experience only a comparatively small number of the greats in a lifetime of wine drinking.

Some years ago I had the pleasure of observing that moment of discovery in a guest who had remained a close friend despite his skepticism about wine. We were eating a lamb dish and the wine was a 1959 Château Talbot (from the commune of St. Julien in the Bordeaux region). As was his habit, he casually lifted his glass during the conversation, but the aroma from the Talbot caught him before he sipped. His hand stopped quite still; he sniffed again and inhaled deeply. "What is it?" I told him, and watched his next move. He sipped the wine, with total concentration, and then his face expressed great pleasure. He remains devoted to Château Talbot and many of its relations.

LABELS Labels identify and describe wines. They also provide a pleasant hobby for people who enjoy collecting them. They range from impressive and pompous through spare and severe up to amusing—some deliberately so, others inadvertently. Who can resist labels such as Château de Clotte, Château La Gore, Cru Junka, or Tongue of the Devil? From Germany we have Krover Nacktarsch, meaning "naked bottom" and depicting a boy being thumped on his rear. Many of the Bordeaux châteaux display their edifices on their labels. For example, the labels of Château Cos d'Estournel have a picture of its impressive turreted castle. Barolo wines come from Piedmont beautifully attired, often with a seal and red ribbon, like an opera singer in uniform.

Corks also provide opportunities for collectors. Many of them display the name of the vineyard and the year of the vintage. They come in various sizes, shrink with age, and provide excellent material for collages. Incidentally, corks help the wine to mature by allowing a limited supply of air to pass into the bottle.

Returning to the serious side of wine labels: ideally they should give the name of the shipper, region (or precise vineyard) of origin, type of grapes used, place of bottling, year of harvest, major qualities (dry/sweet, sparkling/still, exceptional/ordinary), and even the exact bottle number in cases of an exceptional wine produced in very limited quantities. For the purposes of everyday drinking, the best guide is the shipper's name and your own experience of the wine; everyday wines are blended by the producer in order to ensure uniform standards of quality and type. The selection of *fine* wine, which implies a degree of "individuality," demands more information and also a guarantee of authenticity. In most European countries nowadays the production and marketing of quality wines are strictly controlled. In France, for example, labels containing the words *"Appellation Controlée"* ensure that the wine is correctly described and has been prepared in conformity with state regulations. The guarantee does not extend, as in Germany, to ensuring the quality of the wine or to whether you will find it to your liking. Germany recently introduced a new set of wine laws and German wine labels now provide a guarantee of authenticity *and* quality gradings—three major groupings and detailed subclassifications within the superior quality category. In Spain, Italy, and Portugal the wine labels of bottles whose origin is guaranteed are marked "D.O.C.," meaning "Denomination of Origin [is] Controlled."

TYPES OF WINE   There are three major colors of table wines—red, white, and rosé—and these vary not only in appearance but also in taste and in "heaviness." Wines can also be graded according to the amount of sweetness which they contain, with the sweetest ones recommended for drinking on their own or with desserts. The dry wines are on the whole intended to be drunk during a meal. In all, wines are suitable for four types of occasion. They can be drunk as an apéritif (before dining), as an accompaniment to a meal, to end a meal, or on their own (e.g., chilled on a summer afternoon).

Wines are marketed in four categories. First, there are brand-name wines such as the well-known Nicolas brand from France,

Hirondelle wines from Austria, Liebfraumilch from Germany, Mateus Rosé from Portugal and so on. The second type of wine on the market is best described as a blended, regional wine. This type of wine is produced from a region which may or may not be delimited in law. If it is, in France, for example, the label of such a regional wine will contain the words already mentioned, *"Appellation Controlée"* (A.C.). Examples of blended regional wines include Bordeaux Rouge, Mâcon Blanc, Mouton Cadet, and Mosel Tafelwein. The third category consists of wines from a single vineyard, blended from different types of grape. For example, the wines from Château Talbot, a single vineyard in Bordeaux, are made from a combination of two types of Cabernet grape and merlot grape. Lastly, there are wines from a single vineyard and/or wines made from a single grape variety. A single-vineyard wine made from a single grape variety is most commonly produced in the Burgundy or Mosel areas. In the former region, the grape will almost certainly be Pinot (as in La Tache wines, for example). The Rheingau wines from the Schloss Johannisberg vineyard are another example, this one produced from the Riesling grape. A wine may also be marketed as a product of a single grape variety not necessarily drawn from the same vineyard, e.g., a Traminer grape wine from the region of Alsace.

Brand-name wine, like brand-name brandy, nonvintage champagne, and sherry, is intended to give unvarying flavor and quality. These wines tend to be reliable but can also be dull. The blended regional wines are less predictable than the branded ones, but when successful, they are superior to most brand wines. The third and fourth categories, single-vineyard or single-grape wines, include most of the superior types of wine, but needless to say, not all single-vineyard or single-grape wines are of superior quality.

CHAPTER ONE

Sight, Smell, and Taste

There are some wines which have a quality best described as "easy to drink." They have a pleasant flavor and are low in alcohol content. The three types selected for this first Tasting Practice all share this quality of being "easy to drink." Both experienced wine drinkers and newcomers enjoy them. They are wines that can be appreciated on their own or as an accompaniment to a meal.

Tasting Practice No. 1

For your first selection choose a fresh rosé wine—preferably one with a vintage date on it so that you can be assured of tasting a *young* wine. There are many reliable types of rosé on the market and you should encounter no difficulty in obtaining a youngster. Among the more popular types there is Mateus Rosé (which has a slight sparkle), Anjou Rosé, Tavel Rosé, Rosé de Provence. For your second choice select a *Tafelwein* from the Mosel region in Germany. These wines are light, pale yellow, and refreshing. The wine label should say that it is a German *Tafelwein* from the region Mosel-Ruwer-Saar and provide the vintage date and the name of the producer. For your third choice, select a young Beaujolais marketed by one of the better-known firms such as Calvet, Piat, Bouchard, Lebegue, Jadot, Latour, Patriarche, Leger. In recent years I have found the

Piat Beaujolais, in its attractive club-shaped bottle, particularly good. As with the two earlier selections, it is best to choose a young Beaujolais in order to enjoy its fresh fruity quality.

Chill the rosé and the Mosel wines for approximately an hour before opening them. Let the bottles stand open for a few minutes after removing the corks and then pour the wine into clear six-ounce glasses (most wine drinkers prefer tulip-shaped glasses because they help to capture and retain the bouquet). If you wish to test whether Beaujolais tastes better chilled or at room temperature, pour half of the Beaujolais into a decanter and then chill the remaining half in the bottle. Let the decanted wine reach room temperature.

Before drinking each of the wines, take time to examine their colors and to appreciate their aroma. Pour no more than a third of a glassful and then gently swirl the liquid in your glass. This helps to release the aroma. Place your nose close to the rim of the glass and breathe deeply. Try this with each of the wines in turn before you actually drink them. After you have sipped the wine alone, try it accompanied by a plain cracker, and then again accompanied by a piece of mild cheese and/or a light snack (e.g., cold chicken). The flavor of the wine is altered by the accompanying food taste.

———

How would you describe the tasting experiences you have just had? Most veteran wine-lovers appreciate rosé wines for their fruity freshness and clean, light taste. Mildness of flavor and lack of individuality are considered to be weaknesses. With Mosel wines, one looks for refreshing acidity and a flowery aroma, watching out for those that suffer from a lack of flavor or too much acidity. The third wine, Beaujolais, should be fresh, fruity, and light. Common weaknesses are lack of body and lack of flavor.

You will see from the judgments given above that the first problem in developing an appreciation of wines is the extraordinarily limited vocabulary we have for describing the attributes of wine, particularly taste and smell. As we have so few words and concepts to recount olfactory experiences, our descriptions of wine odors rest almost entirely on similes. People differ a good deal in their interpretations of the odors but the descriptions are nevertheless of some value in helping one to label a clear but literally indescribable smell.

A second major obstacle to improving our perception of the qualities of wines is to be found in the fleeting nature of the sensations stimulated by the sight, smell, and taste of wine. To complicate matters, the human senses of smell and taste are both subject to rapid satiation. That is to say, if we are stimulated in a moderate or intense degree, our senses of smell and taste enter a temporary dormant period, which can last for several seconds. During this time our senses are dulled. For this reason it is unwise to attempt to sniff or taste a number of wines in quick succession. Allow time for your nose and your palate to recover their full sensitivity. Take rest pauses of up to fifteen seconds before a concentrated inhalation and pauses of from fifteen seconds to several minutes between tastings, depending on the quality and depth of the wines concerned.

As many of the more delicate wine aromas are easily masked by intrusive smells, it is difficult to appreciate them in the presence of smoke or strong perfumes and the like. Physical impediments, such as colds or blocked nostrils, make satisfactory tasting impossible.

APPEARANCE   Healthy wines are both clear and lively but the colors vary with the grapes used, the region of origin, and the age of the wine. For example, claret (a French word for a light red wine) is generally a pale shade of red, while a Burgundy has a deeper red hue, at times verging on purple. Fine Sauternes or Barsac wines are a golden yellow color and, because of their high glycerine content, cling to the side of the glass. Hocks (Rhine wines) range from straw-colored to those verging on pale golden, whereas their neighbors of the Mosel are a delicate pale yellow. Rosé wines vary from reddish to pale pink and even to pale orange.

The appearance of a wine can tell you a great deal about its quality and origin. You should look at wine against a clean white background, for example, a white tablecloth. Place a lighted candle behind the glass or bottle if the color is of particular interest.

Both white and rosé wines should be quite clear; cloudiness or patchiness is almost certainly a sign of a faulty wine. Cloudiness in a red wine, particularly if it is a full-bodied type, does not necessarily mean that it is faulty. These wines all contain sediment and this is what you might be seeing in a cloudy red wine—particularly if you have inadvertently shaken it up before examining it. The presence of sediment in full red wines is necessary for their continued development.

In white wines the amount of yellow is sometimes a good indicator of its origin. For example, the very pale yellow wines of the Mosel river region can be distinguished from the yellow Sauternes or even from their German neighbors in the Rheingau. Some flinty white wines such as Chablis have a greenish tinge. Many white wines undergo changes in color with increasing age. The most common change is toward a brownish hue. If the process goes too far, the brownish tinges can be a sign that the wine is past its peak.

In the case of red wines the hue is even more important. A purple fringe is a reliable indicator of immaturity, whereas a brown border indicates advanced age—possibly too far advanced. Burgundies can often be distinguished from clarets by the fact that they are more heavily saturated with red; clarets are paler and grow increasingly so with advancing age. A claret that is too pale, however, may be the product of a poor vintage with not much body. These aspects are illustrated in Practice Tastings 2, 3, and 4.

AROMA   The aroma, even more than the appearance of the wine, provides one of the great pleasures of drinking. Not only do different grape varieties express themselves in different aromas, but the same grape variety grown under different climatic and soil conditions will yield noticeably different smells. The aroma is such an important aspect of wine drinking that it is part of every Tasting Practice in this book. In order to capture the often ephemeral aroma of a wine, it is best to leave the glass only one-third full, then swirl the wine gently and take a deep breath with your nose close to the rim of the glass. As suggested earlier, it is best to take rest pauses between inhalations of the wine. By the way, in this book I make no distinction between "aroma" and "bouquet," as it is needlessly complicating.

Although many wines have a fruity or flowery smell, very few have an aroma that is distinctly grapey. Commonly, claret provides an aroma reminiscent of black currants, Beaujolais is said to smell like ripe strawberries, Traminer wines like spices, Mosels like flowers, Burgundy like violets. But wine with an aroma of grapes? Whether or not you experience similar olfactory sensations—and during the course of the book's explorations you will have an opportunity to discover this for yourself—it is not likely that you will come across a wine with an aroma of grapes. The mystery involves not simply the loss of the smell of grapes but also the acquisition of aromas of other types of fruit (or flowers). Incidentally, the fact that some wines give off aromas reminiscent of fruits and flowers is not their main attraction. In the case of fine quality wines, their aroma has a concentrated intensity and attractiveness that will not be met in a garden, or indeed anywhere else.

An intimate connection exists between smell and taste sensations, with the former heralding the latter. Experienced wine drinkers can tell a great deal about a wine, even to predicting its taste, from a careful and repeated (but spaced) inhalation. Unfortunately, the relation between the odor and the taste of a wine can also be unpredictable or misleading. For example, some clarets (especially those from the Cantenac-Margaux area) have a strong and attractive aroma, but in a poor year their taste is weak and anticlimactic. On the other hand, some pleasant-tasting white wines from South Africa are almost odorless. Rating the smell and taste of a wine and the extent to which they correspond is an interesting exercise and introduces the idea of balance. Ideally wines should have a satisfactory balance between their attributes—color, odor, taste, fruitiness, acidity, fullness, and after-flavor.

Despite numerous attempts to develop an elaborate classification system for taste sensations (including one attempt by that archclassifier, Linnaeus), contemporary physiologists appear to be content with a fourfold classification. The four fundamental tastes are saltiness, sweetness, sourness, and bitterness. As saltiness does not enter into wine tasting it can be dismissed for present purposes. Of the others, sweetness is an important characteristic of wine and its presence or absence will determine not only its appeal to drinkers with different predilections, but also the type of food with which it can be combined satisfactorily. The sensation of sweetness is experienced most acutely at the tip of the tongue, where there is a concentration of taste buds sensitive to this type of stimulation. Sourness is experienced most exactly at the sides of the tongue and bitterness most clearly at the back of the throat and the back of the tongue.

TASTING   After noting the appearance and aroma of the wine, taste it. There are seven aspects to tasting and each of them is listed in the specimen Tasting Chart that follows. The seven attributes to look for are dryness or sweetness, softness or harshness, acidity, body, flavor, finish, aftertaste.

Sugar is a natural constituent of grapes. The amount retained in the final product, the wine, depends on the type of grapes used and the soil and climate where they are grown. Some grapes and soils are particularly suitable for the production of sweet wines and others for the production of dry wines (e.g., chalky soils). This quality in the wine, sweetness or dryness, is easily apparent. The Tasting Chart rates the amount of sweetness on a five-point scale, ranging from very sweet through medium dry to very dry.

The next quality, the softness or harshness of the wine, is a little more difficult for newcomers. Softness is a quality of wines characteristically described as "easy to drink"; it refers to an absence of edges or sharp features of any type. At the other end of the scale we have harsh wines, those with an unpleasant edge to them. These abrasive sensations are felt most acutely at the back of the throat. The harshness scale includes rasping, cutting, or biting wines. In the center of the scale, firmness relates to wines that are neither unpleasantly rough nor too blandly soft. The next attribute, acidity, is partly related to softness-harshness. A well-balanced wine needs a certain amount of acidity in it; without it the wine lacks shape and structure. This acidity, which is natural in grape juice, gives to wine the element of tartness that is the basis for its refreshing qualities. A lack of acidity results in a flabby and formless wine—a wine with no kick in it. The best-made wines have just enough acidity to give them the tartness and structure required for a satisfactory drink. Acidity is most easily perceived in German wines, particularly those

TASTING CHART

DATE: _____

NAME: _____   REGION: _____   CLASS: _____

YEAR: _____   MERCHANT: _____

SUPPLIER: _____   PRICE: _____

Cloudy	Dull		Clear, Lively	APPEARANCE

Unpleasant	Nondescript	Clear	Pleasant	Extremely Pleasant	AROMA

Very Sweet	Sweet	Medium Dry	Dry	Very Dry

Extremely Light	Light	Medium	Full	Heavy	BODY

Soft		Firm		Harsh

Acid		Balanced		Flabby

Unpleasant	Flavorless	Light	Moderate	Full-Flavored

Rough Finish		Mild Finish		Smooth Finish

Fades Quickly	Gone within 5 secs.	Lingers up to 1 min.	Lingers 1–60 min.	Lingers + 1 hour

NOTABLE CHARACTERISTICS:

FOOD/OCCASIONS:

GENERAL COMMENTS:

from the Mosel area. In a poor year the wines may have too much acidity because the grapes have not reached maturity. The resulting taste has been likened to that of an unripe apple. At the other extreme, wines lacking in acidity are often extremely dull.

The quality of body refers to the "weight" of the wine as you experience it in the mouth. This quality is the result of both the grape variety and the climate in which the fruit matured. Wines from the cooler climates have less body (being lighter) than those from the hotter areas. The main determinant of the weight of the wine as we experience it is, however, the level of alcoholic content. Wines low in alcohol taste lighter. So, for example, white wines from the Mosel region, which are low in alcohol and mature in a cool climate, are far lighter than, say, white wines from Sauternes, where the wines are characteristically high in alcohol. In red wines the difference in body is clearly illustrated in Beaujolais, which is light, and Hermitage, which is a heavy and more alcoholic wine. The alcoholic content contributes not only to the perceived weight of the wine but also to its durability and the degree to which it can survive transportation. Wines low in alcohol are more likely to lose their good qualities in transport than are the heavier types.

The next attribute, flavor, is in one respect the most important of all, for this determines more than any other single quality whether or not the wine is enjoyable to drink. On the scale provided, the range is from unpleasant (of which more later) through flavorless, a common fault of poorly made wines, to fully flavored wines.

The sixth attribute, finish, refers to the sensation produced by the wine in the act of swallowing it. Some wines, particularly the high-quality examples from Burgundy, have such a smooth finish that there is seldom any hesitation in recognizing and describing it. The use of the adjective "velvety" to describe the sensation is, in truth, not an exaggeration. At the other extreme are the wines which rasp and bite as you swallow them. White wines that have retained too much sulfur in the process of vinification leave an unpleasant prickling sensation at the back of the throat when you swallow them, or indeed even if you simply take a deep sniff.

Lastly we come to the quality of aftertaste. This quality of a wine, which may in favorable circumstances produce the greatest and certainly the most prolonged pleasure, is seldom encountered by people who only rarely have the good fortune to drink a fine wine. The depth and duration of aftertaste is one of the distinguishing qualities of fine wines. Everyday wine is unlikely to produce aftertaste to any marked extent.

The chart also provides space for recording any particularly notable characteristics of the wine under consideration and for making note of the occasions when the wine is likely to be appropriate and/or the food which the wine might complement.

You might wish to make copies of the Tasting Chart as you go along or several hundred all at once. If you keep your Tasting Charts with your assessments systematically recorded, you will be able to observe the emergence of your own tasting preferences and, what is most interesting, the consistency of your judgments over time. As a general guide to choosing wines and the foods to accompany them, the charts are also helpful.

GENERAL REMINDERS   Please attempt to use the full range of each of the scales. With almost all rating scales people tend to stick to the central points of the line. This tendency to use only the central sections limits the value of rating scales, so try to avoid the habit. If you are using the Tasting Charts as a member of a group, you may find it preferable for each member to complete his own Tasting Chart *without consultation* first. Examine the smell and taste the wine, then complete your Tasting Chart, as it were, privately. When everyone has completed the Tasting Charts on the wines of the evening, then is the time to compare your judgments. You will find that this leads to a lively exchange of experiences and opinions, and in turn usually leads to a desire to check by retasting the wines. With this probability in mind, you should reserve a small amount in each bottle for a "second-look" tasting.

How many wines can one assess on a single occasion? Opinions vary because it depends on the extent of one's tasting experience. Newcomers tend to become confused after tasting more than four wines of a similar type, whereas veterans continue to discriminate sensibly even after ten tastings—taking care not to swallow the wine. In most regions of France it is customary to spit out the tasting samples, whereas in Germany one usually drinks them. In all of the Tasting Practices included in this book it is hoped that you will drink the wine and refrain from spitting it out, unless you have made an unfortunate purchase. If you are tasting a range of widely differing wines, say, from a Yugoslavian light white wine to a Burgundy red and then a Sauternes, you will be able to cope well enough with up to as many as ten different wines.

If you intend serving more than one wine at a meal or tasting, try to serve everyday wines before fine-quality ones, dry before sweet, and light before heavy. An everyday wine is made to look shabby if it has to follow a fine wine and in any case it will be an anticlimax. Sweet wines tend to leave heavy traces that distort the taste of succeeding dry wines, and heavy wines tend to produce longer-lived sensations than light wines.

By way of general advice, it should be mentioned that young wines are likely to leave you feeling dehydrated. Forewarned is forearmed, so it is a good idea to have a glass of water handy after you have been tasting young wines. Notice also that green wines (i.e., immature ones) frequently act as a laxative. I will not propose a Tasting Practice to prove this point.

UNPLEASANT AROMAS AND TASTES   Misfortunes occur. You are likely to encounter some of the unpleasant qualities of wine with increasing experience. In the first place, any odious smell is an indication that the wine is off. For example, wine should not smell of metallic substances, paints, or sulfur, or smell sour. The sulfurous smell results from the use of excessive amounts of this cleaner and preservative in the making of the wine. Metallic smells are usually the result of bad storage conditions and sourness may indicate that the wine is turning to vinegar. Some unpleasant smells are transient and therefore of no consequence. These occur most frequently when the cork is removed from an old bottle. For a brief period an unpleasant aroma escapes, but if you allow the wine a minute or so to breathe, then your troubles are over.

Among the unpleasant tastes sometimes encountered in wine are the following. An acidic taste usually indicates that the grapes had not reached maturity before being turned into wine. A sour-tasting wine indicates that it probably is turning to vinegar. A corked taste, which incidentally is far more rare than is commonly believed, simply describes a wine which has the taste of cork because it was bottled with an unsound or damaged cork. Bits of cork floating about in the wine do *not* indicate a corked wine. They are perfectly harmless and almost an inevitable consequence of removing a cork with certain kinds of corkscrews.

A metallic taste is often present in badly made red wines or those of very inferior quality. It is clear and unpleasant and is generally noticed as the wine flows toward the back of the mouth. Closely allied to this metallic taste is one which is frequently described as "inky." This is also found in red wines and it generally means a thick, harsh taste which borders on the metallic. Among inferior or badly stored white wines one may come across a nasty taste which was once graphically described to me as being reminiscent of a wet dog. The taste and smell certainly do occur and I am unable to better that description.

Tasting Practice No. 2

TESTING THE CHART   In order to help you to become familiar with the Tasting Chart and its use, try a selection of wines that will require you to explore the full range of the scale. For this purpose I would recommend a good-quality French sweet wine, preferably from the Sauternes area; a dry red wine from Graves in Bordeaux, and a branded white wine from Germany, Liebfraumilch (medium dry and soft). Of these proposed selections, I suspect that only the Graves will prove a problem for some American readers. If you find it difficult to obtain a suitable example, then substitute a wine from the Médoc (Bordeaux).

For the first choice, the Sauternes, select a bottle from a vintage within the last ten years and ensure that the authenticity of the wine is guaranteed on the label by the words *"Appellation Controlée."* Although it is not essential, the tasting is more likely to be enjoyable if you can obtain a château-bottled wine from a single vineyard (see page 155 for a list of prominent sites). For the second selection, attempt to obtain a château-bottled red Graves from within the last six to twelve vintages. If you are unable to obtain a single vineyard Graves wine, you are sure to have more luck in finding one from the nearby region of Médoc or a regional wine from either the Médoc or St. Emilion. In any event, be sure that it is an A.C.–guaranteed bottle. The third selection, a Liebfraumilch, should pose no difficulties as there are large numbers of these brands on the market. Most of them are sound reliable wines, but it is best to be guided by the name of the shipper or merchant (e.g., Deinhard, Sichel, Kendermann, Hallgarten among others). If you are in doubt, ask your supplier to recommend his best example of Liebfraumilch.

Chill the Sauternes and the Liebfraumilch for approximately an hour before opening and try tasting each of them on their own. Then try the Sauternes accompanied by a dessert, nuts, or nonacidic fruit, and the Liebfraumilch accompanied by a mild cheese, then by a light snack such as a chicken sandwich.

The dry red wine, the Graves or its substitute, is best appreciated at room temperature; decant the wine one or two hours before you anticipate drinking it, leaving the stopper off so that the wine can "breathe." The few simple bits of advice about the handling of wine, which will be discussed in more detail presently, can increase your appreciation and enjoyment of wine considerably. Try the Graves on its own first, then accompanied by a plain cracker, and finally accompanied by a mild cheese.

Complete a separate Tasting Chart on each of these three examples and discuss your assessments with your companions.

The consensus obtained at a small Tasting Practice recently organized is shown in the following completed Tasting Charts. The wines on that occasion were a Piat Beaujolais and a bottle of Château Guiraud, a sweet white from Sauternes.

After giving the Tasting Chart a few test runs, the seven aspects of wine-tasting should take on a clearer significance. As mentioned earlier, the art of tasting wine with sensibility and enjoyment depends primarily on your ability to concentrate your attention on the act of drinking. This includes the approach (appearance and smell of the wine) as well as the aftertaste.

The main purpose of the charts is to direct your attention to

TASTING CHART

DATE: *October 24*

NAME: *Ch. Guiraud (A.C.)*　　REGION: *Sauternes*　　CLASS: *2*

YEAR: *1966*　　MERCHANT: *Château-Bottled (C.B.)*

SUPPLIER: ———————————　　PRICE: ————

Cloudy		Dull		Clear, Lively	APPEARANCE
			x		

Unpleasant	Nondescript	Clear	Pleasant	Extremely Pleasant	AROMA
			x		

Very Sweet	Sweet	Medium Dry	Dry	Very Dry	
x					

Extremely Light	Light	Medium	Full	Heavy	BODY
			x		

Soft		Firm		Harsh	
		x			

Acid		Balanced		Flabby	
			x		

Unpleasant	Flavorless	Light	Moderate	Full-Flavored	
				x	

Rough Finish		Mild Finish		Smooth Finish	
				x	

Fades Quickly	Gone within 5 secs.	Lingers up to 1 min.	Lingers 1–60 min.	Lingers + 1 hour	
		x			

NOTABLE CHARACTERISTICS: *Intense aroma and full flavor.*

FOOD/OCCASIONS: *Sipping, sponge desserts, or nonacidic fruit.*

GENERAL COMMENTS: *Good example from a fine château.*

TASTING CHART

DATE: *October 24*

NAME: *Beaujolais A.C.*   REGION: *Bj.*   CLASS: _____

YEAR: *1969*   MERCHANT: *Piat*

SUPPLIER: _____   PRICE: _____

Cloudy		Dull		Clear, Lively	APPEARANCE
				x₁	

Unpleasant	Nondescript	Clear	Pleasant	Extremely Pleasant	AROMA
				x₁	

Very Sweet	Sweet	Medium Dry	Dry	Very Dry	
		x₁			

Extremely Light	Light	Medium	Full	Heavy	BODY
	₁x				

Soft		Firm		Harsh	
	x₁				

Acid		Balanced		Flabby	
		x₁			

Unpleasant	Flavorless	Light	Moderate	Full-Flavored	
			x₁		

Rough Finish		Mild Finish		Smooth Finish	
			x₁		

Fades Quickly	Gone within 5 secs.	Lingers up to 1 min.	Lingers 1–60 min.	Lingers + 1 hour	
		x₁			

NOTABLE CHARACTERISTICS: *Strawberry aroma, fresh fruity flavor.*

FOOD/OCCASIONS: *Alone, or luncheon wine or cheese.*

GENERAL COMMENTS: *One of the best examples of Beaujolais.*

the significant aspects of wine and to do this in a systematic way. With some experience, you may find that you can dispense with the actual charts, having absorbed their pointers and developed your own system for focusing on the wine's features. Even then, however, the Tasting Charts retain some value. As an aid to the extremely fallible human memory-system for taste, they provide a reliable storehouse and hence, a sound basis for comparative judgments. The use of the Tasting Charts also facilitates an easy exchange of reactions and opinions between tasters. They help to identify common views and those aspects of the wine on which people differ. I hope that they will contribute to your expanding enjoyment of wine.

CHAPTER TWO

Wine at Its Best

With the important exception of red table wines, serve wine chilled but not icy. White wines are best when their temperature approaches that of fresh stream water. Allow them a minute or two to breathe after removal of the cork. Full-bodied red wines require considerably more time in contact with the air in order to bring out their best qualities. The exceptions to this are old red wines, which may disintegrate if left in contact with the air for too long, and some fresh young red wines, which should not be allowed too much contact with the air. Decanting red wines one to three hours before they are to be served ensures that they are at their best when you wish to drink them. The action of air on wine releases its bouquet, improves the taste, and can round off any remaining sharp edges. In a sense, this period of breathing after decanting is a way of bringing the wine to full maturity.

Wine does not take well to being manhandled and red wines especially need to be handled with care. If full red wines are shaken, they can become muddy and harsh to the taste, partly because of the presence of tannin, which is an important constituent of these wines. The tannin and other constituents in full red wines appear as sediment and are more likely an indication of quality rather than faultiness. Leave a full red wine standing upright for several hours, at room temperature, before decanting it. In this way the sediment is allowed to slide to the bottom, and when you decant it by holding the bottle at an angle of roughly forty-five degrees you can avoid pouring the sediment from the bottom of the bottle into the decanter or glass. If, at the last, you pour the dregs from the bottom of the bottle into a clear glass, you can observe the extent and density of the sediment.

Well-flavored sweet wines such as those from Sauternes, Barsac, and late-pickings from the Rhine are robust and can be kept (corked and preferably in a refrigerator) for several days after opening. Lighter wines, white or red, do not last more than a few hours after opening, although there are exceptions to this general rule.

Tasting Practice No. 3

TIME TO BREATHE   Full red wines need time to breathe. Contact with air generally releases the bouquet, improves the taste, and removes rough edges. Select a good-quality red wine, preferably from the Médoc region of Bordeaux (see the list on pages 128–29). Leave the bottle in an upright position, at room temperature, for several hours before use. Remove the cork and pour a third of a glassful. Smell and taste the wine. (Do not replace the cork.) Repeat the procedure thirty minutes later and again at hourly intervals. Record three perceptions at each tasting:

TABLE 1

	Smell	Taste	Rough/Smooth
On opening			
After 30 minutes			
After 1 hour			
After 2 hours			
After 3 hours			
After 4 hours			
After 8 hours			

If you are having a group tasting, use three bottles of the same wine (a good Bordeaux red or Burgundy will ensure the success of this Tasting Practice). Bring all three bottles to room temperature, open the second bottle (B) an hour after the first (A) bottle, and compare the qualities of the two.

TABLE 2

Bottle	Smell	Taste	Rough/Smooth
A (one hour open)			
B (newly opened)			

Then, after a lapse of two hours, open the third bottle (C) and compare the qualities of all three.

TABLE 3

Bottle	Smell	Taste	Rough/Smooth
A (three hours open)			
B (two hours open)			
C (newly opened)			

You will probably find that with successive tastings the wines improve in aroma, taste, and smoothness. The quality known as body should not alter nor should the dryness vary.

Tasting Practice No. 4

HANDLING   Most wines need to be handled with care, particularly full red examples. As in the previous Tasting Practice, select an example from the Médoc region in Bordeaux. If possible, allow the bottle to stand upright for several hours before pouring it into a glass decanter. Avoid tipping or shaking it and hold it at an angle when pouring. The purpose of this care is to ensure that the sediment does not mix into the wine you drink. If you fail to exclude the sediment, the bright and often beautiful colors of the wine are lost and you may instead be left with a muddy, opaque wine. The taste is also affected adversely and harshness can be detected.

If you have been unable to obtain a suitable Médoc wine, use one of the full Burgundy wines such as Chambolle-Musigny or Gevrey-Chambertin at least six years old. Stand the bottle in an upright position for several hours. Then, holding the bottle at an angle, pour three-quarters of its contents into a decanter. Leave the remaining quarter in the open bottle and allow the wine in both decanter and bottle to breathe for an hour.

Then pour some wine from the decanter into a glass. Shake the bottle roughly and pour some of this wine into another glass. Compare the appearance of the wine in the two glasses. Next, compare the taste of the wine in the two glasses.

Finally allow the wine left in the bottle to remain undisturbed for another hour. Then pour off and drink the clear wine at the top. Pour the thick sediment from the bottom of the bottle into a glass and rub some of it between your fingers.

Tasting Practice No. 5

TEMPERATURE   With the exception of full red types, wines are best served cool or chilled. The best temperature for white wines varies. For example, Mosel, Graves, and Sauternes seem to need more chilling than Burgundy white wine.

This Tasting Practice can be carried out either on its own or, perhaps more economically, as part of one of the other practices. In order to demonstrate the importance of temperature on the aroma and taste of the wine, carry out two simple exercises.

1. Chill an example of a dry white wine and a sweet white wine. After removing the cork, allow the wines to breathe for a minute or two before assessing the aroma and tasting them. Pour a third of a glass of each wine and leave them for an hour to reach room temperature. Repeat the assessment of the aroma and taste and compare these with your earlier assessments at the chilled temperature.

2. Repeat the same process with a full-bodied red wine. In order to avoid any risk to the wine, decant three-quarters of the bottle and leave it to reach room temperature. With the remaining one-quarter of the bottle, replace the cork and then put the bottle in the refrigerator for one hour. Carry out assessments of the aroma and taste of the wine at room temperature and chilled.

In the case of the dry white wine you may well find that its pleasant refreshing quality is lost at the tepid temperature. The sweet white wine may become cloying and thickly unpleasant at room temperature. If, on the other hand, your white wine seems to be silent, it might be too cold. Try warming the glass in your palms for a minute or two. Red wines lose much of their flavor and aroma at a cool temperature. The cold seems to "anesthetize" them. When brought up to room temperature, they display their best qualities.

CHAPTER THREE

The Dimensions of Taste

As with so many aspects of wine drinking, you can learn a great deal from comparative tastings. You will find yourself acquiring an increasingly fine discrimination between the different characteristics of wines.

One of the easiest characteristics to detect and interpret is "body." This, you will recall, was described in a previous chapter as the weight of the wine in the mouth. It is determined by the alcoholic strength of the wine and by those constituents that are not filtered out in the process of vinification. Tasting Practice 6 is designed to illustrate this property of body, combined with a closer look at sweetness in wine.

Tasting Practice No. 6

BODY AND SWEETNESS   For the purpose of this tasting select two sweet wines and two dry wines. The choices that I think will make the qualities most evident are as follows: For the sweet white wine, choose a Sauternes of recent vintage, with an A.C. label. The second sweet wine, which should be of a lighter body, might very well be selected from the Mosel area. As with the Sauternes choose a recent bottle carrying the guarantee of a *Qualitätswein* label. Wines from the Mosel may be sweet or dry, so it necessary to choose one that qualifies for the distinction of *Spätlese, Auslese,* or *Beerenauslese* on the label. For purposes of comparison, an *Auslese* might be most suitable. Although the question of labeling of German wine bottles is discussed in Chapter Four, you might note here that from the 1971 vintages onwards, all bottles of high-quality genuine Mosel sweet wine should state on the label that they are *Qualitätswein. wein."*

For the dry wines, choose another example from the Mosel, this time ensuring that it is a dry wine, which it should be unless the label states otherwise, i.e., specifies that it is an *Auslese, Spätlese,* and so on. After the 1970 vintage the better-quality German wines are described on their labels by the terms *Qualitätswein* or *Tafelwein.* The last choice should be a white wine from the Burgundy area. Try to get a Meursault (A.C.) bottle, which is often characteristic of wines from this region.

Chill the wines and leave them to stand for a minute or so after uncorking them. Taste each wine in succession, first unaccompanied and then against a plain cracker or dessert in the case of sweet wines; with the dry wines, try a plain cracker and then a mild cheese. Complete your Tasting Chart without consultation in the first instance. Then take a second tasting after you have exchanged your opinions and assessments.

In the comparison between the sweet Sauternes and the sweet Mosel wines, it should be plain that the French example has far more body than the German. The clear-cut differences in weight are partly attributable to the fact that the Sauternes is relatively high in alcohol while the Mosel is comparatively low. Turning to the dry wines, notice first the marked differences between the sweet and dry bottles. There should be no mistaking this property. The French Meursault is a fuller wine and should demonstrate more substantial body than the Mosel dry. If you compare the two Mosels, it is probable that the sweet example will have more body than the dry. A comparison between the two French wines, the Sauternes and Meursault, will very likely show that the former has greater body than the latter. The Sauternes are generally of a higher alcoholic level than the Meursaults.

Tasting Practice No. 7

RED, WHITE, AND ROSÉ Moving from the dimension of sweet-ness/dryness, see if there is a difference in the amount of body possessed by wines of different colors. Do red, white, and rosé wines differ in "heaviness?" If you and the other members of your group have a weakness for mysteries, you might try tasting this selection of wines blindfolded in order to see whether you can guess their colors.

With the exception of sweet wine, most whites are lighter than reds. Rosé wines are, as a result of the way they are produced, inevitably fairly light. With no further clues, see if you can guess the colors blindfolded.

Select a dry white wine either from the Mosel or Rheingau area of Germany, or from the French region of Graves, Sancerre, or Muscadet. Choose your rosé wine from France—either Anjou, Provence, or Tavel. For your red, choose a big solid wine from a hot region, e.g., the Rhone valley in France (Hermitage or Châteauneuf-du-Pape) or a Chianti Classico from Tuscany. Finally, to illustrate the exception, choose another sweet wine from the Sauternes region of France.

Chill both white wines and the rosé for approximately an hour before opening them. Leave the red wine bottle standing upright at room temperature for as many hours as is convenient and then open it about two hours before use. Decant it and leave the stopper off so that it can breathe for two hours before use. As before, taste each wine in turn on its own and then accompanied by a mild cheese or light snack. In the case of sweet white wine try a sponge dessert of some sort. Complete the Tasting Chart as before, and after the blindfolds have been removed discuss your assessments with each other, then carry out your second tasting.

It is most probable that the heaviness of the wine will turn out something like this, in ascending order: rosé, dry white, sweet white, red. You will also notice at the same time that, although the sweet white and the red wines are both full of body, their other qualities are strikingly different, i.e., aroma, flavor, etc. The rosé wine, although light in body and alcohol, should be refreshing and fruity.

As a variation on this Tasting Practice, you might care to compare a Beaujolais (A.C. bottle) with the Hermitage. Although both are red wines, they differ markedly in body, the Beaujolais being considerably lighter than the wine from the Rhone valley.

OTHER DIMENSIONS   The next dimension of tasting, softness/harshness, does not make a convenient Tasting Practice and in any event it is likely that you will unfortunately come across some harsh wines by accident rather than by design. The qualities of acidity and flabbiness are best illustrated in the section on German wines in Chapter Four. I am not inclined to recommend wines whose flavor is either unpleasant or absent, and again you will regrettably come across examples of these inadvertently. The next dimension on the Tasting Chart, roughness/smoothness, can be illustrated without difficulty.

SMOOTHNESS   If you have never tasted a sound Burgundy or St. Emilion wine which has reached maturity, then this Tasting Practice may hold a pleasant surprise for you. If you have already had this pleasant experience, here is an opportunity to repeat it.

The smoothness of a wine is determined partly by what goes into making it, partly by the skill with which it is done, and lastly by whether it has reached maturity by the time of opening the bottle. It requires raw materials (i.e., grapes) coupled with skilled labor to produce a smooth wine. Rougher wines can be produced more easily and more cheaply by a combination of prolific grapes and gross methods of production. The only reason someone might set out to produce a wine of rough quality is that it can be produced in sufficiently large quantities to obtain a satisfactory return. In some wine regions of the world the soil and climate preclude the possibility of producing high-quality wines and the producers opt for inferior wines which can be turned out in great quantity. It should not be thought, however, that rough wines have no place; quite the contrary, they serve extremely well as everyday wine. The purpose of the present Tasting Practice is merely to acquaint you with the extremes of difference that you might encounter—and in the process, to further the development of your discrimination between the two extremes.

Tasting Practice No. 8

For this Tasting Practice, select a mature St. Emilion red wine, preferably from the vintages 1959, 1961, 1962, 1964, 1966, 1967, 1970, or 1971. Then choose a Burgundy of mature years. If you are lucky enough to obtain a good example of the 1959, 1961, or 1969 vintage, then use that. Otherwise a bottle from the good 1962, 1964, 1966, 1970, or 1971 years will do very nicely. Again, if you are sufficiently fortunate to obtain a Burgundy from a single vineyard (see Chapter Ten for further details), then do so. However, a good Burgundy commune wine (A.C., of course) such as Chambolle-Musigny, Pommard, Fixin, or Gevrey-Chambertin will do very well. For the third selection try to obtain a bottle of Algerian, Moroccan, or Tunisian red.

Leave all three bottles in an upright position to attain room temperature for several hours before use. Decant the wines a few hours before use. Taste them briefly on their own and then against snacks (especially meaty ones). Complete the Tasting Charts in the usual way, discuss them, and then carry out a second tasting.

––––––––

Among the other differences which you may detect in this comparative tasting, one of the major ones will be the smoothness or roughness of the wine. The two French examples, both of sound quality, should be and very likely are far smoother than the bottle from North Africa, which is renowned for its rough red wines. The smoothness of the French examples, sometimes described as "silky" or "velvety," is expressed by an absence of edges and the way in which they produce the sensation of gently enfolding themselves in the mouth. The roughness of the North African wines is revealed, as is generally the case with most rough wines, at the back of the throat and the back of the tongue. It can be a rasping sensation experienced as the wine is swallowed and for a short period thereafter. Although there are those hardy types who drink rough wines with impunity, people who are not addicted to them find them more agreeable if they are accompanied by strongly flavored foods.

You might, in the course of conducting this Tasting Practice, also pay attention to the last dimension—the length of time the taste lingers—as it may well mark a prominent difference among the three wines. In the case of quality wines the flavor commonly endures for some little while after you have actually swallowed the wine. In remarkable cases the aroma and flavor can still be sensed quite clearly more than twenty-four hours after drinking the wine. Such a prolonged aftertaste is almost always associated with wines of a deep flavor.

ROSÉ WINES   Having compared the body of the three main color categories of wine, move on to a closer inspection of each category. Rosé wines are made to be drunk, not sipped. At their best they are pleasant and refreshing wines which are hard to better on a summer day. They range in color from pink such as the popular Mateus Rosé to pale red and even orange types (e.g., Tavel Rosé). There are dry rosé wines and sweet ones. Although many rosé wines have a slight prickle or fizziness in them which adds to their refreshing quality, others are still. Because of the way they are produced, rosé wines are never substantial in body. The grapes are squeezed and the fermenting juice is drained from the skins, which contribute the color to wines, after only brief contact. In the case of full red wines, the skins are left in the fermenting juice for long periods, thus contributing to the body of the final product as well as to its color.

Rosé wines should have a lively and clean appearance and a fresh taste. If not drunk when young, the wines lose their fresh quality. The main drawback to rosé wines is their lack of individuality—a consequence of the early separation of juice from grape. The aims of the practice tasting on rosé wines are two: to acquaint you with the range of rosés and to give you the opportunity to judge their suitability as luncheon accompaniments and summertime drinks.

Tasting Practice No. 9

FOUR ROSÉS Although France produces some of the best rosé wines available, for the present tasting it may be better to restrict your French selections to no more than two of the four bottles. In this way you will have the opportunity to compare rosés from different countries, although you may find surprisingly slight differences among them. For a sound rosé, attempt to obtain an Anjou Rosé. (The various names used for these products from the Loire almost always include "Rosé" and "Anjou" so there should not be any problem in identifying them.) For your second French choice try to get a rosé from Provence. In view of its great popularity and prickling freshness, the Portuguese Mateus Rosé is a good choice for the third bottle. For your fourth bottle select one from a country other than France or Portugal—perhaps Spain, Italy, or Yugoslavia.

Chill the wines for approximately forty minutes before opening them and taste them on their own—they should be satisfactory when drunk in this way. Then try them with a mild cheese, and lastly with light snacks such as cold meats. After completing your Tasting Charts, discuss them in the usual way and then carry out your second tasting.

Rosés at their best are clean, pleasant-smelling, refreshing light wines. You may find the Provençal example to be drier than the others. The Mateus Rosé should have a pleasant prickle and fresh taste. The Anjou will probably be still, dry, and pleasant. The common weaknesses of rosé wines are predominantly negative in character, i.e., lack of flavor, dullness, thinness, and the like.

THE RANGE OF WHITE WINES White wines are more versatile and more varied than rosés, ranging from very pale yellow to golden in color, from bone dry to richly sweet, and from still to semi-sparkling.

Tasting Practice No. 10

For the quality of dryness, you would be quite safe in choosing a Graves or, failing that, a Chablis. For the sweet white a

Sauternes or Hock, made from late-picked grapes (e.g., *Spät-lese*) would do very well. Although the wines from the Vouvray region of the Loire valley vary between medium dry and medium sweet, they almost always lie somewhere in the middle of the dimension of sweetness/dryness and there-fore can be used as a central point for the present Tasting Practice. They often share the same prickling (pétillant) qual-ity which should have been evident in the Mateus Rosé of the previous Tasting Practice.

Chill the wines for approximately an hour before opening them and allow them a minute or two to recover after uncork-ing. Try each of the wines on its own, then with a mild cheese, and finally with a light snack. Complete Tasting Charts on each of the wines and then discuss them with your companions before having your second tasting.

———

In general, dry wines have a paler color than sweet ones, i.e., there is more yellow in the sweeter varieties. (Incidentally this is a useful guide for estimating the sweetness of a wine.) Sweet wines almost always have a higher alcohol content than dry and frequently have more body than the dry examples. In the present tasting you may well find that the Graves is drier and lighter than the Vouvray, with Chablis somewhere between the two. The sweet wines, Sauternes or Hock, will probably be fuller in the mouth and may leave a longer aftertaste.

THE RANGE OF REDS   The production of red wines, particularly those of quality, is a more complex process than that involved in making rosé or white. The end products are also more complex and to a considerable extent less predictable than whites or rosés. What-ever their attractions, and there are many, neither rosés nor whites can surpass the pleasures provided by a fine red wine, particularly when it is combined with an appropriate meal. None of this means that red wines are the choice for all occasions—far from it. The in-appropriate selection of a red wine can be a misfortune.

In color, red wines range from the pale clarets through the ruby-red Burgundies up to the purple young Rhone wines. They range from very dry Graves to the dry Médocs, from the medium dry Pomerols to the slightly sweet Beaujolais and the frothy, sweet Lambrusco.

Tasting Practice No. 11

Select a red Graves of a sound vintage, not more than fifteen nor less than five years of age. For the dry example choose a Médoc wine, from a commune such as St. Julien, Pauillac, or St. Estephe, once again making quite sure that the bottle is an A.C.-guaranteed product. Do not select a bottle with less than seven years of age and attempt to get one from a sound vintage (1955, 1959, 1961, 1962, 1964, 1966, 1967, 1969, 1970, or 1971). If you can afford it, choose a château-bottled Médoc from a good year. Lastly, to offset the power and dryness of the first two selections, select a more frivolous red wine. Lambrusco is one of the few sweet red wines of any quality. Produced in Italy, it has the distinction of being one of the rare red wines that benefit from being chilled (for half an hour or so) before drinking. Vintages play little part in the Italian wine regions as the weather is reliably hot year after year.

Leave the two French wine bottles standing in an upright position for as many hours as is convenient before decanting them. In most cases it is best to leave them in the open decanter for at least an hour before drinking them. As mentioned, Lambrusco needs to be chilled to be at its best. Taste the two French examples on their own, then accompanied by a plain cracker, and lastly with mild cheese or a light snack. Complete Tasting Charts on these two wines and then turn your attention to the Lambrusco. This wine drinks very easily on its own but can also be taken with a light snack or dessert. Complete a separate Tasting Chart for it. After comparisons carried out among your group, conduct a second tasting.

The two French examples should have a full, fruity aroma and deep flavor. Their characteristic dryness should distinguish them sharply from the Italian example. In comparisons of this kind the dryness of the Graves, sometimes severe, should be evident. At its best Lambrusco is a refreshing, fruity drink.

The weaknesses of these types of dry French wines are occasional touches of harshness, absence of flavor, or lack of
depth. The Lambrusco may be relatively flat or oversweet.

CARAFE, EVERYDAY WINES   Fine wines are for gourmet dining or
special occasions. For the rest there are everyday wines, also known
as carafe wines, monopole wines, or *vin ordinaire*. For the silliest of
reasons, these perfectly useful wines are treated with disdain by
some wine drinkers. This unfavorable attitude may be traced in
part at least to a misconception about what you should expect from
them.

Nonsweet white wines and rosés should be refreshing drinks.
The aroma and taste should be pleasant. Sweet white wines should
be fuller, pleasantly flavored, and, of course, sugared without being
cloying. Light red wines should be easy to drink, of pleasant flavor,
and refreshing. Fuller red wines should have more substantial body
and greater penetration. Some common faults and weaknesses of
everyday wines are roughness, cloying heaviness in the sweet wines,
thinness and sour tastes in the whites, and a general lack of flavor.
In addition, you are far more likely to come across some of the serious faults described on pages 18–19—bitterness, a smell of foreign
substances, metallic tastes, the aroma of wet dog, etc.

There are so many branded carafe wines on the market that it
would be invidious for me to select only four for your Tasting
Practice, or at most eight for two such practices. A number of full
and light red wines are available at moderate cost, including some
Beaujolais and some from the Burgundy region. There are many
reasonably priced Italian wines, and particularly those in the Chianti
group provide agreeable and reliable drinking. Although there is an
entire chapter devoted to the red wines of Bordeaux, at this stage it
is sufficient to know that there are many good regional and commune wines from this area and you should be reasonably safe provided you select those which have an A.C. label. In the sweet wine
categories, there are many branded German sweet wines which are
entirely satisfactory. The Spanish and Portuguese also produce
quantities of sound sweet wine. In the dry white wine range are

many good varieties of German branded wines. Sound dry white wines are produced in Spain and Portugal, but many of the best come from France—in particular, the wines from Graves, Chablis, Muscadet, and Pouilly-Fuissé. Apart from the usually reliable Spanish and Portuguese rosé wines, the major French regions for this product are Provence, Tavel, and Anjou.

Keep on hand a small stock of carafe wines, with each of the five main types represented. In this way you will learn to enjoy them with meals and on occasions when you would not previously have thought of opening a bottle. It is surprising how a wine, no matter how plain, can contribute to a meal. It is like a change from feeding to eating. In carrying out Tasting Practices with everyday wines, try using the Tasting Charts on occasion. You may be surprised how satisfactorily you rate some of them. The major discovery in carrying out Tasting Chart assessments on everyday wines may well be the fact that the gap between carafe and fine-quality wines is not so great as many people believe.

A DIGRESSION ON EXPENSES   If the price of fine-quality wine continues to increase at the rate that it has in the recent past, I can foresee a time when the men at Fort Knox will register international trade deals by moving cases of Château Latour or La Tache from chamber to chamber. The price of everyday wines has been increasing at approximately the same pace as most food and drink but the superior wines, such as château-bottled claret and single vineyard Burgundies have become items of considerable luxury. It is an interesting thought, albeit not a sobering one, that at current prices one can choose between six bottles of Scotch whiskey or a single bottle of a first-class claret of good vintage. The prices of fine wines have almost trebled within the past two years. Many merchants have had to cease publishing price lists because they are out of date before they leave the printer. If stable, sensible prices do not return, then the growers, producers, and merchants will find their market limited to a smaller and smaller minority, eventually only a tiny plutocracy. Nothing short of a return to stable prices can prevent this from happening in the near future.

One way this prospect can be postponed is for producers and

merchants to market a far greater proportion of their wines in half-bottles, despite the unsubstantiated assertion that big bottles are *better* for the wine. While it is true that they may age sooner in half-bottles, this could be prevented, should one wish to do so, by the use of smaller openings and corks. Another argument for the use of half-bottles is that in Bordeaux they carry the charming nickname of "little girls" (*fillettes*).

I am afraid you will find that, as your interest and enjoyment in wine increases, you become less constrained by prices. You may even find that within a year you are unhesitatingly buying wine at a price which would have appalled you when you started. There is not much one can do about this except that by becoming aware of the process, it is possible to exert a measure of self-restraint. One way of helping yourself to live with the growing desire is to seek the lesser or less well-known wines which live in the shadow of the great products. For example, in the Bordeaux region there is a fourfold classification of lesser wines (e.g., *cru bourgeois*) which sell at prices well below those of the great classified growths. In the Burgundy area you will be more or less restricted to purchasing commune wines—although this is by no means a hardship. Many of them are exceedingly good. Another dodge you might practice, one which, when successful, brings in its train particular pleasure, is to seek out good bottles from poor vintages. Success at this game requires a combination of skill, experience, good advice, and luck.

It is difficult in discussing the price of wines to avoid mentioning the villainous practice by which the price of any wine served in a restaurant is automatically doubled. As a result all but the very well-heeled are forced to "drink down" when eating in a restaurant, since the price of a wine appropriate to a special restaurant occasion is virtually prohibitive.

In order to continue drinking wine despite the inflated prices of the finest bottles, you should experiment with products from lesser-known regions and countries and search for the best of the lesser wines hidden in the expensive regions. The countries worth exploring are Austria, Portugal, Spain, and Italy. The French regions are those of Loire, Jura, Provence, and Roussillon, while the lesser wines are the *cru bourgeois* and *cru artisan* bottles from Bordeaux.

❧❦❧

CHAPTER FOUR

The White Wines
of Germany

Although Germany produces a comparatively small amount of wine, the overall quality is consistently good and a substantial fraction is superlative. Most German wines are medium-dry whites. The principal grapes used are the Riesling, Sylvaner, Traminer, and Muller-Thurgau. The two most important regions for wines of superior quality are the Mosel valley and the Rheingau.

The wine producers are unceasingly occupied with standards of quality and they grade their products into numerous classes. In a successful year as many as six grades of wine can emerge from the same vineyard. In other European countries fewer gradations are used—broad classifications are the rule and although vineyards and even whole areas and regions are classified into grades, the wines from a particular vineyard are seldom sorted into more than two classes: those acceptable for marketing under the vineyard label (e.g., Château Lascombes, 1961) or under a district label (e.g., Médoc, 1961).

In Bordeaux all of the highest-quality vineyards are owned by a single proprietor or single group. In Germany, as in Burgundy, many vineyards are shared among several owners and for this reason the name of the producer or merchant is an important indicator of quality and indeed of authenticity. One of the main consequences of the German wine laws introduced in 1971 has been the unifica-

tion of small vineyards into larger units. This should help to improve standards and ensure honest dealing. It will also make the
choice of wine far simpler. Under the old system a single village
might produce and market as many as thirty different wines, each
with a different name. Many of these labels have now disappeared
and the *quality* wine areas have been reduced to a mere 154.

The production of fine *sweet* wines involves a sacrifice of quantity, considerable additional effort, and the courage to refrain from
picking ripe grapes off the vine. The final product, which is expensive, often achieves perfection. These wines are best sipped on their
own.

Most German wines are sold in tall, elegant bottles—green in the
Mosel region, brown in the Rheingau. Franconian wines are bottled
in glass flagons.

Try drinking German whites (especially Mosels and Rhein-
gaus) on their own. They do combine well with some foods but
many people prefer them as nonfood wines. Food wines include
some of the particularly dry wines from Franconia or Baden. Experiment on food-wine combinations; you may find that salty foods
make the wines appear sweeter, and sweet dishes may neutralize a
wine's taste. At any rate, it is probable that you will agree that fine
wines are more easily "put out" by certain foods than are their more
mundane, everyday relations.

LIEBFRAUMILCH   Liebfraumilch is a brand name for blended German wines from the regions of Rheinhessia, Rheinpfalz, and Nahe.
It was originally applied to wines from the vineyard of the Lieb-
frauenkirche (Church of the Beloved Lady) in Rheinhessen, but in
time became a generic term. The wines, which are generally of
sound quality, are made predominantly from Sylvaner grapes.

There are so many different types of Liebfraumilch on the mar-
ket that the only available guide, apart from one's own choice based
on tasting experience, is the name of the producer or merchant.
Among the well-known brands are those of Muller, Blue Nun
(Sichel & Co.), Crown of Crowns (Langebach), Goldener Oktober
(Grants), Blackfriars (Hallgarten). The best of them are soft, me-

dium dry, or slightly sweet pale-yellow wines that are easy to drink and readily enjoyed.

Tasting Practice No. 12

Select four branded Liebfraumilchs, chill them for sixty minutes. Let the wine breathe for five minutes or so after removal of the cork. If the wine is too cold, warm the glass in your palm.

A major attraction of German wines is their outstanding aroma so it is worth paying attention to the smell before tasting. Pour a small quantity of wine into your glass, swirl it gently and then take a deep breath with your nose close to the rim of the glass. Try a few such inhalations before tasting the wine, but be careful to allow your senses time to absorb and then recover from each deep breath. Approximately thirty- to sixty-second intervals should be sufficient. Provide at least two glasses per person so that you can compare the successive sips of different wines and then check backwards and forwards at will.

These hints about allowing wine to breathe, concentrating on the aroma and so on are applicable to *all German white wines* and therefore they will not be repeated in each Tasting Practice of this section. Save some wine from each bottle for the second tasting.

Try each of them on their own, and then each with a plain cracker and mild cheese. Without consulting your companions, complete a separate Tasting Chart for each wine, keeping in mind the good and poor qualities described below. Attempt to grade your choices.

Now open your Tasting Charts and compare your assessments with those made by your companions. After discussion, use the remaining wine to check and compare your assessments once more.

The qualities to look for in selecting a Liebfraumilch are flowery smell, clear pale-yellow color, freshness, grapey flavor. Common weaknesses are lack of flavor, flabbiness, too much acidity, thin and watery, sulfurous smell (preservative).

BRANDED MOSELS   In addition to Liebfraumilch and the common Niersteiner Domthal brands of Hock (the British term for Rhine wines), Germany produces a range of moderately priced blended wines from the Mosel valley. Common brand names include Deinhard Green Label, Moselblumchen, Moselspezial (Dominics), Piesporter, or Piesporter Goldtropchen, or Piesporter Michelsberg, and Bernkasteler (Riesling).

Tasting Practice No. 13

Select four branded Mosels, chill them for approximately sixty minutes, and taste each in turn. Try each of them on their own and then with a mild cheese. Without consultation, complete a separate Tasting Chart for each wine and pay attention to the good and poor qualities mentioned below. Attempt to grade your choices. After comparing Tasting Charts with each other, use the remaining wine to clear up outstanding queries.

Mosels are light, pale wines made mainly from Riesling grapes. At their best they have a flowery smell and delicate fruit flavor. They should be drunk young and taste clean and fresh. Common weaknesses are thinness and lack of flavor.

Tasting Practice No. 14

From the two previous tastings select the two most enjoyable Liebfraumilchs and compare them with the two most enjoyable Mosels.

Chill them for approximately sixty minutes and taste each in turn. Try each of them on their own and then again with a mild cheese. Complete a separate Tasting Chart for each wine and see if you can detect the differences and similarities between the two groups. As before, complete your charts without consultation in the first instance. Then discuss the assessments of the group.

If you are having this comparative tasting at least a few days after having tried the wines from the two groups separately, it might be instructive to keep your earlier Tasting Charts out of the way until you have completed this, the third in this series on German wines. Once you have completed the charts for this tasting, compare your appreciation of the Liebfraumilchs and Mosels with your ratings of them made on the earlier occasions. They should be reasonably similar. In passing, it is worth mentioning that the consistency of one's assessment of the same wine on different occasions has been found to increase with experience.

The wines will probably share the following characteristics: flowery smell, freshness, and a clean taste. They will probably differ in color, with the Mosel being paler. The Liebfraumilch will probably feel fuller in your mouth. The Mosel may have a thinner quality.

FINE SWEET WINES   An introduction to German wines is incomplete without a taste of some of the fine-quality sweet wines. Unfortunately they are expensive, some prohibitively so. However, as they can provide a startling and rare experience, try them—even if it means exploring only two or three wines instead of the customary four or more. Regrettably few of these special wines are sold in half-bottles, so that one can only economize by buying fewer examples. On the other hand, they are full, alcoholic wines which should be sipped, not quaffed. A smallish amount suffices. For some readers, the search for an ideal wine will reach its climax with this tasting.

The sweetness is achieved by leaving the grapes to "rot" on the vine. Water is lost and the sugar content is concentrated. Hence, when the wine is made it is sweet, but in short supply. Wines made from late pickings are called *Spätlese;* those made from selected bunches are termed *Auslese;* those made from selected grapes are termed *Beerenauslese;* and finally, those made from selected over-ripe grapes are called *Trockenbeerenauslese*—a word which resembles the silhouette of an oil supertanker.

Germany and France produce incomparably the best sweet wines in the world. The relative attractions of the two types are often debated and a comparison between them is attempted later in the book. Here we are concerned with the qualities of the great German products.

The sweet wines generally have a darker color than the dry ones, often a yellowish gold. They have an intense aroma, are smooth and rich, and yet manage to retain their freshness. They generally have a delicious flavor which lingers in the mouth; some of them are reminiscent of warmed raisins. These outstanding wines are easily recognized and recalled.

Tasting Practice No. 15

If you can afford it, buy one bottle of *Trockenbeerenauslese* or *Beerenauslese*. Then, to complete your day, select an *Auslese* and a *Spätlese* for comparison. In order to make the characteristics of each grade explicit, it would be ideal to choose the three wines from the same district and the same vintage. As this is difficult to arrange, do not insist on it.

If tasting a *Trockenbeerenauslese* must remain a hope for the future, try a comparison between two *Spätlese* and one *Auslese* wine, sticking to the same region or area and preferably to the same vintage if this is at all possible.

Chill the bottles for approximately one hour and taste each one with concentration. As other tastes and smells tend to interfere with one's enjoyment of these special wines, it is probably best to avoid taking them with foods. Many people do seem to prefer having something to eat with any and all wines and if you do, try a mild dessert (e.g., something with a sponge-cake base). This has been found to be a satisfactory combination for many people.

After tasting the wines and completing your Tasting Charts, compare your assessments with those of your companions. Clarify doubtful points or apparent conflicts by the second tastings of the wine remaining.

The qualities of the best sweet wines are easily perceived, and in the case of the *Trockenbeerenausleses* they can be overpowering. They should have a deep, rich, fruity smell which escapes as you draw the cork. They are a deeper yellow than their dry counterparts and should taste full, smooth, and honey-sweet. An underlying raisin flavor will often emerge in the middle of tasting a mouthful. Their smell and taste often linger for some hours. Poor examples will be either cloying and dense or disappointingly lacking in flavor.

GOLD MEDALS? There is no argument about which country produces the greatest red wine. Although the competing claims of Bordeaux and Burgundy will never be resolved, these regions unquestionably produce the world's greatest reds. The gold medal for white wine is, however, a matter for debate. France's candidates are wines from the Sauternes and Burgundy regions, but protagonists of German wines can readily answer with examples from the Rhine or Mosel. Moreover they can appeal to a wider range of wines as German wine producers have a tradition of grading their products into a large number of categories, according to quality, whereas Sauternes growers use all of the acceptable grapes in producing their annual wine output.

The best of the German wines achieve a superb balance of fruitiness supported by a backbone of acidity. If this balance is not achieved, the wine is flabby and dull (too little acidity) or if tilted in the other direction, it is thin and sourish (too *much* acidity, unripe). The harmonious balance can be tasted with ease and pleasure in many of the wines produced in the harvests of 1959, 1964, 1966, 1971, and 1973. The better German wines have a distinct flavor; and the poor ones tend to be thin and watery.

The vineyards of Germany have a long history. Some can apparently be traced back to the early Christian period. Many of the superior German vineyards were created by monks and some of them today, although secularized, retain their ecclesiastical names. Most of the important vineyards are to be found in cool, northerly latitudes. The success of the harvest depends greatly on the sunshine and warmth experienced during the ripening period. In a year of bad weather the grapes simply do not ripen sufficiently. In warm years the greater part of the grapes ripen and in achieving maturity produce successful vintages. The wines produced from naturally ripened grapes are called *Naturwein* whereas those which fail to ripen have to be improved by the addition of sugar. In all, a great deal depends on the question of warmth and the ripeness of the grapes. The most successful and expensive wines are those made from overripe grapes and the least successful and cheapest wines are made from underripe, green, and sour grapes saved only by the addition of sugar.

In seasons blessed with good weather the grower will make several sweeps through the vineyard, harvesting only part of the crop at the normal time of year. As long as the good weather lasts, a portion of the grapes will be left on the vine for late harvesting. These late pickings are of a richer and better quality and hence produce a superior grade of wine. These dried, late pickings consist of intensely sweet, almost raisin-like grapes full of concentrated sugar. Because of the loss of water involved in the process, the quantity of this exceptional wine is inevitably limited.

The success of the German wine growers depends very largely on the Riesling grape—a small, round yellow grape with green veins, which grows in tight bundles. When fully ripe they turn a reddish brown and have a thick, fleshy skin. The grape juice has a sweet perfume and a delicate flavor. Its success in the difficult conditions of German vineyards rests on its ability to thrive even in poor soil (e.g., slate in the Mosel valley), its resilience in cold weather, and late ripening. From the point of view of a wine drinker, its most remarkable quality is the balance which it can achieve between sweetness and acidity. Riesling wines mature moderately quickly and can survive for between six and twenty years, depending on the quality of the harvest. The higher-quality grades, such as *Spätlese* and *Auslese*, can survive for thirty or more years if stored under good conditions.

Although the Riesling vine survives transplantation from its natural habitat better than most other vines, it does, of course, produce different wines in different conditions. For example, within the boundaries of Germany itself it produces the firm, emphatic yellow wine of the Rheingau and only a short distance away, in the Mosel valley, a light, prickly, pale, and delicate wine.

Its fine wine-producing qualities coupled with its resilience have made it popular among wine growers in many countries. Riesling vines are cultivated with success in Austria, South Africa, California, Alsace, Yugoslavia, and Hungary, among other places. A comparison of its performance under these widely differing conditions is a rewarding and pleasant enterprise.

The Sylvaner grape is widely cultivated in Germany, particularly in Rheinhessia, where it prospers and produces abundant yields. The wines are mild, smooth, and pleasant. They mature quickly but age within a few years of bottling. Like the Riesling, it is cultivated in other European countries including Austria (under the name of Zierfandler), Hungary, Yugoslavia, and Alsace. A comparison of the performance of this grape in Austria, Alsace, and Germany is also of interest.

The other major white-wine grapes of Germany are the Traminer and its close relation, the Gewürztraminer. The wines produced from these grapes are full and have a pronounced spicy aroma. Traminers are prominent in Baden, Franconia, Rheinpfalz, and Hessia, while in Austria they are found in Burgenland and Wachau. Just across the German border in Alsace, it is a popular and productive vine. After contrasting the Traminer products from Austria, France, and Germany, compare the wines produced in Germany from these three main grape varieties, the Riesling, Traminer and Sylvaner.

OLD WINES IN NEW BOTTLES   Under the wine laws introduced in 1971, an entirely new classification of wine and wine regions was made in an attempt to put order into chaos. Under the old system, with its multitude of regions, vineyards, and labels, it was a major task to understand and remember the different varieties and their qualities. Now, with the new labels, so much information is given that almost nothing is left to the imagination.

Although Germany is responsible for only five percent of European wine production, it produces the highest *proportion* of quality wine. Three-quarters of the distinctive wines come from the regions of the Mosel valley and the Rheingau. In both of these regions the Riesling is the major grape variety. Although the wines from these two great areas share important qualities, such as juicy acidity and freshness, some clear differences exist which are largely attributable to the constitution of the vineyard soil. Mosel wines tend to be lighter and paler—almost white at times. They often produce a slight prickle and are noted for their superb flowery perfumes. They can be drunk while still young and do not last as long as the Rheingau wines. These are firmer, contain more alcohol, are slower to develop, and last longer than the Mosels. They are straw-colored, tending to deep golden yellow. Their fullness is often accompanied by an extremely pleasant aroma.

The Rheinhessen region is planted in the prolific Sylvaner grape and in Riesling. The abundant wines from this area are softer and have less emphatic aromas and tastes than those of the two supreme areas. They develop quickly and have a shorter life span. Much of the blended, branded wines come from this region. Another region productive of large amounts of sound white wines is the Rheinpfalz, whose soft wines have more body than those of Rheinhessen. A few of the areas in this region produce outstanding wines. The Nahe region, planted mainly in Sylvaner and Riesling grapes, produces light, crisp wines which can be drunk young.

Both the laws and the 1971 reclassification, desirable reforms in themselves, were hastened by the development of the European Common Market. Among other things, the reclassification attempted to facilitate understanding of the different types and qualities of German wines and to bring many of their wine regulations into line with prevailing European practices. The regulations are enforced by a large number of inspectors.

The main consequence of the reclassification is that the multitude of German wines have now been reduced to four groups. They are:

Blended, branded, everyday wines.

Tafelwein (table wines of sound quality and authenticity)

Qualitätswein (quality wines, giving details of the area)

Qualitätswein mit Prädikat (quality wines with distinction)

The blended, branded, everyday wines are generally superior to the cheap monopole or *ordinaire* wines found in other parts of Europe such as Spain, Italy, or France. Some, such as Liebfraumilch,

Moselblumchen, and Goldener Oktober have already achieved considerable popularity, and are in general sound, agreeable wines.

In order to qualify for the second category, *Tafelwein*, the product must meet with firm minimum standards as to authenticity and quality. The origin of the wine has to be indicated on the label and for this purpose six regions have been designated. The six *Tafelwein* regions are Mosel, Rhein, Main, Neckar, Oberrhein (Romertor) and Oberrhein (Burgengau), shown in the map below. The wine label must indicate the type of grape used, the producer, the vintage date (i.e., the year in which the grapes were harvested), and the district in which the grapes were grown and the wine produced.

The third category, quality wines, consists of superior products drawn from one of eleven areas. The label on the bottle must give a good deal of information including vintage, region, district, grape variety, producer, and finally the official inspection number. This number, consisting of a row of digits, indicates the content and grading of the bottle (on a twenty-point scale, in which eleven points are given to quality wine, fourteen points to a *Spätlese*, fifteen to an *Auslese*, and so on). The digits also indicate on a three-point scale the appearance of the wine. Thus a white wine which is considered to be too pale receives a score of zero whereas a wine with typical color for its type is given a score of two. Red wines which are too light are given a score of zero, red wines which are plain red are given a score of one, while "appropriate" redness is given a score of two (one can foresee problems here). The clarity of the wine is scored zero for cloudiness and opacity, one for clear, and two for clear and lively. Smell is graded in five categories. If there are faults present, a score of zero is given, one is allotted to nondescript wine, two to wines with clear distinct smell, three for fine smell, and four for a flowery perfume. Taste is graded in a twelve-point scale, ranging from faulty wine (zero) through nondescript (one to three), small but distinctive (four to six), harmonious (seven to nine), to mature and noble (ten to twelve).

This system, with its digits displayed on every label of quality wine or quality wines with distinction, leaves little to chance. It seems to be overdoing things and may undermine the individuality of one's experience with the wine itself. Contrary to the fears of

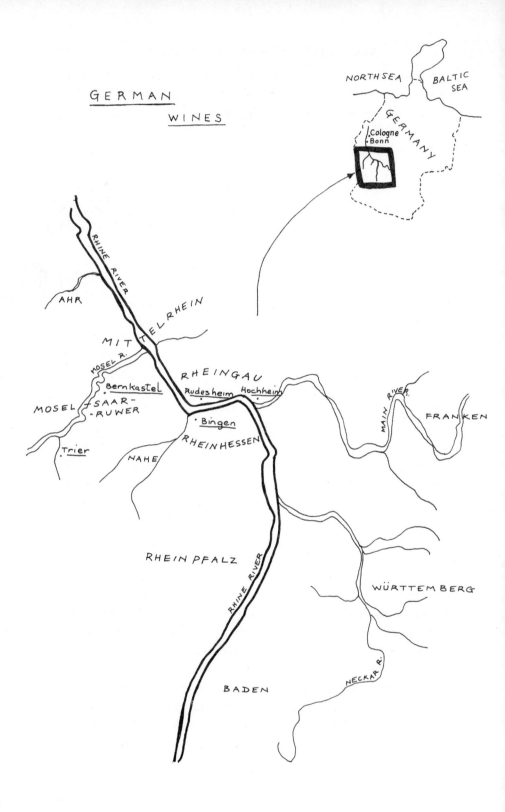

some wine drinkers, however, it will not necessarily lead to the disappearance of famous and popular vineyard names. Most of these are permitted to include their familiar name on the label.

TAFELWEINS (TABLE WINES)   Wines can only qualify for the grade of *Tafelwein* if they meet strict minimum standards of quality, level of alcohol, etc. If they meet these standards, then the merchant may label the wines as official *Tafelwein*, stating the region and district of origin as well as the vintage and his own name. Bottles bearing these labels can be relied upon; the information will be accurate and the wine of sound construction. These wines are of moderate price, trustworthy, and a step above everyday wines. They should provide reliable, easy drinking.

WINES OF QUALITY AND DISTINCTION   Wines which meet the stricter standards demanded for classification as *Qualitätswein* or *Qualitätswein mit Prädikat* are guaranteed to be of superior quality. They must look better, smell better, and taste better than even the sound *Tafelweins*—by no means an easy matter. If a wine is graded by the official inspectors as a *Qualitätswein*, then the producer or merchant may label and sell it as a superior product. He is, however, obliged to supply a full pedigree on the label of the bottle. Name, rank, and number may suffice for a *Tafelwein*, but the actual *Qualitätswein* must contain nine points of information, including region, district and local area, grape content, and quality grading. At the end of all this, I am happy to report, you will find a fine, satisfying wine.

The new classification will protect the standards of the great vineyards and gradually raise those of the nearly great. The German quality wines are precisely that.

In the new groupings there are eleven *Qualitätswein* regions —Rheingau, Mosel-Saar-Ruwer, Rheinpfalz, Mittelrhein, Nahe, Rheinhessen, Hesse Bergstrasse, Franken (Franconia), Baden, Ahr, and Württemberg. People who were accustomed to drinking German wines before the new classification was introduced will recognize some of their old favorites, such as the Rheingau, Mosel, Rheinhessen, and Rheinpfalz regions. As before, the outstanding wines come from the Rheingau and Mosel areas. Many of the other regions, such as Ahr, Mittelrhein, and Nahe, produce a great deal of agreeable blended wine but little that falls into the category of quality or distinctive wines. As few wines from the lesser areas are exported, opportunities for comparison and cross checks are limited. However, the six or seven regions that do produce wines for export offer sufficient opportunity for regional comparisons.

CHAPTER FIVE

The Mosel Valley

Drinking a fine, fresh Mosel wine, chilled, has been likened to drinking from a cool and perfumed mountain stream. At their best, these medium-dry, light, pale-yellow wines have a flowery aroma. They achieve a desirable balance of acidity and a trace of sweetness and should taste both tart and fruity.

Inferior Mosels can be thin or flabby or dull. In unsuccessful years, when the weather fails to bring the grapes to a full ripeness, they are on the thin side and may have a sour touch. Like many German wines, Mosels are a pleasure to drink on their own. They provide a satisfactory apéritif, afternoon drink, or a wine for sipping throughout the evening. Providing that care is taken not to overwhelm their delicacy with heavily flavored food, they can be enjoyed equally well as a complement to a meal. They combine well with fish (e.g., sole), chicken dishes (especially cold), and mild cheeses. Ordinary Mosels should be drunk within six years of bottling, but the late pickings can last fifteen years or more.

It is only by dint of untiring manual labor that the Mosel vineyards can be made to yield their delicate wines. The vines are perched on steep slopes of the snaking Mosel valley, where the soil is slaty and the cool latitude is as northerly as Winnipeg. In these unpromising conditions, hard work, skill, and the Riesling grape have been combined in an unlikely victory over circumstances. Apart from this compensation, the growers can enjoy the tranquil beauty of their valley.

Most of the wine is produced by firms and institutions with large wine holdings. In purchasing German wines it is helpful to know something about the producer whose name appears on the wine label. Although there are very many more sound and honest producers than unreliable ones, the names of some of the larger establishments might be helpful. In this Mosel area the products of the various branches of the Prum family are notably good; so are the wines of Thanisch and Christoffel. Among the institutional producers the German government (Staatsweingut), the Trier Cathedral (Hohe Domkirche), the Catholic seminaries, St. Nikolaus Hospital, United Hospitals, and Friedrich Wilhelm Gymnasium (a school) are well represented and wholly reliable. (Incidentally, Karl Marx was a pupil at this school.)

The most outstanding wines come from the middle section of the Mosel valley and the prominent wine villages are Wehlen, Bernkastel, Piesport, Graach, and Zeltingen. There are twelve major vineyards in the district of Piesport village and one of them, Goldtropfchen (Little Gold Drops), achieved a doubtful renown because some producers took to marketing Mosel wines under a branded label called Piesport Goldtropfchen. Although many of the branded bottles are pleasant drinking, misuse of the vineyard's name devalued the label of the genuine article. Misleading labels of this type will, however, disappear under the influence of the new laws. Invented (fantasy) names will replace inaccurate place names. In the nearby village of Bernkastel a similar misuse of a vineyard name occurred. The Badstube vineyard was incorporated in a branded label, Bernkasteler Badstube; most of the bottles carrying this title did not contain wines from the vineyard of that name. The most famous vineyard in this area goes by the name of Doktor. One of the justly famous Graacher vineyards, Josephshofer, is still owned by a single proprietor. Other prominent vineyards are Himmelreich, Homberg, and Munzlay. Wehlen has acquired the reputation for being the supreme village of this fortunate stretch of river. The

Prum family owns large holdings in this area and their wines are reliable and often outstanding. The leading vineyard is called Wehlener Sonnenuhr and I have a personal fondness for the nearby vineyard, called Nonnenberg. There are six other major quality vineyards in this area. The district of Zeltingen is the largest producer of quality wines and boasts its own Sonnenuhr vineyard. Other fine vineyards include Zeltinger Schlossberg and Zeltinger Himmelreich.

Two everyday Mosel wines which acquired some fame through the use of comic names and labels are worth mentioning. From the village of Krov we have the "naked bottom," in which a boy is depicted being spanked. The wine is called "Krover Nacktarsch." The brand name of Black Cat helped the wine from Zell to acquire considerable popularity—the full name of the wine is Zeller Schwartze Katze. As a consequence of the new regulations, more branded wines are entering the market and we can expect a proliferation of "bare bottoms," "black cats," and variations thereon.

SAAR The Saar river, largest tributary of the Mosel, is an active wine-growing area. The premier wine town is Wiltingen and its most important vineyard is Scharzhofberg. Other valuable vineyards here are Wiltinger Kupp and Wiltinger Dohr. The nearby village of Ayl is particularly noted for the wine from the Kupp vineyard, which is, of course, marketed as Ayler Kupp. This area, which borders Luxembourg, was a strategic zone during World War II and part of the antitank defenses of the Siegfried Line ran through some of the vineyards.

It is said that the Saar wines fluctuate between the extremes of good and bad. In poor years the wine is hard and unpleasant or, as the Germans describe it, "steely." Their best products are exceptionally fine and the steeliness is transformed into a clean, austere, and fruity wine. The opportunity to taste an authentic Wiltingen vineyard wine of a good harvest should not be missed.

As we have seen, German wines are grouped according to quality. The areas and vineyards of Mosel which can qualify for *Qualitätswein* are as follows:

WEINBAUGEBIET (Region)

Mosel-Saar-Ruwer

Bereich Zell / Mosel

Einzellage Lay	Rosenhang
Grosslage Weinhex	Grafschaft
Goldbäumchen	Schwarze Katze

Bereich Bernkastel

Vom Heissen Stein	Kurfürstlay
Schwarzlay	Michelsberg
Nacktarsch	St. Michael
Münzlay	Sonnental
Beerenlay	Probstberg
Badstube	

Bereich Saar-Ruwer
Rümerlay
Scharzberg

In selecting a Mosel wine, as indeed any German wine nowadays, your first decision is whether you want a blended wine which is sold under a brand name or whether you want a classified regional wine (*Tafelwein*). Or, if you have a particular liking for a wine from a specific region, you may prefer to try the higher-quality wines which are described in terms of the local area from which they come. At a higher level of quality you can opt for a Mosel wine from a specific vineyard. Naturally the price increases as you climb up through the scale of quality.

To begin with, let us compare two branded wines with two blended wines which have met the standards required of a Mosel *regional* wine, i.e., a Mosel table wine (*Tafelwein*).

Tasting Practice No. 16

MOSEL TAFELWEIN Select a Piesport Goldtropfchen or Michelsberg (if still obtainable), Moselspezial, Moselblumchen, or other variety. Then select two Mosel *Tafelweins*, preferably from the same year but from different wine producers. All four are blended wines, but the regional wines have satisfied officially controlled standards whereas the branded wines may or may not have done so.

Chill the four wines for approximately an hour and then taste each in turn. Taste each of the wines on their own and then with a mild cheese, as before. Complete separate Tasting Charts for each of them, paying attention to the characteristics listed above. Attempt to grade your choices and notice whether the classified regional wines seem to you to be markedly different from the branded types. Discuss your assessments and retaste the wines.

Attractive Mosel characteristics are a pleasant flowery smell and a delicate fruity flavor. These are precisely the characteristics one would hope for in a regional table wine. The weaknesses to watch for are lack of flavor and/or a thin quality.

Tasting Practice No. 17

MOSEL QUALITÄTSWEIN   Moving up the scale, let us turn to some wines which have passed stringent state standards—the Mosel district quality wines. Select one wine from the Zell/Mosel district (Bereich) and one from the adjoining district of Bernkastel. Then compare these two *Qualitätsweins* with your two most favored wines from the previous tasting, regardless of whether they were from the branded or *Tafelwein* group. If none of the four wines in the previous tasting appealed to you, then select two new *Tafelweins* from the Mosel region and try them against the two *Qualitätsweins*.

As before, chill the wines for an hour and try them with and without the accompaniment of a mild cheese. Enter your assessments on the Tasting Charts as before, and attempt to conclude whether the differences between the *Qualitätsweins* and the others were evident, and if so, whether they were of significance for you. Were the differences sufficiently pronounced to matter to you?

The *Qualitätsweins* should retain a general similarity to the other wines but should be without faults. The balance between fruitiness and acidity should be correct. The wines should have a mature and full flavor.

THE AGE FOR MOSELS   With the exception of the *Qualitätsweins* with distinction (*Prädikat*), Mosel wines should be drunk when young, i.e., within approximately six years of bottling. In old age the Mosels lose their most appealing characteristics and can turn dull. A comparison between young, fresh Mosels and aging examples is worthwhile, but the changed labeling conventions and classifications make it difficult to match up new and old vineyards and districts. In a few years it will be easy to make these comparisons. Meanwhile, you might discover the difference in an unexpected and perhaps unwanted way. Branded Mosel wines which fail to indicate the year of bottling may have been left unsold for too long. On opening them, you find a wine that is dull and flat.

CHAPTER SIX

The Rheingau

This small wine area, situated along the Rhine river between Mainz and Rudesheim, produces some of the acknowledged greats of the German wine world. The south-facing hill along this short stretch of river provides excellent conditions for the slow-ripening Riesling grapes. The vineyards are maintained with meticulous care; in one famous vineyard you are requested to take off your shoes when passing through certain sections. Some vineyards conceal outstanding bottles in specially constructed small vaults.

The Rheingau wines are full-bodied and characteristically reveal a delicious, fruity acidity. Most of them have a fine aroma, recalling for some people the smell of pear drops and for others, the smell of fresh dough. Produced mainly from the Riesling grape, they take longer to develop and survive longer in bottle than other German wines. They have more yellow in them than the Mosels and may have a deeper smell and flavor. The specially selected wines, including those made from late pickings, are without doubt among the most outstanding wines produced anywhere in the world.

A curiosity of this region is that some of the largest producers still carry aristocratic names. In fact, by comparison with almost any place other than Portuguese coastal retreats such as Estoril, there seem to be more names of nobility in this district than anywhere else.

There are the estates of Prince Heinrich of Prussia, of Prince Lowenstein, Duke Schönborn, Duke Matuschka, Baron von Ritter zu Groenesteyn, Duke von Kanitz, to name only a few. Some other large producers in this area whose names appear on wine labels are Eltz, Weil, Engelmann and von Brentano, Mumm, and Erben. In addition, there are many reliable small producers and good cooperative cellars (*Winzervereine* or *Winzergenossenschaften*).

QUEENS AND CASTLES   Some of the most famous vineyards in the world are to be found in the Rheingau region. They include Schloss Vollrads (Castle Vollrads), Schloss Johannisberg, Steinberg (Kloster Eberbach), Marcobrunner, and Koningin Viktoria Berg (Queen Victoria). Unlike the other vineyards in this list, the last-named acquired its fame from the fact that Queen Victoria expressed a preference for the wines from this area and as a return tribute the owners named it in her honor. The two Schloss vineyards are famous for the excellence of their products and their impressive sites.

Schloss Vollrads is a large and attractive vineyard which has been owned for several centuries by the Matuschka-Grieffenclau family. It produces rich, fruity wines of distinction which the producers classify into six grades, each identified by a different colored capsule bottletop. This unusual form of labeling indicates the ascending order of quality—green followed by red, blue, pink (*Auslese*) and white (*Trockenbeerenauslese*).

The Metternichs are neighbors. Their famous Schloss Johannisberg is a dramatic hillside vineyard, beautifully kept. The wines are consistently fine, well balanced, and full of fruit. The vineyard was for many centuries the property of a Benedictine monastery but was confiscated in 1801 and given to Prince William of Orange. After the fall of Napoleon, the Congress of Vienna ceded it to the Austrian emperor who donated it to Prince Metternich. It remains in the Metternich family to the present.

Another interesting Rheingau vineyard, Steinberg, also has a religious history. As at Clos Vougeot in Burgundy, this vineyard was created by Cistercian monks several hundred years ago. Like its French counterpart, the Steinberg vineyard is a walled site, but unlike Vougeot this Rhine property has been maintained as a single parcel (owned by the German state). Thus it has been possible to maintain a uniformly high standard on this valuable site. The wines are full and of penetrating flavor. The property is worth visiting not only for its product but also for a look at the well-preserved aged Gothic monastery constructed in a wooded valley near the vineyard. The monastery, Kloster Eberbach, doubles as a wine museum and a storehouse for the aging wines.

The village of Hochheim produces consistently agreeable wines which are slightly softer than those made in the downstream villages. In addition to the Queen Victoria Hochheimer wine mentioned above, the notable vineyards of this area include Kirchenstuck, Neuberg, Domdechaney, and Raaber. Wines from the Rauenthal area are exceptionally good and noted for their ripe and fruity aroma and flavor. The Baiken vineyard is believed by many to be among the top four wines in Germany. Other celebrated vineyards include Herberg, Gehrn, and Kesselring. At their best, single-vineyard Rauenthal wines display those very characteristics which most German white-wine producers strive year in and year out to achieve.

The Marcobrunner vineyard in the adjoining district of Erbach is a narrow strip of land divided among several producers. The Marcobrunner wines, like those from the Baiken vineyard, are included in most lists of Germany's outstanding wines. They have a deep, full flavor and a superb aroma. Some other important vineyards in the Erbach district include Herrenberg, Steinmorgen, Sielgelsberg, and Honigberg.

The adjoining district of Hattenheim is dominated by the Steinberg vineyard and its ancient monastery, mentioned earlier. The superior vineyards in the Hattenheim district include Hassel, Mannberg, Nussbrunnen, and Moxberg. The district of Winkel is similarly dominated by a supreme vineyard, Schloss Vollrads. Some of the best vineyards in the Winkel area include Hasensprung, Klaus, and Ansbach.

If many German wine producers strive to achieve the qualities and standards of the Rauenthal wines, even more of them take the wines from Schloss Johannisberg as their model. Indeed, wine growers in many different countries where the Riesling is cultivated use the Johannisberg wine as the paradigm of excellence. Although dominated by the wines from the great castle, the Johannisberg district contains other outstanding vineyards. These include Erntebringer (a personal favorite), Vogelsang, Klaus, Sterzelpfad, and Kochsberg. Rudesheim, on the western outskirts of the Rheingau area, combines its attractions as a tourist center and a producer of substantial quantities of superior wine. Like all of the quality wines from the Rheingau, they have a richness and depth of flavor coupled with a clear golden color. The outstanding vineyards include Burgweg, Rottland, Bronnen, Zollhaus, Lay, Platz, and Hainterhaus.

Those wines from the Rheingau which fail to meet the standards required for classification as quality wines but are sound nevertheless are marketed as table wines from the Rhine region. Under the new classification the quality wines from the Rheingau have been grouped into two districts: Bereich Johannisberg and Bereich Hochheim. The full list follows:

WEINBAUGEBEIT RHEINGAU

Bereich Johannisberg

Burgweg	Mehrholzchen
Erntebringer	Deutelsberg
Steil	Heiligenstock
Honigberg	Steinmache
Gottesthal	

Bereich Hochheim
Grosslage Daubhaus
Einzellage Lorberger Hang

Tasting Practice No. 18

RHEINGAU QUALITY WINES The pleasures of becoming acquainted with wines from the Rheingau are surpassed only by the pleasures of becoming *familiar* with them. For the sake of pleasure and at the same time to establish for yourself some knowledge of the major characteristics of these outstanding wines, the first of the Rheingau tastings concentrates on grades of quality wines. Select four quality wines from a successful year, such as 1971. Try to ensure that you have at least one from the Hochheim district and attempt to include a bottle from one of the outstanding vineyards (Vollrads, Johannisberg, Marcobrunner, Steinberg, or Baiken). From the Johannisberg district the Burgweg or Erntebringer wines are characteristic and enjoyable.

Chill the selected wines for approximately an hour and then taste each in turn. Try each of the wines alone and then again in combination with plain crackers and/or a mild cheese, as with the earlier German wine tastings. Complete separate Tasting Charts for each wine, paying attention to the list of qualities given below, and then attempt to grade your choices. They are quite likely to resemble the official gradings but they may not reflect the different prices you have paid. Retain your Tasting Charts for later reference as these wines will be used in subsequent practices, and it is always interesting to see how consistent your judgment is.

If you enjoyed this tasting of Rheingau wines (and most people do), repeat the pleasure using the wine that received your most favorable rating; then select three new wines. As before, complete Tasting Charts on each and this time compare your notes on all seven wines, i.e., the first four (from Tasting Practice No. 18) and the three new selections.

The wines will probably share the following qualities: a fruity aroma, deep, fresh flavor, and clean taste. They should have a sound balance between fruitiness and acidity and their color should be a pale yellow. In appearance the wines should be clear and lively. You can expect the higher grades to display the characteristics listed here in marked degree. The finer the wine the fuller the body and deeper the flavor. Common weaknesses are lack of flavor and flabbiness.

Tasting Practice No. 19

RHEINGAU TABLE WINES (TAFELWEIN) The Rheingau *Tafelweins* are pleasant and easy-to-drink wines which can accompany a wide range of foods or be drunk happily on their own. Select two table wines from the Rheingau area, preferably from the same area but produced by different growers or merchants. Then for purposes of comparison choose a table wine from the Mosel (a previous choice or a new one, depending on your inclination), and a table wine from either the Main or the Neckar wine region.

As before, chill them for approximately an hour and then taste each in turn. Try each of the wines alone and then accompanied by a plain cracker, and then by a mild cheese. Complete a separate Tasting Chart for each wine, paying attention to the list of qualities mentioned.

The wines will probably share the following qualities: an attractive smell, freshness, and a clean taste. They will probably differ in color, with the Rheingau containing more yellow than the others. The Rheingau wine will probably have a fuller body, but the others may well be more crisp.

LESS EXPENSIVE ALTERNATIVES   Having by now paid out a sizable sum for these quality Rheingau wines, you might be wondering if it is possible to obtain less expensive wines which approximate their attractions. There are three main possibilities: Rhein *Tafelwein;* wines from other German regions; and Riesling wines from other countries.

Tasting Practice No. 20

RHEIN TAFELWEINS   Select the Rheingau wine or wines you have most enjoyed, as a standard for comparison. Now add two or three Rhein *Tafelweins,* preferably from the same district and year as your selected standard.

Prepare the wines by chilling in the usual way and carry out the tasting accompanied and unaccompanied by cheese or crackers. Complete the Tasting Charts as usual.

Restricting our search for the moment to wines produced in Germany, those from the Mosel region are likely contenders. As the predominant Rheingau grape is the Riesling, it seems reasonable to look toward the Mosel, which specializes in the cultivation of this grape. The drawback to this tactic is that Mosels generally fall into a similar price range as Rheingau wines. The Mosel search is not entirely without purpose, however, as the comparison between the wines of this region and those from the Rheingau is endlessly interesting. Moreover, by including a branded Mosel wine, you may succeed in finding the cheaper alternative you seek.

Tasting Practice No. 21

RHEIN AND MOSEL   Select a branded Mosel wine such as Moselblumchen or Moselspezial. Then obtain a Mosel *Tafelwein* and a Mosel quality wine. Compare each of these with your Rheingau standard.

Chill the wines as usual and taste them with and without the plain cracker and cheese. As we are concerned in this Tasting Practice with wines that might substitute for the Rheingau standard, set aside one glass of the standard. In this way you can compare each of the three Mosel wines with the standard in turn. Record your assessments on the Tasting Charts.

You may well find that the Rheingau wine is heavier and fuller than those from the Mosel, as well as being of a deeper color. The Mosels are likely to be less intense and more crisp than your standard.

RIESLINGS   Of the three great wine-grape varieties, Riesling, Pinot, and Cabernet, none has done so well outside as it has in its home environment, despite the fact that all three have been transported to most parts of the world at one time or another. The Riesling, however, manages to maintain its general identity in a variety of sites and countries.

With the exception of the Mosels, few of the German wines outside Rheingau contain a large proportion of Riesling grape. But since the Riesling has been grown in so many different countries, a wide choice is possible. The most accessible, reasonable alternatives come from Austria, Yugoslavia, Hungary, and Alsace.

The special interest of the Austrian and the Alsatian wines is that in both of those countries the vine and its cultivation were strongly influenced by German practices. The Alsatian wine industry was for some time under the direct influence of German growers and it is interesting to see how the former satellite compares to the parent. The Austrian wines are well cultivated and carefully produced, yielding bottles of consistently good quality. In my opinion they are underrated at present and for many occasions are a thoroughly acceptable alternative to German quality wines.

The Hungarian and Yugoslavian wines are inexpensive and easy to drink. They vary from medium-dry to moderately sweet. You can find out about their qualities only by direct experience, as the labels are rarely informative. The drawbacks to these otherwise satisfactory wines are that many have only mild flavor and a tendency to contain too much sulfur.

Tasting Practice No. 22

Select a Riesling wine from Austria and one from Alsace. Then add another from either Hungary or Yugoslavia.

As in the previous tasting, retain a separate glass for the Rheingau standard wine and taste it against each of the other three wines in turn. All of the wines should be chilled in the usual way, allowed to breathe for three minutes, and sampled on their own and then accompanied by a plain cracker and some mild cheese. Please complete the Tasting Charts as usual.

It would not be surprising if the Rheingau wine displayed a clear superiority. It should. Try to discern the qualities of the Rheingau wine that make it superior.

SWEET RHEINGAU AND MOSELS   The best German sweet wines are so outstanding that it is worth considering a second tasting of them even at the risk of financial embarrassment. The highest-quality sweet wines, such as the *Trockenbeerenauslese*, are exceptionally expensive. There can be very few people indeed who are in a position to buy one of these bottles except on rare occasions. Even within the wine trade itself there are many experienced people who can recall on the fingers of one hand the occasions on which they have sipped these wines. Although out of the reach of the private purchaser, there is no reason you should not consider them as special gifts or prizes donated by a group. Many of the "lesser" varieties, such as *Spätlese* and *Auslese*, are just within reach.

Tasting Practice No. 23

Select two *Spätleses* or *Ausleses* from the Rhein and two from the Mosel region. In addition to comparing the sweet wines produced in these two important areas, pay heed to the variations in different harvests. For this purpose, select your two Mosels from different years and then match up these two vintages with similar ones from the Rheingau area. For example, you might compare a 1969 Mosel *Spätlese* with a 1969 Rheingau *Spätlese* and a 1971 Mosel *Auslese* with a 1971 *Auslese* from the Rheingau.

Chill the wines in the usual manner and take particular care to give them a few minutes to breathe after removal of the cork. Do not miss out on the aroma of these wines and notice also how the taste lingers after you have swallowed. These wines are best drunk on their own, but they can be combined satisfactorily with unobtrusive desserts or plain crackers. They do not go well with cheese.

———————

The wines will probably share the same intensity of aroma and richness of flavor. You may find that the Mosel examples, even in this sweet form, retain their lightness relative to the Rheingau bottles—perhaps like the relationship between young sister and big brother. You may find the Rheingau examples are headier than the other two.

YOUNG OR MIDDLE-AGED? Unlike most of the classic red wines, whites tend to mature within one to two years. The reason for the difference lies in the constitution of the reds. They require time to develop, in either barrel or bottle, because they contain not only the juice of the grapes but also some contributions from the skin and stalks. The greater complexity and heaviness of the red wines takes longer to resolve itself into an acceptable form for drinking. White wines, on the other hand, consist predominantly of the juice of the grape, which is pressed out shortly after the fruit has been picked from the vine. The juice is not in contact with the whole grapes, seeds, and stalks for more than a short period of time. So, one way and another, white wines are ready for drinking far sooner than most red varieties.

Although white wines are *ready* for drinking at an early stage, it does not follow that this is the most propitious time to enjoy them. There is no universal agreement about the best drinking time for white wines, and this is as it should be because the wines from different areas and grape varieties vary a good deal. A general rule would inevitably be misleading. We cannot avoid the question altogether, however.

If we restrict ourselves to particular types of German wines, we can then ask questions which may produce some kind of answer. For example, we may inquire as to the best drinking time for Rheingau wines. In order to increase the likelihood of obtaining a useful reply, we would have to specify that the wines are either dry or sweet. We would also have to ensure that the wines are selected from vintages of comparable status.

Tasting Practice No. 24

With these considerations in mind, select an easily obtainable medium-dry Rheingau wine of sound quality (e.g., a Johannisberger, or Winkler, or Mittelheimer, or Hallgartner—consult the lists on pages 62–64). In order to control for the quality of the harvest, choose one bottle from each of the 1964, 1966, 1969, and 1971 vintages. If it is not possible to obtain this full selection, choose two bottles of *Qualitätswein* with at least five years' gap between them.

Incidentally, if you prefer Mosel wines, carry out this Practice Tasting with four wines from that region, using the same harvest years. As to the choice of wines, consult the lists given on pages 56–58 (e.g., a Wehlener, Piesporter, Bernkastler, or Graacher).

Although the main question is whether these classic German wines are best for drinking early in their life or in their "middle age," you should realize that they fade after about twelve years. Be well advised and drink them before they reach senility. This suggestion will have to be taken on trust as the older German wines are extremely difficult to obtain. If you can obtain one or two examples from the older vintages, then by all means include them in the Tasting Practice.

Chill the wines and prepare them for tasting in the usual fashion, taking care to retain some wine for the second tasting. Taste each in turn, first on its own and then accompanied by a plain cracker and/or a mild cheese. Complete your Tasting Charts without consultation and then compare and discuss the outcome. As before, use your second tastings to confirm or deny differing claims.

Bear in mind that any differences which you have detected between the wines are most probably attributable to aging— that is, if you have been successful in holding the factors of quality and area constant. What, in your opinion, are the differences, and what is your conclusion? Most important of all, did you discover a preference for the young or for the more mature examples of these wines?

The wines may be similar in some respects: a fruity aroma, smoothness, clarity of appearance, full flavor, and pleasant after-taste. You may notice differences of this type: the younger wine is lighter in color and fresher in the mouth. The older wines *may* have a more intense aroma and a deeper flavor.

"STONE DRY" Before completing the exploration of the superior wine areas of Germany, it may be well to digress a little. As we have already seen, the country excels in medium-dry and sweet wines. Some useful *dry* white wines are also produced, and for these we turn to the area of Franconia (Franken). The wines in this area are produced on stony soil, mainly from Sylvaner grapes but Riesling and Traminer are also grown. The most famous of the Franconian vineyards is Wurzburg Stein, and partly because of the fame of this plot, Franconian wines were commonly referred to as *Steinwein* ("stone wine"). The use of this generic term has been altered by the new labeling conventions.

The wines are sold in glass flagons and are long-lived and markedly dry. They often have a flinty and spicy flavor that brings to mind some of the French dry wines. In my opinion they can be classed with the French wines of Sancerre, Chablis, Pouilly-Fuissé, or Pouilly-Fumé.

Tasting Practice No. 25

FRENCH AND GERMAN DRY   Select two Franken *Tafelweins* and compare them with two wines from the list of French types given above. Chill the wines for approximately an hour and allow them a couple of minutes to recover after removing the corks. Compare the appearance, aroma, and taste of each of the wines in turn. Then repeat the tasting accompanied by fishy snacks, or cheese, or a selection of hors d'oeuvres.

After completing your "closed" assessment on the Tasting Charts, you will probably find a good deal to talk about. Then check your views on the second tasting.

The wines will probably share a penetrating aroma and a flinty, fresh taste. They may differ in body (French examples fuller), color (German examples containing more yellow), and aftertaste (French lingers longer).

RHEINHESSIA AND RHEINPFALZ   These two areas are responsible for the bulk of German wine production and both of them rely largely on the prolific Sylvaner grape. The wines are in consequence soft, mild, and comparatively short-lived. Small areas in both regions produce wines of superior quality.

In Rheinhessia the two districts concerned are Nierstein and Nackenheim. The former district, like so many others, suffered from the fame of one of its best vineyards—Domtal. The name

Niersteiner Domtal was debased and became a generic term describing mild, soft wines from the general area of Rheinhessia. The best vineyards in the area of Nierstein are Rehbach, Hipping, Auflangen, and Kehr. In Nackenheim the best vineyards include Rothenberg and Engelsberg.

In the Rheinpfalz the gems are the villages of Forster and Deidesheim. This restricted area has an unusual type of soil and the Riesling grape flourishes there, where it would be less successful in other parts of the region. The combination produces wines of superior quality and a renowned aroma. They are considered to be among the greatest in Germany and you would be doing yourself a service by arranging to taste them. In the Forster district the most famous of all vineyards is called Jesuitengarten. Other famous names are Kranich, Kirchenstück, and Pechstein. The adjoining area of Deidesheim, which produces wines of equal greatness, is particularly noted for the vineyards called Hohenmorgen, Grainhubel, and Kieselberg. The best-known of the numerous reliable producers in this area include Wolf, Deinhard, Pioth, and Erben.

Weinbaugebeit Rheinhessen

Bereich Nierstein

St. Alban	Güldenmorgen
Domherr	Vögelsgarten
Gutes Domtal	Krötenbrunnen
Rehbach	Petersberg
Spiegelberg	Rheinblick
Auflangen	

Bereich Wonnengau

Gotteshilfe	Burg Rodenstein
Bergkloster	Domblick
Pilgerpfad	Liebfrauenmorgen
Sybillenstein	

The most important quality areas in the Rheinpfalz include the following:

Weinbaugebeit Rheinpfalz

Bereich Mittelhaardt

Schnepfenflug	Hochmess
Goldgrube	Schenkenböhl
Hollenpfad	Mariengarten
Schwarzerde	Schnepfenzug
Rosenbühl	Hofstück
Saumagen	Meerspinne
Kobnert	Pfaffengrund
Honigsäckel	Rebstöckel
Feuerberg	

VINTAGES   Comparisons of vintages can provide some interesting tasting experiences, but the procedures are so straightforward that they will not be the subject of a formal tasting here.

CHAPTER SEVEN

The Wines of Alsace

Alsatian wines bear a strong resemblance to German wines. Virtually all the wine is white. The methods of vine care, wine production and bottling, and indeed the grapes are similar to those used in Germany. The reason is not hard to find. From 1870 until 1914 the province was occupied by Germany, and viticulture in Alsace was strongly influenced by German practices. Whether by chance or by design, the wines of Alsace were inferior to German wines and were bought in bulk by German producers for blending.

With the return of the province to France after World War I, Alsatian farmers and merchants determined to improve the quality of their wines. One way to make this determination explicit was to indicate the grape variety on all bottles of wine. The practice has continued. An Alsatian wine label characteristically states the name of the grape or grapes used in the production of the wine. However, the use of district names is uncommon and therefore in selecting Alsatian wines one must be guided largely by the merchant's label. There are a number of large and reliable merchants in the area. Among the most prominent are Hugel, Dopff, and Schlumberger. You may choose, for example, Hugel's Alsatian Riesling or Dopff's Alsatian Traminer. The elegant wine bottles are long, thin, and tapering and come in green or brown.

The principal grape varieties are familiar to German-wine

drinkers: Riesling, Sylvaner, Traminer, and Gewürtraminer (a slightly elevated relation of ordinary Traminer).

Although they are similar to their German neighbors, the Alsatian wines are not identical to them. The Alsatian wines can be described as firm, lean wines which are uncomplicated, at least in comparison to Bordeaux, Burgundy, Mosel, or Rheingau varieties. They are at their best when taken with food and in this respect are different from many of the German wines. They are not quaffing wines; rather, they are made to complement food and are especially useful at lunchtime, when their dryness is an advantage. They have an incisive, dry, and clean taste. The aroma varies, of course, with the type of grape used; for example, the Traminer grape gives off a distinctive spicy aroma. In color they are pale yellow and cannot be distinguished from the German wines.

Although they succeed in maintaining a sound level of quality, the Alsatian wines seldom rise above their customary standards. They cannot compete with the *superior* German products in quality or in range. The best of the wines are made from the by now familiar Riesling grape and the interesting Traminer. The wines from the Sylvaner grape are soft and drinkable as in Germany, while the Muscat grapes untypically produce a dry wine.

The Alsace shares with the Loire the beauty prize for French wine regions. Many of the wine villages are romantically picturesque and Colmar is the site of an entertaining annual wine festival. The towns of Riquewihr, Kayserberg (good wine-tasting facilities), and Ribeauville are particularly attractive.

As in nearby Germany, the harvests are very much determined by weather conditions and for this reason vintages are of importance. It is also worth bearing in mind that the wines reach maturity reasonably quickly. Since one of their main attractions is their fresh quality, it is recommended that they be drunk while young, that is, within six years or so.

There are three ways of approaching Alsatian wines. One can use them as a basis for making comparisons with their mentors in Germany. Or one can use them to illustrate and explore the performance of different wine grapes under different conditions

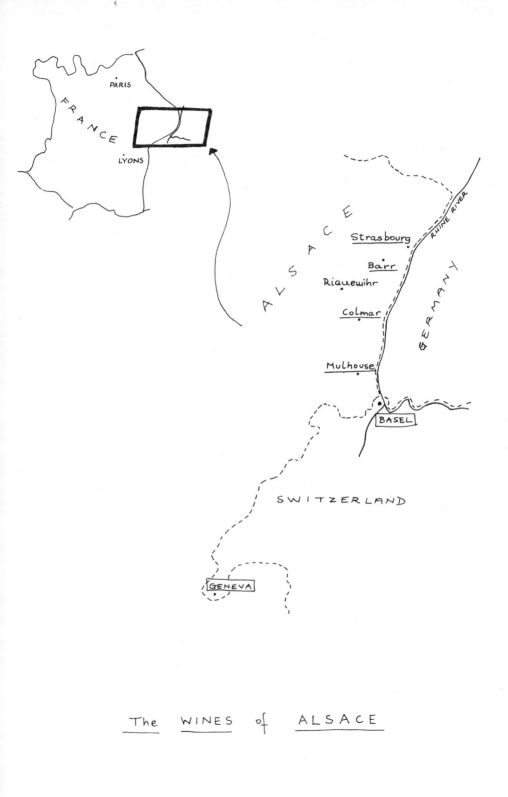

The WINES of ALSACE

(e.g., Sylvaners in three different countries). Or, finally, one can become acquainted with them as wines in their own right. To begin with, try looking at the range of Alsatian wines.

Tasting Practice No. 26

ALSATIAN WHITES Select four bottles of Alsatian wine, making sure to include at least one Riesling and at least one Traminer or Gewürztraminer. The Sylvaners and muscats are of less appeal. You might consider instead obtaining two Rieslings and two Traminers from different vintages or from different merchants. Incidentally, in carrying out your search for these wines, you might find it useful to know that the words *Zwicker* or *Edelzwicker* indicate blends of different grapes. The former name refers to blends of common varieties and the latter to blends of superior grapes.

Chill the wines for approximately an hour and allow a couple of minutes for them to breathe after you remove the corks. Try out some initial tastings of the wines, unaccompanied by food, and then repeat with some snacks, preferably of a salty or fishy type. Paying attention to the characteristics described below, complete the Tasting Charts and then discuss them with your companions. Carry out the second tasting and determine whether you agree with my description of them as "food wines" rather than "quaffing wines." If you do agree, what sort of meals might they complement?

The prime qualities of these wines are usually dry, clean, and fresh taste, pale-yellow color, and firm constitution. The grape varieties may produce wines that differ in aroma (Traminer more spicy) and may be more or less dry and more or less strong. If the comparison is between Riesling and Traminer, the former may well be stronger and firmer. It will probably have more acidity than the Traminer.

Tasting Practice No. 27

FOUR RIESLINGS After your introduction to Alsace, compare two brands of Alsatian Riesling, a Rheingau Riesling and a Mosel

Riesling. A comparison of this kind will probably show the superior qualities of the German wines without reflecting adversely on the Alsatian examples. At the same time you will increase your experience of Rieslings.

Chill and taste the wines in the customary way, first without and then with some light food. As before, complete your assessments on the Tasting Charts without consultation, then, after discussing your judgments, return for a second taste.

The wines are likely to share a clean, fresh quality—both in smell and in taste. The Alsatian wine will tend to be more dry and stronger than the Mosel (certainly) and the Rheingau. The Mosel will probably be the palest of the three and you may detect little difference in the amount of yellow contained in the Rheingau and Alsatian examples. The German wines will probably have a fuller flavor and a more lasting aftertaste.

Depending on your particular choice of snacks, you may find that the Rheingau and Mosel wines are strongly influenced by the accompanying food. Alsatian wines tend to be more resilient in this respect and, although they cannot complement all kinds of food, they do seem to survive most of them.

THE MUSKY TRAMINER   The Traminer grape has unusual and interesting qualities and, like its cousin the Gewürztraminer, is difficult to cultivate. Hence Traminer wines appear less frequently than their attractive smell and taste would lead one to expect. It is grown with moderate success in Austria, Germany, and Alsace.

Its distinctive aroma is most often described as "spicy"; some people prefer "musky." Personally, I am reminded of the smell of cinnamon.

For those who enjoy this aroma and the accompanying flavor, the Alsace Traminer wines are a gift. Unfortunately the quality of these wines is not as consistent as it might be. If, on your first attempt, you are unable to capture the aroma and flavor of this quite distinctive wine, try again with another example—perhaps from a different vintage or shipper. The aroma is particularly easy to miss in cheaper brands or in aging wines, so attempt to obtain young fresh Alsatian wines of a good vintage, bearing the label of a prominent producer. It is said that the bigger cousin, the Gewürztraminer, expresses the spicy aroma and flavor more emphatically. On the whole I have found that the Gewürztraminer is slightly more reliable. Perhaps it might be best to include a Gewürztraminer in your comparative tasting.

Newcomers to these unusual wines may find it easier to discern their special aroma by sniffing first at a can of allspice or a can of cinnamon. Try it.

Tasting Practice No. 28

TRAMINERS   Select two Traminer wines from the same vintage, but from different wine merchants. Add to this a Traminer wine from Germany (try the Rheinpfalz region) and an Austrian Traminer.

Chill and then taste the wines in the usual manner, **paying** attention to the particular characteristics mentioned below. When, after completing your Tasting Charts separately, you discuss the qualities of the wines, you might care to consider some of the questions posed here.

———————

The wines will probably share the characteristics of being mild, easy-to-drink, light wines. They are likely to be dry to medium dry, pale yellow in color, and spicy in flavor.

Does the aroma emerge from all four examples, and if it does, can it be described as "musky"? If not, what alternative description can you offer? Does it resemble the aroma of Rieslings or Sylvaners? The likely weaknesses are those common to whites, namely, a tendency to thinness, little flavor, too much sulfur.

ALSATIAN SYLVANERS   If the previous Tasting Practice has afforded you some entertainment and/or instruction, you may care to repeat the exercise with the Sylvaner grape. This, too, is grown in Alsace, Germany, and Austria, as well as in other countries in Europe and elsewhere. Wines from this grape have a soft, mild quality that makes them ideal for everyday drinking. They complement most light foods, but are also refreshing and pleasant to drink unaccompanied. Their major attraction should be their freshness. In the absence of this quality, they can be dull. The weakness of wines made from Sylvaner grapes are the common white-wine problems: little flavor, thinness, and oversulfuring.

VINTAGES   In seasons of poor weather when the Alsatian grapes fail to ripen adequately, the wines are thin and watery. Some of them are rescued by the addition of sugar but others are consigned to the manufacturers of sparkling wines. In the good years Alsatian wines have a full, fruity fresh flavor and attractive aroma.

CHAPTER EIGHT

Beaujolais

In general, the impact of white wines is immediate and one can form an opinion quite readily. Complex red wines, especially those of fine quality, defy a quick assessment. The aroma, flavor, and other characteristics are subject to many changes, some of a subtle nature. For these reasons you should not try to approach fine reds until you have sufficient experience of less complex wines. Unfortunately this means that the unsurpassed joys of fine red wine must be postponed. To console yourself, try Beaujolais as an intermediate step.

Beaujolais is an extremely popular, fruity (mostly), red light wine produced in a forty-five- by nine-mile strip between Lyons and Mâcon, from the Gamay grape. Its freshness is a great attraction and hence most types of Beaujolais are best drunk young, that is, within three to four years of bottling. It is a relatively uncomplicated wine which has the immediate appeal characteristic of white wine and the flavor of red wine; it therefore provides a bridge between the colors. In addition to the delights of its fruitiness and freshness, Beaujolais combines with a wide selection of foods (from cheese to cold meats, from sandwiches to roasts) and can also be drunk with pleasure unaccompanied by food. A wine that is so pleasant in itself and also versatile might be expected to attract a large following. In the case of Beaujolais, its advocates have become, if anything, too numerous.

The region of Beaujolais is inviting and the people, hospitable. The sight of all those vines busily producing is a great reassurance. During the holiday seasons, wines are offered along the roadside and throughout the year many pleasant tasting centers are open (see Chapter Twenty).

Although it is permissible in French law to stretch Beaujolais by the addition of *minor* quantities of other wines, a thorough investigation carried out some years ago revealed that widespread frauds were being perpetrated. Many bottles purchased on the open market were judged by infuriated Beaujolais men to be wholly fraudulent. Despite the undoubted damage to the reputation of Beaujolais caused by these imitations, the enormous demand for the wine enabled it to survive comfortably. As the demand will always exceed the supply, the situation is custom-built for crooks—and unfeeling crooks at that. Consequently it is necessary to select Beaujolais with some caution. The best assurance of authenticity is, of course, the A.C. label—in those countries which have agreed to respect the French controls. Other useful guides are the name of the shipper and the reputation of the merchant selling the wine.

Beaujolais draws its name from the village of Beaujeu. It is a wine with a distinctive fruity aroma that is difficult to describe in words. Some refer to the smell of peaches, apricots, or strawberries. My own choice is ripe strawberries; sometimes it is closer to the smell of canned strawberries, and in unsuccessful bottles it approaches the aroma of oversweet strawberry jam.

With some exceptions, notably the wines from the communes of Morgon and Moulin-à-Vent, Beaujolais is a light wine—light in color, light in body, and light in alcohol. The lightness is a natural consequence of the widespread use of the Gamay grape, which yields a pale juice, low in alcohol, and the methods of vinification in the Beaujolais area, which favor quick fermentation. Some Beaujolais are so light as to risk being mistaken for rosé wines. One variety of Beaujolais, called *vin de l'année* (made and bottled within six months) is so light and slightly prickly that it might be pink lemonade. This wine is a popular thirst-quencher and is drunk chilled and in large amounts. Drinking large quantities of any young wine raises the danger of stomach upsets and Beaujolais Nouveau (*vin de l'année*) is no exception. The temptation is hard to resist as the wine is most refreshing.

Although there is virtually universal agreement that this exceptionally young Beaujolais is best drunk chilled, when it comes to other wines from this region disputes arise. In the end it is a matter of personal preference. My own preference is to take the lighter varieties cool and the heavier ones at room temperature. The advantage of having young Beaujolais chilled should become apparent in Tasting Practice No. 29. For the rest, give yourself an opportunity to discover your own preference.

Although it is said, quite correctly, that Beaujolais is characteristically a light wine, in the wine trade outside France it is frequently reported that people prefer their Beaujolais full-bodied. Whether the claim is justified or not, a great deal of wine sold as Beaujolais is far heavier than the home-tasted product. Authentic light Beaujolais is preferable. The heavy products available so widely outside of France are too thick and cloying for my taste. Poor Beaujolais, false or genuine, is harsh, thick, and heavy. As with other wines, the producers attempt to disguise poor types by the addition of sugar. Oversweetened Beaujolais is distasteful and all too common.

The best of the Beaujolais wines have a fresh and enticing aroma of fruit, a refreshing lightness, and a pleasing flavor. A few of the commune wines, such as Morgon and Moulin-à-Vent, are of greater weight (and durability as well) but nevertheless retain the typical Beaujolais aroma and flavor. These heavier but genuine examples of Beaujolais resemble the wines of the southern Burgundy area and can profitably be treated as such. Unlike the lighter types of Beaujolais, they can be regarded as *food* wines— as wines that need decanting and that should be allowed at least four to six years in the bottle before drinking.

The Beaujolais area is divided into two sections: Haut-Beaujolais, lying between Mâcon and Villefranche, produces the higher quality wines. Bas-Beaujolais, lying between Villefranche and Lyons, produces lesser Beaujolais, which is generally marketed under the generic name. Within the forty-five-mile stretch of vineyards four grades of wine are produced. The standards required for these four grades are controlled and are based on minimum levels of alcohol, quantity of grapes used, methods of cultivating the vines, and so on. Approximately half of the total output is entitled to use only the generic name "Beaujolais." Approximately one-sixth of the total is entitled to use the label of "Beaujolais Supérieur" or "Beaujolais-Villages." Finally, the best quality wines, comprising the remaining third of the region's output, are entitled to describe themselves as being the product of one of the nine designated communes: Chenas, Julienas, St. Amour, Fleurie, Moulin-à-Vent, Morgon, Chiroubles, Brouilly, and Côte de Brouilly. Exploring the differences between the wines of these communes is an entertaining pastime, particularly for lovers of the Beaujolais style. If in the Tasting Practices to be proposed you discover in yourself a passion for Beaujolais, indulge it.

Bearing in mind that the wines from the nine communes have a great many more similarities than differences, these are some of the characteristics I have detected and other writers have described. Moulin-à-Vent, as mentioned above, is a darker-colored Beaujolais with a full flavor and the smoothness reminiscent of Burgundy wines. It requires a minimum of three years of bottle age and can last satisfactorily for up to ten years without deteriorating. Fleurie is believed by many people to be the most typical of Beaujolais wines. In my experience it is extremely fruity, smooth, and delicious. Julienas is another of the longer-lasting wines with a pleasant fruity quality. Brouilly and Côte de Brouilly are lighter-colored wines with a fresh flavor, best drunk young. Morgon is one of the harder wines, full-bodied and long-lasting. Chenas resembles Moulin-à-Vent in being full-bodied, darker, and smooth. Chiroubles and St. Amour are both light, soft, fruity wines that are best drunk young.

Within the communes there are single vineyards or estates that have acquired a reputation for producing superior wines. The list given is far from extensive. It is worth bearing in mind that

single-vineyard or estate bottles of Beaujolais are good value—
they cost not much more than the commune names and some of
them are difficult to obtain (few merchants carry them), so
throughout this book I have referred to Beaujolais commune wines
rather than single-estate wines. If you have access to estate or
vineyard bottles, please substitute them in the Tasting Practices.

Some of the prominent vineyards are as follows:

Commune of Morgon—Château Pizay and Château Bellevue
Fleurie—Clos de la Roilette and La Madone
Julienas—Château Capitans and Les Fouilles
Moulin-à-Vent—Les Carquelins, La Rochelle, Château des
    Jacques
Côte de Brouilly—Château de la Chaise

As the climate in Beaujolais is reliably sunny, the quality of
the wines does not fluctuate greatly from year to year. Vintages
are of lesser importance than the age of the wine. With the exceptions mentioned, try to drink your Beaujolais before it ages.
Plainly, the vintage *date* on a Beaujolais label is desirable.

Tasting Practice No. 29

TASTE AND TEMPERATURE   As an introduction to the pleasures
of Beaujolais it might be best to choose an example of the lighter
wines and, for contrast, one of the fullest wines. Try to obtain
a bottle of *vin de l'année* and a bottle of Moulin-à-Vent (from
the vintages of 1966, 1967, 1969, or 1971). To complete the
tasting, select two bottles of plain Beaujolais (A.C.), each from
a different shipper. In order to discover your preferences for
chilled or room-temperature Beaujolais, pour half of each bottle
into a decanter, replace the corks, and then chill the remaining
contents of each bottle. With the exception of the decanter
containing Moulin-à-Vent, place a stopper or cork in the mouth
of the decanters. The bottles in the refrigerator should be chilled
for between thirty and sixty minutes before drinking. You have
no need to worry about sediment as Beaujolais seldom has much
of it.

This Tasting Practice consists of two comparisons—between

chilled and nonchilled wines and between wines of different maturity and fullness. Taste each of the wines at both temperatures and complete separate Tasting Charts for each type of wine, but not necessarily for the same wine at different temperatures. After tasting each wine on its own, try each of them accompanied by a mild cheese.

The wines should share a fruity aroma and a fresh pleasant taste. The *vin de l'année* will probably be extremely light, bordering on a nonalcoholic drink, whereas the Moulin-à-Vent will have a full, rich depth. These two wines should also illustrate the differences in color, with the Moulin-à-Vent several shades darker than the *vin de l'année*. The Moulin-à-Vent should have a deeper and longer-lasting flavor than the slightly frivolous *vin de l'année*. The *vin de l'année* should go down far more easily when chilled, while the Moulin-à-Vent may lose some of its flavor when chilled. When drunk at room temperature, the *vin de l'année* may well lose its attractive liveliness whereas the Moulin-à-Vent will probably display its depth of flavor to advantage.

Tasting Practice No. 30

THE FOUR GRADES   To illustrate the differences in gradation, select one plain Beaujolais A.C., a Beaujolais Supérieur, the slightly better Beaujolais-Villages, and a Beaujolais commune wine (or if you can obtain it, a single-vineyard wine). The purpose of this Tasting Practice is to acquaint you with the fourfold classification of Beaujolais, based on the official quality controls mentioned earlier. In theory you should notice a step up in quality with each gradation, from the humble Beaujolais A.C. to the pride of the single vineyard. In practice the differences are usually but not always easily detectable.

Depending on the preferences which you discovered in the previous Tasting Practice, take the wines at room temperature or chilled—with the exception of the commune wine or single-vineyard wine, which may be tasted to better advantage at room temperature. After tasting each wine on its own, try it accompanied by a mild cheese and/or light snack. Complete Tasting

Charts on each of the wines without consultation, then carry out your second tasting.

———

The wines should share the typical characteristics of Beaujolais—a pleasant, light fruitiness and agreeable flavor. They may well differ in body as you go up the scale and should certainly differ in the amount of alcohol they contain—but this may not be detectable. As you go up the scale, the depth of flavor of each wine should increase, as should the duration of aftertaste, although this is seldom prolonged in Beaujolais.

Tasting Practice No. 31

BEST VERSUS TYPICAL It is said by many that the Fleurie and Julienas communes produce the most typical and attractive wines. Some of them certainly are extremely pleasant. Try examples from each of these communes and compare them with the two bottles of Beaujolais from previous Tasting Practices that have given you the greatest pleasure.

As before, taste the wines at room temperature or chilled according to your preference. Taste each wine on its own, then accompanied by cheese or a light snack. Complete separate Tasting Charts on each wine, without consultation. Then discuss your assessments with your companions and carry out your second tasting. Any blue ribbons?

———

The Fleurie and Julienas should both be pleasantly fruity, smooth, light, pleasant-flavored wines. They may not differ from each other in any obvious respects—particularly if you have been successful in obtaining wines from the same vintage. If you have been unlucky in your choices, the wines may be dull or sluggishly heavy.

Tasting Practice No. 32

COMMUNE DIFFERENCES It has already been suggested that a thorough exploration of commune differences is intriguing.

In the present Tasting Practice my purpose is to demonstrate some of the more obvious differences between two extreme groups of commune wines. For this purpose I suggest that you select two bottles from communes producing fuller-flavored, long-lasting wines, i.e., choose one bottle each from Moulin-à-Vent, Morgon, and Chenas. At the lighter end of the scale, choose two bottles from any of the following four communes: St. Amour, Chiroubles, Brouilly, or Côte de Brouilly. Attempt to select the wines from the same vintage if at all possible.

Drink the wines at room temperature or chilled, according to preference. As before, try each of the wines unaccompanied and then with cheese and/or light snack. Complete separate charts on each of the wines without consultation and then discuss your assessments with your companions before carrying out a second tasting.

The bottles from the first group of communes will probably be darker in color and fuller in flavor. They may also be slightly smoother than the wines from the second group. The wines from St. Amour, Brouilly, etc., will probably be lighter in appearance and body, softer and easier to drink, but less fully flavored. They may fit the description of "clean and brisk."

Tasting Practice No. 33

OTHER LIGHT WINES The comparison of Beaujolais with light red wines from other regions is an interesting experience. For this purpose select two commune wines from the light group described in the previous Tasting Practice, i.e., St. Amour, Brouilly, etc. Compare these two with a wine from Bourgueil in the Loire valley and one from Italy, Bardolino.

As neither the Loire nor the Italian wines are taken chilled, it might be best for the present Tasting Practice to have all four bottles prepared at room temperature, even though you may prefer your Beaujolais chilled on most occasions. As in the earlier practices, taste each wine on its own and then accompanied by cheese and a light snack. Complete Tasting Charts on each of the wines without consultation and then have a second tasting after you have discussed your first assessments.

All four wines will probably share the characteristics of lightness of color and body. The three French examples will probably have a more distinctive fruity aroma, but the Beaujolais
examples are unlikely to have as much body as the Italian or
Loire wines. You may find that the Beaujolais wines are more
satisfactory when drunk without the accompaniment of food.
Your opinion of the other two wines may differ on this point.

Tasting Practice No. 34

OTHER FULL WINES   The purpose of this Tasting Practice is to
compare some of the fuller Beaujolais wines with full reds
from other regions. In order to carry out the comparison, select
two Beaujolais bottles from the full-bodied areas mentioned
earlier, i.e., Morgon, Chenas, or Moulin-à-Vent. Compare these
two wines with one from Burgundy (preferably a Volnay,
Pommard, Mercurey, or Santenay). Finally choose a Chianti
Classico from Tuscany.

Prepare all these wines by decanting them one to two hours
before drinking. Allow them to reach room temperature before
drinking. Try each one of the wines on their own and then
accompanied by cheese and a light snack. Complete Tasting
Charts without consultation and discuss them before carrying
out your second tasting.

Although the Beaujolais wines will probably have their distinguishing aroma, you may be surprised to find how closely
they resemble the Burgundy wines in smoothness, depth of
flavor, and aftertaste. The Beaujolais wines will probably differ
from the Italian example in being smoother, of sweeter aroma,
and more lightly flavored. You may find the Italian wine to be
less smooth but stronger in flavor and aftertaste.

＊⊰§⊱＊

CHAPTER NINE

The Valley of the Loire

Grapes flourish along almost the entire length of the Loire valley. It is gentle countryside, often suffused by a soft river haze. In a region dotted with fairytale châteaux and a romantic history to match, the hazy scenery is suitably enchanting. With careful planning you can achieve an internal haze to match the external one.

There can be few more enjoyable wine trips than those which combine vineyard explorations with scenic and architectural beauty. Trickling one's way down the Loire valley is one of the best of them. The superb châteaux include Amboise, the contained perfection of Azay-le-Rideau and Chenonceaux, the grandiose chaos of Chambord, and the grisly fascination of Loches, where they specialized in frightful methods of torture. In the dungeons of Loches you can see some relics of their instruments, including a small iron cage suspended from the ceiling of one of the dungeons. The prisoner was cramped into the cage and left hanging, often for years. The horrors of the damp, dark, and icy dungeons are augmented when you leave the château grounds in bright sunlight and realize what monstrous prisons lie beneath your feet. The only sensible use for chilly, dark cellars is the storage of wine.

Apart from the brisk, dry white wines produced at either end of the valley, the Loire wines are pleasantly soft and easy to drink.

A good deal of Loire wine is medium-dry to medium-sweet white wine, with a fair proportion being converted into the sparkling wines of Saumur and Vouvray. The Anjou area produces large amounts of popular, attractive rosé wine and some delicious light red wines are made in the area of Tours.

Loire wines are appetizing and extremely enjoyable but do not rank among the greats. In general they are intended to be drunk young and, for the most part, locally. Because of their low alcoholic content, they suffer when transported. The dictum that wines always taste best in the region where they are produced can be applied especially to the wines of the Loire. A distinctive feature of many of the softer wines produced in the central area of the valley is their tendency to be slightly prickly (pétillant).

Although some sections of the Loire vineyards qualify for A.C. recognition, they are in the minority. A proportion of the wines do, however, qualify for the second ranking title of V.D.Q.S., indicating that they are quality wines which satisfy state-determined and controlled standards. This second-rank grading is common in the area of Provence.

A curious aspect of the Loire wines is their general similarity despite the employment of a variety of different vines in different areas. The four main regions of wine production are Sancerre, Anjou, Tours, and Muscadet.

Sancerre and Muscadet wines are produced at opposite ends of the Loire valley and from different grape varieties, yet manage to retain some measure of similarity. Both of these white wines are crisp and dry, quick to reach maturity, and at their best when drunk young. By comparison with other dry wines, they are relatively light in body. Presumably one has to attribute these similarities to a common climate and methods of viticulture as Sancerre is produced from the Sauvignon Blanc grape while Muscadet is produced from the grape of the same name. Both wines have become increasingly popular during the past ten years and are preeminently drinks to accompany fish dishes. Slim Muscadet has less body and less alcohol than Sancerre wine and is more suited for drinking at lunchtime or during the summer. The tart Sancerre wines are of a superior quality, with a fuller and richer flavor, and an aftertaste which is rarely detected in Muscadet. They are severe wines and unfortunately in some bottles this severity is not redeemed by the fruity flavor—in which case the wine approaches an astringent mouthwash. Most bottles are entirely satisfactory.

Tasting Practice No. 35

DRY WHITE The major purpose of this Tasting Practice is to introduce the dry white wines of this region, their similarities and differences, and their attractive qualities. Choose two bottles of Loire wine, one a Sancerre, one a Muscadet. At the same time you can take a look at some other dry white French wines, made from different grapes. In Burgundy the quality white wines are made from the Chardonnay grape and the end product is softer and fuller than Loire whites. For the purpose of this tasting attempt to obtain a bottle of Meursault (A.C.) or Pouilly-Fuissé (A.C.). Although an interesting comparison can be made with wines from another French area, Chablis, reserve this for the next Tasting Practice. As a fourth choice for the present Tasting Practice obtain a bottle of Graves wine. These wines are made from the Sauvignon Blanc grape (the basis of Sancerre wines) combined with the Semillon grape, which produces a softer and less acidic wine.

Chill all of the wines for at least an hour before use and attempt in your selection to obtain wines of a recent and comparable vintage. Allow the wines to breathe for a couple of minutes after removing the corks and then taste each of them unaccompanied, accompanied by mild cheese, and then by fish snacks. Complete your Tasting Charts on each of the four examples, without consultation. After discussing your assessments, carry out a second tasting.

––––––––––

You will probably find that all four examples are emphatically dry, with the Sancerre the most extreme. The Burgundy choice will probably be the least dry. The two wines from the Loire and the Graves example will share some characteristics which distinguish them from the Burgundy example. They will probably have a pale-yellow color and a crisp, dry taste. The Muscadet will be lighter and have less flavor and aftertaste than the other three wines. These features of the Muscadet bottle will be plainest in the comparison with the Burgundy wine. This one will probably be darker in color than the other three bottles, fuller in body, stronger in aroma, and more enduring in aftertaste. The interesting comparison between Sancerre and Graves may show that they share a light, fruity aroma and full flavor, but the Graves is rounder than the Sancerre. The latter may also have greater acidity than the Graves.

The weaknesses in the Loire dry white wines may be a lack of aroma and flavor, and a tendency to contain a little too much acidity. Unsatisfactory Graves wines will have similar weaknesses, whereas poor bottles from Burgundy are more likely to be dull and flavorless rather than overacidic.

Tasting Practice No. 36

LOIRE VERSUS THE REST   In this Tasting Practice the major comparison is between Sancerre and Chablis, both high-quality, crisp, dry white wines, bordering on the severe. They provide a perfect accompaniment to many types of fish dishes and most particularly shellfish. A satisfactory comparison depends on your success in obtaining genuine Chablis. Almost more than for any other Tasting Practice, make sure to obtain an A.C. bottle of Chablis and, if possible, one from a single vineyard.

As the third bottle in this Tasting Practice, choose one of the Italian dry white wines. One of the best for this purpose is Frascati, made from the Trebbiano grape, in a region near Rome. In the absence of Frascati, try a bottle of Soave. Although most Frascati is dry or even very dry, some medium-dry to sweet bottles are also produced. Try to get a bottle labeled dry (*secco*). The fourth bottle for this tasting can be German, and what better than a Riesling wine from the Rheingau area? This wine, particularly if tasted last in the sequence of four, should remind you of the pleasures of a full-bodied *medium*-dry white wine.

Despite the joy of drinking Rheingau wines unaccompanied

by food, this is not a Tasting Practice for unaccompanied drinking. The Sancerre and Chablis wines, and even the Frascati,
do not perform well on their own. After chilling the bottles
for at least an hour, taste them against a variety of snacks (including several of fish) and some well-flavored cheeses. The
hardy and more curious among you may prefer to ignore my
advice and taste even the cold Sancerre and Chablis unaccompanied by food. Complete your Tasting Charts without consultation and then discuss them in the usual way before checking
your reactions on a second tasting.

———————

The Sancerre and Chablis wines will probably be lighter in
color than those from Italy and Germany; Chablis occasionally
has a discernible green tinge. The Rheingau wine may have
a soft and faintly sweet aroma, with the French examples showing a penetrating, clean smell. The Frascati may have only a
light aroma. The two French bottles will almost certainly give
you a drier, crisper drink than the other two. The Rheingau
wine is likely to be the heaviest and fruitiest of the four. The
Chablis and the German wine leave the most lasting aftertaste.
All four wines run the risk common to whites of excessive
acidity, thinness, or lack of flavor. Their best qualities are their
fresh, astringent fruity flavor and the way they pleasantly swell
when accompanied by light foods.

TOURS RED   In the center of the Loire valley the growers produce
some red wines with slight to medium body, among the most
delicious of which are Bourgueil and its close neighbor, St. Nicolas
Bourgueil (which will not be distinguished henceforth), and
Chinon. These soft, light, well-flavored red wines make a welcome contrast to the austerity of the crisp whites. Although they
provide excellent accompaniment to poultry, meat, and cheese
dishes, their pleasures are only slightly diminished when taken
unaccompanied by food. Unfortunately these attractive wines are
precisely the sort which suffer in traveling and many people who
have not had the good fortune to taste them where they are
produced search unsuccessfully for the attractive qualities other
people describe. If in the Tasting Practices and thereafter you

find them to be on the disappointing side, postpone a final assessment until that happy time when you can taste them with your
evening meal after having spent a happy day wandering around
Chenonceaux or Amboise.

The major grape is the Cabernet Franc and it produces a
soft, light, immensely fruity wine. Some people find in these wines
the aroma and taste of raspberries, others say strawberries; I agree
with both simultaneously. The smell and taste of Chinon and
Bourgueil evoke in me a powerful sensation of fresh berries, but
I can't identify *which* berries. I suspect that for me the smell and
taste do not correspond to any existing berry but rather to some
common attribute I am unable to describe. Suffice it to say that
these attractive light-red wines are extremely easy to drink and
in the right circumstances cannot fail to bring one a glow of
pleasure.

Talking of wines for meals reminds me that the Loire area is
one of the most productive agricultural regions in France. The
regional specialties are too numerous to be gone into here, but
the fish dishes served with a special butter sauce are exceptionally
fine. The fat, locally grown asparagus spears (you will see the
sandy mounds shielding them in the fields as you pass by) combine superbly with hollandaise sauce.

Tasting Practice No. 37

SOFT AND FRUITY REDS   In the proper surroundings, that is, the
Loire valley itself, one can happily spend several Tasting Practices sniffing, swirling, and swigging these wines. As they do
not travel well and are seldom exported in any quantity, for
the present Tasting Practice we will have to be content with
one or two examples only. The Cabernet Franc grape, which
is the basis for these wines, is also cultivated in the Bordeaux
area, where it is used as a supplementary grape in the production
of claret. The Loire wines, lacking the other Bordeaux grapes
and with a different soil and climate, mature far more quickly
and reach their peak within a few years. They are slighter in
body, have a lower alcohol content and more transient aftertaste than clarets or Burgundies. On the correct occasion, how-

ever, their light, fruity qualities more than compensate. In this Tasting Practice compare two Loire reds with one from the St. Emilion area of Bordeaux and another bottle from Beaujolais.

Attempt to obtain one bottle of Chinon and one bottle of Bourgueil, preferably between three and eight years of age. Wines from older vintages, no matter how successful at the time, will probably have lost their vitality by now. Compare these two wines with a single vineyard St. Emilion wine (A.C. bottle) from a slightly older vintage, say five to ten years old. For the fourth bottle choose a Beaujolais A.C. of vintage within the last four years.

Decant the St. Emilion wine at least one hour before drinking time. The Loire and Beaujolais wines may not need more than thirty minutes in the decanter to reach their peak. Try tasting each of these wines on their own and then accompanied by a mild cheese and finally by a light snack. Complete separate Tasting Charts on each of the wines as before and discuss the outcome with your companions. Clear up any obscure points or disagreements by the second tasting.

The wines may differ in the extent to which they are saturated with redness, with the Bordeaux wine having the darkest hue, followed by the Loire wines, and lastly the Beaujolais. With good fortune in your selection you should enjoy attractive aromas from all four bottles—all fruity and probably bearing some resemblance to berries, strawberries, raspberries, and so on. All four wines should be at least moderately smooth, with the Bordeaux leading. The Loire wines should be of light to medium body and fall somewhere between the fuller Bordeaux wine and the lighter Beaujolais. All four bottles should yield wines with attractive flavor and the Bordeaux will in all probability have a deeper and longer-lasting, though not necessarily more attractive, flavor. The wines may well differ as to dryness, the Beaujolais being the sweetest and the Bordeaux wine, the driest. The weaknesses you might encounter in any or all of the wines are a lack of flavor, traces of hardness after swallowing, absence of aroma. In a happy selection all four bottles should give you considerable pleasure.

VOUVRAY Cave dwellers reside only a few miles outside the city of Tours. The village of Vouvray, which has given its melodious name to the by-now famous white wine from this area, is situated in a district with large chalky hills. These provide excellent cellar space for the production and maturing of wines and, as it turns out, for the families of some wine makers to live in. The rooms of the dwellings have been cut into the chalky cliffs and faced with wood or brick, windows, front doors, and all. One of the more curious aspects of this odd housing is the sight of curtains covering the windows of a façade stuck into the face of the cliff. I have not been able to discover how the formal address of these cave houses is given. Third cave on the right after you pass the interchange?

More to the point, the extremely pleasant, soft white wines of Vouvray, commonly with at least a touch of sugar in them and a slight prickle, make agreeable drinking. Unlike the wines of Sancerre made from the Sauvignon grape or the Muscadet wines from the Muscadet grape, Vouvrays are produced from the Chenin Blanc grape. The wines are quick to reach maturity and the dry ones seldom retain their fresh qualities for longer than six years. They are appetizing and refreshing wines which appeal to almost all drinkers and even to people who do not ordinarily enjoy wine. The wines are always soft and, depending on the year, range from medium dry to medium sweet. Despite the fact that Vouvray must by law contain a minimum of eleven percent alcohol, to the taste it remains a light wine. What Vouvray wines lack in depth of flavor and duration of aftertaste is balanced by their undemanding attractiveness and immediate appeal.

It is a peaceful area to explore on foot for a day or two and has the added advantage of a plentiful supply of tasting caves and bureaus. A good deal of sparkling white wine is also made in this district and serves as a substitute for champagne.

Vouvray wine is produced in eight communes, none of them mentioned with any frequency in the labels or descriptions of the bottles. Most of the wine is marketed as Vouvray, with the date of the vintage given, an indication of how sweet or dry it is, and the name of the producer. Similar conventions of description and labeling apply to the red wines of Chinon and Bourgueil described in the previous Tasting Practices.

Tasting Practice No. 38

VOUVRAY AND OTHERS In this introduction to Vouvray, first compare its qualities with the light to medium-bodied red Loire wines featured in the earlier tasting. In this way you may be able to discern the qualities contributed by the climate, soil, and methods of viticulture employed in the central Loire. Then, stretching eastward, compare this medium-dry to medium-sweet Loire wine with the severe Sancerre. Lastly taste it against one of the German or Alsatian wines, which bear some resemblance to Vouvray in that they also are of medium dryness and medium body.

Select a Vouvray (A.C.) from a vintage within the last three to eight years. For the red example try one of the wines you enjoyed in the previous tasting or an entirely fresh example from Chinon or Bourgueil. Lastly obtain a bottle of Alsatian or German medium-dry white wine. My own preference would be to compare the Vouvray with a Traminer wine from Alsace.

Chill the white wines for approximately sixty minutes before use and remember to allow them a couple of minutes to breathe after removal of the corks. Decant the red wine approximately thirty minutes before use and drink at room temperature. Taste each of the wines on its own and then accompanied by a mild cheese and finally with a light snack. Complete separate Tasting Charts on each wine without consultation, then discuss your assessments and carry out second tastings.

――――――

The red and white varieties from the Loire may share a pleasant, light aroma and refreshing taste. They should both be smooth and of a pleasant, fruity flavor, although not necessarily deep. Neither of them is likely to have a prolonged aftertaste. By comparison with the Sancerre example, the Vouvray will seem full and rather sweet. In respect to both fullness and sweetness, the Vouvray will probably come closer to the Alsace Traminer. The major difference between these two wines will be in their aroma, the Traminer showing its characteristically spicy smell. In flavor the Vouvray and Traminer will vary in the way that fruity and spicy flavors contrast. The Vouvray is the only one of the three white wines likely to have a prickly taste to it.

The weaknesses of unsuccessful Vouvray bottles are lack of flavor, too much sulfur, excessive acidity, and, rarely, the smell of wet dog. Broadly, the quality of Vouvray is consistently sound, but there is little doubt that it weakens after being transported. Good examples of Vouvray make extremely pleasant summer drinking.

ANJOU ROSÉ   A great deal of rosé wine is produced in the Anjou area. The best of it is described as Rosé de Cabernet, made entirely from Cabernet grapes. These wines tend to have a better and stronger fruit flavor, a livelier color, and a cleaner taste. Like most rosé wines, they make for pleasant drinking on their own and are a welcome help in washing down lunches or other light meals. They are particularly suitable for drinking on a hot day. As the most attractive attribute of rosé wines is their freshness, try to purchase wines with a date on the label. This simply ensures that the wine is of recent vintage—as is usually the case with rosé wine. It is recency of vintage rather than a particular year which is of consequence.

CHAPTER TEN

Burgundy

Many superb wines, both red and white, are produced in Burgundy. The reds are big wines with a penetrating aroma and full flavor. The concentrated aroma of a great Burgundy red can almost knock your head back. The whites are dry with a big fruity flavor. First and last they are food wines.

Burgundians like to joke about those unenlightened souls who drink water—actually *drink* it. My favorite is a story told by Samuel Chamberlain, about a Burgundian who was expounding on the iniquities of permitting water to pass one's lips. "But, monsieur, what about cleaning your teeth?" The reply: "Invariably I use a light, dry, unpretentious white wine."

Burgundy is shapeless, a narrow stretch of land between Dijon and Lyons in east central France that has no clear boundaries. Tracing the vineyards by car or by map is a process of wiggling one's way southward. The area has a spectacular history and a unique one in that it treats menus as historical documents. Perhaps because they were dukes aspiring to be kings, the successive rulers of Burgundy attempted to make extravagance appear commonplace. Banquets were arranged for the slightest reason and were known to last up to four days. As a result of this extravagant style of life, or perhaps because of it, the chefs of Burgundy developed a repertoire of astonishing dishes and meals. The efforts

of both chef and consumer were and still are inspired and complemented by the great wines produced from the Burgundian soil.

The popularity of Burgundy wines has led to the inevitable
imitations that have come from many parts of the world. Far
more Burgundy is drunk than is produced. In addition to imitations that are fraudulently labeled Burgundy, one has to contend
with Burgundy wines that have been stretched by the addition
of inferior wines, and with the silly practice of labeling bottles
"Spanish Burgundy," "Australian Burgundy," and the like. To
combat the illegitimate exploitation of their fame and at the same
time to improve and maintain standards of quality, the Burgundy
wine producers operate under a state-controlled A.C. system. The
supervising inspectors ensure that only the appropriate grapes are
used (Pinot Noir for the superior Burgundy reds), that the sites
are not overused, that the wines contain a high proportion of the
wine which appears on the label, and so on. From the point of
view of the purchaser, Burgundy wines whose labels state that
they have been prepared according to A.C. regulations are the best
for authenticity.

Broadly speaking, Burgundies are prepared and presented as
single-vineyard wines, commune wines, or regional wines. In
the case of single-vineyard wines, the label should state the commune of origin as well as the name of the vineyard and the wine
producer and/or merchant. One unusual feature of the Burgundy
wine region is the multiple ownership of single vineyards, which
had its origin in the postrevolution confiscation of clerical vineyards and their distribution among the peasantry. This fragmentation has been maintained and extended by the French laws of
inheritance. In consequence one may find that the several wines of
a single vineyard are quite legitimately produced by different
owners. Many of the commune names are double-barreled affairs
in which a local village name is combined with the name of the most
famous vineyard in its area. So it is that the village of Gevrey calls
itself and its commune wines by the grand title of "Gevrey-Chambertin" after the famous vineyard which goes by the name of Chambertin. In the nearby commune of Chambolle-Musigny, the village
of Chambolle appends the name of *its* famous vineyard, Le

Musigny. These Burgundian commune wines are what most of us drink, since the single-vineyard bottles are so expensive that they are usually reserved for special occasions. Authentic commune wines (i.e., those with the A.C. label) should reflect the distinctive qualities of the great single vineyards of the commune, but in a minor key. The wines are gathered from different growers in the area, blended by the merchant, and then distributed. It follows that the name of the merchant is of critical importance in the selection of Burgundy commune wines, and indeed of single vineyard wines as well. A list of wine merchants whose products are well-known is given on page 108.

The greater part of this chapter discusses the great wines of Burgundy, particularly its reds. Although I am aware that the commune wines are more easily purchased, I decided to center my discussion on the greatest products of the region both because of their intrinsic interest and to provide a clear account of the best attributes of Burgundy's wines. You should regard the descriptions of the great single-vineyard wines as the ideal and then in your own drinking attempt to obtain commune wines which come closest to these ideal characteristics.

The Burgundy wine region is customarily divided into four sections, running from north to south. They are Côte de Nuits, Côte de Beaune (these two comprising Côte d'Or, the "golden slopes"), Côte de Chalon, and Mâcon. The glory of Burgundy reds derives from a felicitous combination of soil, climate, and the perfectly suited grape, the Pinot Noir.

This grape, less prolific than other wine grapes, rarely prospers in other regions. In Burgundy, however, it produces some of the greatest red wines in the world. They are rich, smooth, and deep red. The wines have a penetrating fruity smell which some say reminds them of raspberries, while others say that it is reminiscent of violets. The color of the wine, which has itself become an adjective, is a deep ruby red. The taste qualities of the wine are characterized by softness and, above all, by an amazing smoothness. They are full-bodied, round wines which swell and fill one's mouth. They have prolonged aftertaste. They are assertive wines.

The great white wines of Burgundy are made from the Char-

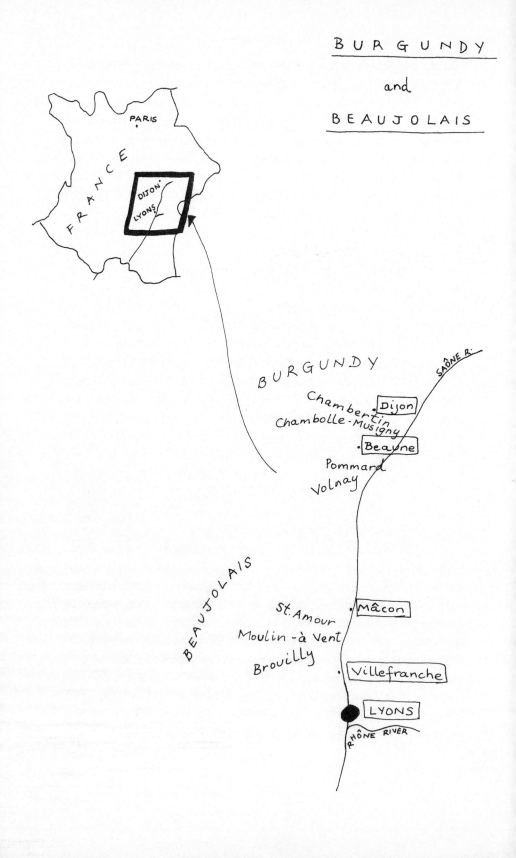

BURGUNDY

and

BEAUJOLAIS

PARIS

FRANCE

DIJON
LYONS

BURGUNDY

SAÔNE R.

Chambertin
Chambolle-Musigny

Dijon

Beaune

Pommard
Volnay

BEAUJOLAIS

St. Amour

Mâcon

Moulin-à-Vent

Brouilly

Villefranche

LYONS

RHÔNE RIVER

donnay grape. They have a full and fragrant aroma, are fat with flavor and dry to the taste. Many people detect a nuttiness in the flavor. They share with the red wines a remarkable smoothness and also have a sustained aftertaste. All of the classical white wines are made from this grape. The Aligote grape, which is a prolific producer, is used in Burgundy to produce mainly carafe white wines. The fourth grape encountered in the region, or to be more exact in the southern Burgundy region bordering on Beaujolais, is the Gamay, which as we have already seen in Chapter Eight, produces light, fresh, and fruity red wines. French law prohibits the use of this grape in the production of the quality red wines of Burgundy.

The Great Reds

The fine red wines should reflect the best qualities of the Pinot grape, especially its smoothness and depth of flavor. They mature within three to ten years and are best drunk younger than the fine red wines of Bordeaux, that is, preferably within four to fifteen years after bottling depending on the area of origin and quality of the particular vintage. The wines are noted for their full flavor and are most enjoyable when accompanied by food. In the main their best complements are red meats and flavored cheeses. The major communes are Fixin, Gevrey-Chambertin, Morey-St. Denis, Chambolle-Musigny, Clos de Vougeot, Vosne-Romanée, Nuits St. Georges, Pernand-Vergelesses, Aloxe-Corton, Savigny les Beaunes, Pommard, Volnay, Meursault, Auxey, Puligny-Montrachet, Chassagne-Montrachet, and Santenay.

GEVREY-CHAMBERTIN   Well over a thousand years ago the monks from the monastery of Beze were given the plot of land which is today known as the commune of Gevrey-Chambertin. They planted vineyards in the area and the best known of the surviving plots is called Chambertin Clos de Beze—one of the two supreme vineyards in the commune. The other is called simply Chambertin and is said to derive its name from a farmer by the name of Bertin whose newly acquired plot was called the "field (*champs*) of Bertin"—hence, Chambertin. These two outstanding vineyards, their slightly lesser neighbors, and the best of the commune wines are characterized by the depth of their color and flavor. They have a full aroma, smoothness, and power. Gevrey-Chambertin produces strong wines.

Chambertin is renowned as having been Napoleon's favorite wine. What is less well known is the fact that he adulterated it, and other wines, with water. Although this is an exceedingly common and indeed sensible habit when drinking coarse wines, nowadays a debasement of Chambertin by the addition of water would merit ten black marks.

Among the thirteen superior vineyards in this commune are the following (bottle labels will always have the word "Chambertin" preceding or following the name of the vineyard): Latricières, Mazys, Mazoyeres, Charmes, Ruchottes, Clos St. Jacques, Griotte, Chapelle, Foucherc.

In drinking the commune wines, you can legitimately expect a deep-ruby (burgundy) color, a penetrating fruity aroma, smoothness, and full body—a strong wine. If you have made an unfortunate choice, the wine may be lacking in flavor, oversugared, inky, or harsh.

CHAMBOLLE-MUSIGNY   The wines of this commune share many of the attributes of the Gevrey-Chambertin products but are softer and more delicate. The great vineyard of this commune is Le Musigny, which is capable of producing wines of surpassing excellence. The smoothest wine I have ever tasted came from this vineyard. I also had a curious experience with a Musigny wine from the 1961 vintage. The wine was as perfumed and smooth as can reasonably be expected from any bottle, but within a few minutes of having drunk a few mouthfuls of it, I began to experience a curious sensation in my knees and legs. It seemed as if the wine had gone directly into my knee joints. Although the sensation was genuinely felt, I only became aware of it after one of the other people at the table remarked on it. The same experience recurred on the next two successive drinkings of Musigny 1961.

The other outstanding vineyard in the commune of Chambolle-Musigny is called Bonnes-Mares. The major vineyards include Les Amoureuses, Les Charmes, Les Cres, Les Noirots, Les Sentiers. The commune wines from this area have a large following and understandably so. The best examples of them provide excellent drinking. They combine the strength and full flavor of red Burgundy with a smoothness and light delicacy that are enormously appealing.

The commune of Morey St. Denis lies between Gevrey-Chambertin and Chambolle-Musigny both geographically and from the point of view of flavor and body. The outstanding vineyards are Clos de Tart and Clos des Lambrays, while the major vineyards include the larger plots of Clos de la Roche and Clos St. Denis. Perhaps this is the point at which to mention that many of the Burgundian vineyards are small and hence their annual output of wine is limited. A famous vineyard such as La Tache, in the commune of Vosne-Romanée, consists of only fifteen acres. In consequence it is not surprising that the prices asked for bottles from outstanding single vineyards in Burgundy can be astronomical. The commune wines from Morey St. Denis are none too common, but in view of their high quality and comparatively moderate price, they are good value.

CLOS DE VOUGEOT   At roughly the same time that the Cistercian monks in the Rheingau were establishing the monastery of Kloster Eberbach and the accompanying Steinberg vineyard, a group of their fellows were building the monastery and vineyards known as Clos de Vougeot. The extensive walled enclosure has been maintained until the present time, but the 125-acre vineyard was fragmented into many separate plots. No fewer than sixty owners share a piece of the action here. The Chevaliers du Tastevin, a trade organization masquerading as a cross between an esoteric college and a branch of the Freemasons, purchased the monastery building and hold their bimonthly banquets in it.

It is difficult to be sure of the Clos de Vougeot wines because of this extraordinary fragmentation. There is no alternative but to be guided by the name of the merchant on the label. Among the proprietors whose products are highly regarded and from whom I have rarely had a disappointment are Drouhin, Ramonet, Latour, Gros, Engel, Jaboulet, Piat, Ponelle, Vocoret, Thevenin, Ropiteau, and Thorin. The best of the wines are heavily perfumed and have the characteristic smoothness and depth of flavor which one expects from the great Burgundy reds. The commune wines, like those from the walled enclosure itself, can only be assessed by the merchant's name and personal experience of the particular product.

VOSNE-ROMANÉE   This small commune produces a disproportionately high number of the great wines of Burgundy and is said to contain the most expensive vineyards in the world. It is extraordinary to find that the outstanding vineyards in this commune, whose names are familiar to everyone interested in superior wines, may be no larger than two, four, or ten acres. At their best, these wines are supreme examples of red Burgundy; many would say they are the greatest red wines in the world. Their qualities are fullness of body, velvety rich taste, and an enduring aftertaste. A spicy overtone in the aroma is occasionally remarked, but I have not had that experience.

The five outstanding vineyards are Romanée-Conti, La Romanée, La Tache, Les Gaudichots, and Les Richebourg—the last named with its twenty acres is almost the size of the other four vineyards combined. Only a small proportion of the annual produce from this extra-special small area ever reaches the open market. Most of the wine is allotted privately and well in advance of its actual production.

NUITS ST. GEORGES   This familiar-sounding commune produces excellent wines—leading to the seemingly inevitable sequence of popularity followed by widespread imitation. It is by now a much-abused label. Remember once again that your best protection is the A.C. label, the name of the merchant and/or supplier, and, in the case of single-vineyard wines, the correct name of the vineyard.

The wines are a deep-red color, have a mouth-filling full body, and a powerful aroma and depth of flavor. As you might expect from a wine with these emphatic qualities, it has a prolonged after-taste. The wines can be on the hard side in youth and are among the more slowly maturing of the Burgundy reds.

The outstanding vineyards include Les St. Georges, Les Cailles, Les Porrets, Les Pruliers, Les Vaucrains, and Aux Boudots. A popular vineyard from the subsidiary commune is Clos de la Maréchale.

CÔTE DE BEAUNE   As you travel south toward the wine capital of Beaune, the red wines become lighter in color, less penetrating in aroma, and less emphatic in flavor. In his book on Burgundy wines, Yoxall wittily summarizes the transition: "The nearer the Beaune, the sweeter the wine." Beaune red wines mature earlier than those of northern Burgundy and are drunk younger. The commune wines from Côte de Beaune, combining a fine flavor with smoothness and a delicacy of balance, are deservedly popular. The white wines are among the most outstanding produced anywhere in the world.

Beaune itself is an old walled town replete with wine shippers, growers, buyers, and lovers. It contains a fine museum devoted to wine and the curious, attractive, and interesting institution known as the Hospice de Beaune. The Hospice functions as a hospital, provides a hostel for the aged and a charitable foundation for children. All of its functions are financed by the proceeds from the annual wine auction, in which the produce from thirty-two superior vineyards is publicly sold at a spectacular sale. The vineyards themselves have been donated over the years as acts of charity and retain the name of the donor. Hence one speaks of the Dumay vineyard of the Hospice de Beaune. Among the best known of the vineyards are those of Peste, Muteau, Blondeau, Salin, Rolin, and Baudot. Twenty-four of the thirty-two vineyards produce red wine and the remainder produce whites. The auction is part of a three-day annual celebration and is known as the "candle auction" because the bidding continues until a small taper extinguishes itself. It is widely acknowledged that prices obtained at the auction are excessive and reflect the occurrence of auction-mania. Nonetheless the prices do show the general market trend and help in this way to set the prices for each Burgundy vintage. The wines themselves, with their special appellation, are not without souvenir value.

CORTON, POMMARD, AND VOLNAY In the commune of Aloxe-Corton, smooth and balanced red wines with a lively ruby color are produced. They are well flavored and some people detect an aroma of violets emanating from them. The outstanding vineyards in the commune are Le Corton, Les Bressandes, Le Clos du Roi, Les Renardes, and Charlemagne.

One of the principal owners in this commune is Louis Latour, who also owns and markets a number of other quality wines from Burgundy. Within the commune there are five vineyards belonging to the Hospice of Beaune and they include Dumay and Peste.

In addition to the fine red wines made in this area, some outstanding whites are also produced. They are big and fruity dry whites. The best of them comes from a vineyard called Corton-Charlemagne. The name derives from one of the original owners not only of this vineyard but of a large chunk of the entire commune. Like many of his successors, Charlemagne donated a large part of his vineyards to the church. The qualities of the white Corton wines are discussed in company with other white Burgundies on page 116.

The vineyards in the commune of Pommard are prolific and their products, popular. Like those of the nearby commune of Volnay, these reds are extremely pleasant and on the lighter side for Burgundy. They achieve a balance of body and flavor and are generally fresh to the taste. An Arizonan friend of mine describes Volnay wines as "cosmic." There are other light, red wines which I prefer, but not many of them.

The outstanding vineyards in the Pommard area include La Clos Blanc, Charmots, Les Bertins, Les Fremiers, Les Epenots, and Les Rugiens-Bas (and Hauts). In the Volnay area the outstanding vineyards include Les Caillerets, Les Champans, Les Fremiets, Les Santenots, Grand Champs, Les Lurets, Clos de Chenes, Chanlin, En Ronceret.

REDS FROM CHALON AND MÂCON   Between Beaune and Mâcon some useful light, red wines are produced. Although their lightness is consistent with their geographic situation, between the paler reds of southern Burgundy and those lightest of all reds in Beaujolais, the Chalonnais wines are made from Pinot grapes. Consequently their aroma and flavor differ from Beaujolais wines, which are made from the Gamay grape. The three best communes for red wines are those of Givry, Mercurey, and Rully. All three are covered by A.C. regulations. The wines mature quickly and are meant to be drunk young, between two to eight years after bottling. These light red, fresh, and pleasant wines complement white and red meats and mild cheeses. As their price is moderate, they make a sound purchase. People who find Beaujolais too superficial for their inclination may find an apt alternative in Chalon. Another choice is provided by the abundant Mâcon-Rouge, which is less reliable than the Chalon reds but worth exploring from time to time in expectation of good fortune—some are tasty and agreeable wines, sold inexpensively. They are similar to Beaujolais, but rougher. Like Beaune, Mâcon sports a charitable hospice.

The Mâcon region also produces large amounts of sound white carafe-type wines, usually sold simply as Mâcon-Blanc. The A.C.-labeled bottles are, as always, more reliable. The Chalon commune of Montagny produces useful small white wines and five Mâcon communes market their better grades of white wine under the name of Pouilly-Fuissé. This popular drink is a pale-yellow wine tinged with green and provides excellent company for fish dishes. The wines often have a nutty aroma and are consistently dry. They are meant to be drunk within two to five years of bottling.

Tasting Practice No. 39

VERTICAL REDS   The Burgundy region produces wines of different varieties and a range of qualities. One can approach them by examining the similarities and differences between the various areas and communes (horizontal tasting). Or you may prefer to become familiar with the products of a single commune and concentrate on differences in the grades of wine (vertical tasting). The third possibility is to carry out vertical *and* horizontal tastings. To begin, why not concentrate on either the Gevrey-Chambertin area or the Chambolle-Musigny area? Having decided on which of these two you would prefer to explore, obtain one single-vineyard bottle, one commune bottle (i.e., Gevrey-Chambertin A.C. or Chambolle-Musigny A.C.), and third, a wine carrying the label of one of the communes but no A.C. guarantee. For your single-vineyard bottle select one from the lists provided on pages 106 and 107, attempting to choose from vintages with between five and fifteen years of age.

Both of these communes produce strong red wine of a deep color and an attractive fruity aroma. The Chambertin wines may be slightly heavier and a touch drier than those from Chambolle, but both communes produce exceptionally smooth, full-bodied wines.

Decant the wines at least one hour before you intend drinking them. Take a sample of each wine on its own before tasting them accompanied by a full-flavored cheese and/or some meaty snacks. Complete Tasting Charts on each of the bottles without consultation and then return for a second tasting after having discussed your initial assessments.

The single-vineyard wine will have a deep, rich color and fruity aroma which presage a penetrating and full flavor, followed by a lingering aftertaste. It should be a smooth drink. The commune wine will probably resemble the single-vineyard wine in small print. It should have the same characteristics but may be considerably less intense. The third of your choices is a bit of a gamble and you may find that it bears little resemblance to the first two wines. On the other hand, with a bit of luck you may have landed a sound smaller version of Burgundy. The weaknesses you may come across in these bottles, and particularly the last of the trio, are harshness, thin quality, lack of flavor, excessive sugar, and hence dullness.

Tasting Practice No. 40

MORE VERTICAL REDS The main contrast among Burgundy reds is between those produced in the north, characterized by a deep color and fullness of body, and those in the south, with a lighter color, medium body, and a suggestion of sweetness. Many people prefer these lighter-bodied wines from the southern region. Whether this becomes your preference or not, you will probably enjoy drinking some of these pleasant wines. This vertical tasting is similar to the previous Tasting Practice but the subject is slightly different. For your commune I suggest that you choose either Volnay or Pommard.

Select a single-vineyard bottle from one of the lists provided on page 110 above and at least five years of age. Then obtain a commune wine from Volnay or Pommard which has the A.C. guarantee. Try to get one from the same vintage as the single-vineyard wine. Lastly, choose a wine labeled Volnay or Pommard but with no A.C. guarantee on the label. Prepare the wines by decanting them an hour before tasting and first try each of them unaccompanied. Then drink them accompanied by a mild cheese and/or a meaty snack. Complete Tasting Charts for each of the wines, without consultation. After you have discussed your initial assessments, return for a second tasting.

Volnay and Pommard wines are lighter Burgundies which generally maintain a good balance between body and flavor. They have the smoothness characteristic of a Burgundy and are fresh to the taste. They are easy to drink and leave a pleasant, lingering aftertaste. All of these characteristics should be seen at their best in the single-vineyard wines. Similar qualities should be evident in the commune wine but, as in the previous Tasting Practice, they will be less intense. As in the previous practice, your third choice is a gamble. It may be a recognizable approximation of the single-vineyard Volnay or it may be wholly different. The weaknesses of these wines, probably most evident in the third of your choices, are those of blandness, excessive sugar, and harshness.

Tasting Practice No. 41

HORIZONTAL REDS Now you can move on to a direct comparison between the wines of different areas. If you enjoyed the wines of either or both of the previous Tasting Practices, you could continue with these two areas—that is, compare Chambertin or Chambolle with your choice of Volnay or Pommard. If one or other of the previous Tasting Practices was somewhat disappointing or if you prefer to extend the range of your acquaintance with Burgundy reds, substitute for the first grouping a wine from the commune of Morey St. Denis or Vosne Romanée. The Volnay/Pommard group may be replaced by a bottle from Aloxe-Corton.

The present tasting compares two wines from the Côte de Nuits area with two from the Côte de Beaune. Choose an A.C.-guaranteed commune wine and a single-vineyard wine from each of these two areas. Attempt to obtain a single-vineyard wine from the lists provided in this chapter and preferably use wines from the 1961, 1962, 1964, or 1966 vintage. In view of the price of Burgundy wines, especially reds, this may be an appropriate point at which to remind you that you should attempt to purchase half-bottles wherever possible. Unless you are carrying out the Tasting Practices in a group of eight or more, half-bottles should be quite sufficient to provide adequate tasting experiences for everyone in the group.

Decant all four wines at least one hour before drinking them. To begin, taste the wines unaccompanied and follow this with a tasting accompanied by cheese and then by a meaty snack. Complete Tasting Charts on each of them. After making your assessments without consultation, discuss the outcome and then carry out your second tasting as usual.

The wines from the northern section (Côte de Nuits) will probably be a darker red than the other two, fuller in body and stronger as well as drier. The Volnay wines or their substitutes will be a paler red, lighter in the mouth, perhaps fresher to the taste, and almost certainly a little sweeter. The commune wines used in this Tasting Practice will probably bear the same relation to the single-vineyard wines as in the previous two Tasting Practices. That is, they should show the same characteristics as the single-vineyard wine, but in lesser degree. As in the previous tastings, the weaknesses found in these wines are harshness, thinness, blandness, or excessive sugar.

Tasting Practice No. 42

AGING REDS   The better-quality Burgundy red wines undergo interesting changes with aging. Rough in their early youth, they gradually become smoother and acquire their attractive aroma while softening their color from purple to deep red. You can get some idea of this organic process by carrying out a vertical tasting based on age differences. In order to do this satisfactorily, obtain a single-vineyard or commune wine from the same merchant covering different vintages. So, for example, you would attempt to get an estate-bottled Volnay Les Santenots. It is by no means easy to obtain an adequate sampling of the same producer's wine for several different vintages, but the attempt is worth making, especially if you live in one of the larger cities. If you are unable to match up the vineyards or communes and producers for the different years, then make the best compromise possible.

Decant the bottles an hour before use and carry out tastings on each of them unaccompanied by food in the first instance. Then repeat the tasting accompanied by cheese and a meaty snack. Complete separate Tasting Charts on each of the wines, without consultation. Then carry out your second tasting after discussion of your assessments.

The main changes which occur with aging are those affecting the color, aroma, and body of the wine. The youngest wines have a purple tinge, poorly developed aroma, and an off-key fullness. At their peak these wines have the deep clear-red color typical of Burgundy, a penetrating fruity aroma, and mouth-filling constitution. In old age they take on a brownish tinge, the aroma weakens and falters, and the wine tends to become thin.

The Great Whites

The white wines of Burgundy, which many claim are the greatest dry wines in the world, are produced in the southern half of

the region. All of the classical types are produced from the Chardonnay grape. They have a remarkable fruity perfume which has
been likened to ripe peaches or apricots. Unlike so many dry white
wines, the great examples from Burgundy are full-bodied. They
have a freshness and depth of flavor rarely come across in the
whites. Moreover, the mouth-filling flavor lingers for a prolonged
period. The wines also have the qualities of firmness and a sound
balance between sugar and acidity; they combine well with white
meats, poultry, fish, and cheeses. It would be a pity to judge the
quality of these excellent wines on the basis of imitations or bottles
of excessive age. In order fully to appreciate their finest qualities,
you should ensure that you have a fresh and genuine example.

Corton-Charlemagne, previously mentioned, is a pale-golden
color with a slightly spicy smell and a full flavor. The small
production from this vineyard has restricted its fame, and worse,
it means that only a small number of people ever have the opportunity to enjoy it.

The straw-colored wines of Meursault are dry, soft, and mel-
low. In the best examples the nuttiness in the flavor is discernible.
The aroma is softer than that of the Corton whites. These wines
can last up to eight years after bottling, but the majority of them
are at their best within three to four years. The range of quality
is from the finest products of single vineyards to blends from
several vineyards near the village. The commune wines are moderately reliable and tend to be in the middle range of prices.

In former years the Comte Lafon donated a barrel of Meursault wine to the author of the year's best book on Burgundy. The
time for magnanimous gestures seems to have passed and the custom
is no longer practiced. The outstanding vineyards in Meursault are
Clos des Perrières and Les Perrières, Les Charmes, and Les Gene-
vrières.

The wines of Montrachet are universally regarded as being the
best of the white Burgundies and often are rated as the best dry
whites in the world. There are several Montrachet vineyards.
Their acknowledged leader is called plainly "Montrachet." As
the average annual production of this vineyard is merely 1,000
cases, the demand greatly exceeds the supply. Consequently, if

you plan to buy some of this expensive wine, it is essential to use a reputable merchant and ask for an estate (*domaine*) bottling. Prominent owners include Lafon, Thenard, Bouchard, de Laguiche, and Prieur and their names should appear on the label of the bottle.

The premier vineyards which rank immediately below Montrachet are Chevalier Montrachet, Batard Montrachet, and Pucelles. Other famous wines produced in and around the adjoining village of Chassagne come from the vineyards of Cailleret, Morgeot, Les Ruchottes, Criot, and La Maltroye. These dry, full Chassagne white wines are of similar quality to other members of the Montrachet group. In style the Montrachet wines are similar to those of Meursault; fragrant in aroma, dry and full-flavored, firm, and well-balanced.

One of the most popular vineyards of the Chassagne-Montrachet area is called "La Maltroye," which produces a fine white wine and an equally good red one. A short while ago some Irish friends sent me a generous gift of wines among which were two bottles from this vineyard, one red and one white. They were from the successful vintages of 1966 (red) and 1969 (white) and were both first-rate examples. We decided to drink them on the same occasion in order to carry out a comparison of the red and white products. They were soft and round and both had a persisting aftertaste, the red longer than the white. What was most striking, however, was the fact that both wines were understated. They crept up on one; the red was fuller than the white, as expected.

CHABLIS In former days, before they became so earnest, psychologists derived harmless amusement from word-association tests, a modern form of teacup reading. They pronounced a word and the willing subject replied with the first word that came to mind. So, for example: champagne—slipper; Chablis—oysters. Although the superbly flavored dry wines from this area are an agreeable complement to many types of food, they do combine particularly well with oysters. Genuine Chablis, produced from the Chardonnay grape, has a greenish tinge to it and is best drunk within two to six years after bottling, when it is at its freshest. It is a particularly dry wine, tending in the direction of hardness. Its flavor has been aptly described as "flinty," which is what makes it combine so very well with shellfish. What the wines lack in aroma they make up for in their rich aftertaste.

The fruitful area of Chablis is extremely small and conditions for cultivation are difficult. The wine is produced in four grades: single-vineyard wines, A.C. commune wines, Petit Chablis, and fake Chablis. As always, one is most likely to get the genuine article, and the best of it at that, from a single-vineyard wine with a reputable label. The commune wines, properly guaranteed, are blends made from various vineyards in the district, while the Petit Chablis label indicates a blend of vineyards from outlying districts and a lighter type of wine. The fake bottles far exceed the genuine ones; many of them are thin and watery, not to say acidic. In order properly to assess the qualities of Chablis it is wisest to spend a little extra in order to obtain the genuine article from a single vineyard.

VINTAGES   Although the red and white Burgundies from a particular year are generally of comparable quality, occasionally differences occur within the same year. Among the white Burgundies one has to look to more recent vintages because the older wines have now passed their peak—if indeed there are any left to do so. The reds should, of course, have five to twenty years in which to mature.

Among the many reliable shippers of Burgundy wines, my experiences with the products of the following have been satisfactory —but this, of course, does not mean that names omitted from the list are unreliable: Bouchard (two firms by the name), Calvet, Drouhin, Doudet-Naudin, Jadot, Latour, Lebegue, Mommesin, Piat, Ponnelle, Ropiteau, Sichel, Leger, Thorin, Thevenin, Ramonet, Vocoret.

Tasting Practice No. 43

VERTICAL WHITES   As with the red Burgundies, it is useful to become acquainted with the different grades of quality from a single area. Meursault is a commune particularly suited for this Tasting Practice as it produces a good deal of wine, easily available. Attempt to obtain a single-vineyard Meursault, preferably three to seven years old. Try for a bottle from one of the vineyards listed on page 116. Then add to this a Meursault commune wine carrying an A.C. guarantee on the label. Finally compare these two with a wine which carries the label of Meursault but no guarantee of origin.

The wines should be chilled for thirty to sixty minutes before use and are appreciated best when accompanied by light snacks or mild-flavored cheeses. Even so, it is best to taste the wines unaccompanied before drinking them with food. Complete separate Tasting Charts on each of the wines without consultation, then discuss your assessments and complete your second tasting. Generally Burgundy whites do not need to be quite so cold as many other whites. If you overchill them, they can turn dumb: try warming them gently by holding the glass in your palms.

The best and foremost qualities of white Burgundies can be summarized in three words—fresh, full, fruity. The best of the Meursault wines display these three qualities in abundance. They often have an aroma of peaches and many people detect in their flavor a nutty quality; some say that it is reminiscent of almonds. These attributes will probably be discernible in the single-vineyard wine. The commune wine should have similar attributes but in lesser degree. The third wine, your gamble, may or may not display the same characteristics depending on your fortune.

The weaknesses of Burgundy whites, seen in examples from Meursault on occasion, are excessive acidity, an overliberal use of sulfur, silent aroma, and dull flavor.

Tasting Practice No. 44

HORIZONTAL WHITES This Tasting Practice compares the qualities of different types of Burgundy whites. Select a commune or single-vineyard wine from each of three areas: Meursault (include one of the bottles from the previous practice or choose a new one if you prefer), Montrachet, and Pouilly-Fuissé.

Chill the wines for approximately half an hour before use and remember to allow them a minute or two to recover after removal of the corks. Taste each of the wines unaccompanied. Then try them again with mild cheese and a light snack, preferably some with fish. Complete separate Tasting Charts on each of the wines, without consultation. Carry out your second tasting after discussing your initial assessments.

The wines should share a freshness and a fullness of body. They may differ in color with the bottle of Pouilly-Fuissé a paler yellow with a green tinge, while the other two will likely have a yellowish appearance somewhere between straw and gold. The Pouilly-Fuissé will probably be lighter in body than the other two, which may have a mouth-filling fullness. The Meursault and Montrachet wines may have a rich, fruity aroma while the other may have only a slight aroma. The Pouilly-Fuissé is likely to have only a brief aftertaste while the other two may linger for up to an hour. Finally the Pouilly-Fuissé will almost certainly be drier and thinner than the other two.

The possible weaknesses are a dullness of flavor, thinness, and acidity.

Tasting Practice No. 45

DRY WHITES   For addicts of dry white wines, Burgundy can be bliss. In Chablis they produce the flinty, stone-dry, yet full-bodied wines which are such a fine accompaniment to fish. Pouilly-Fuissé has similar attributes in lesser degree but is produced in greater quantity and hence is less expensive. Sancerre, although not strictly speaking in the Burgundy area, is close enough to it geographically and in construction and taste to merit inclusion in the present Tasting Practice.

Finally, to emphasize the essential dryness of these three wines, include another bottle of your most successful Meursault encountered in the two previous tastings.

Chill the wines for approximately an hour before use (Meursault half an hour) and leave the wines to recover for a couple of minutes after removing the corks. Taste each of them unaccompanied to begin with. Then try them against a fishy snack. Fill in separate Tasting Charts for each of the wines, discuss your assessments, and then complete the second tasting.

———————

Although the wines from Chablis and Sancerre will probably be equally dry, the former is likely to have a fuller body than the Sancerre, which is a little inclined to thinness. The Chablis and Pouilly-Fuissé are both pale wines which sometimes have a greenish tinge—notice the contrast to the yellow Meursault. The Chablis and the Meursault bottles, while differing in the quality of dryness, are likely to be similar in their fullness and enduring aftertaste. All four wines should have a pleasant, refreshing quality.

The possible weaknesses in these wines are thinness, acidity, dullness of flavor, and excessive sulfur.

Tasting Practice No. 46

BURGUNDIES FOR EVERYDAY DRINKING Exploring the heights of Burgundy wines is expensive. Most of the Burgundy we drink is of more humble quality, which is not to say that one cannot get many pleasant and agreeable wines from this region at a reasonable price. Many of them are marketed plainly as Mâcon-Rouge or Mâcon-Blanc. Your guide in purchasing these is the name of the producer given on the label or perhaps the advice of the supplier. The element of uncertainty makes the search for a reliable Mâcon somewhat entertaining and you are likely to have success sooner or later. I hope that it is sooner rather than later, and if sooner, then why not in this Tasting Practice?

In addition to two Mâcon wines try to obtain a Côte de Beaune (*village*) and a bottle of Mercurey. Each of these wines should be relatively inexpensive, with the last two being fifteen to thirty percent dearer than carafe wines. It might be worthwhile decanting the red wines about half an hour before use despite, or some people would say because of, their lesser quality. Chill the white wine for half an hour before use. Taste each of them on their own and then accompanied by mild cheese and a selection of snacks. Complete your Tasting Charts on each of them without consultation, discuss the results, and carry out a repeat tasting.

From these everyday red wines you can reasonably expect to obtain a smooth, moderately strong, deep-red wine with a slightly sweetish edge to it. From the everyday whites you can reasonably expect to get a fresh and full wine with a clean taste.

The unpleasant attributes which crop up in the everyday reds are coarseness, dullness, and an inky quality. The weaknesses of poor white carafe wines are excessive sulfur and acidity, but perhaps most common of all, they are plain dull.

CHAPTER ELEVEN

Bordeaux—Médoc

Now we arrive at my special favorite. I owe a boundless debt to Bordeaux, having enjoyed many exceptionally fine wines from that remarkable region. Although my recollection of most of them is no more than a diffuse glow of pleasure, I can recall a few of the most outstanding bottles. A 1959 bottle of Château Léoville-Las-Cases oozing with fruitiness, a perfectly balanced Château Ducru-Beaucaillou 1961, an astonishingly rich Château Petrus of 1952, the beautifully perfumed Château Margaux of 1953, the deep and full Château Haut-Brion of 1957 and many other absent friends. It is such an interesting and extensive subject that one could write a book on Bordeaux alone—and, of course, many people have done just that.

Apart from that most important area, know as Médoc, which has been described as a tongue of land between the Gironde and the Bay of Biscay, the Bordeaux wine region has an untidy shape. The 300,000 acres of vineyard produce more than eighty million gallons of wine each year (110 million in 1962) and of this staggering amount no less than three-quarters of it meets the requirements necessary for classification as A.C. quality wine. To put the matter in proper perspective, one in three of the world's bottles of fine-quality wines comes from Bordeaux.

Much of the land in this region is flat and gravelly and unattractive to anyone but a wine partisan or native. Looking at the bleak, cropped vines in midwinter you find it hard to believe that within less than a year they will once more, for the several hundredth time, produce millions and millions of berries. It is as if the soil has a reservoir of wine which passes each summer through the pipes of the vines to yield, in September and October, those millions of gallons of wine when the taps are turned on.

Bordeaux has had its share of drama, but from an English point of view perhaps the most interesting single historical fact is that from the middle of the twelfth century until the middle of the fifteenth century—for 301 years to be exact—Bordeaux was English. It went to England or, more correctly, the English went to it when in 1152 King Henry of England received the title as part of his bride Eleanor's dowry. It reverted to French hands in 1453, when the English commander, John Talbot, was defeated. Château Talbot, which consistently produces tasty wines, is named after him. It should not be thought, however, that the picture of the natty gentleman portrayed on the bottles depicts John Talbot. You will find the same portrait on bottles of Château Gruaud-Larose. Both these vineyards are owned by the firm of Cordier and the portrait depicts the founder of this family concern.

The city of Bordeaux has a spacious, civilized, and prosperous air to it and so it should; it is all of these things. Wine enthusiasm apart, the harbor section is especially interesting. With the cellars stretched out along the quayside and the barrels piled up outside them, it is a photographer's delight. Naturally a good deal of the commerce of Bordeaux is associated with the wine trade and the producers, brokers, and merchants are a major presence and influence in the city. Some of the more prominent firms, among others no doubt equally reliable, are Cruse, Calvet, Lichine, Sichel, Delor, Bouchard, Cordier, Barton and Guestier, Dubos, Lebegue, Eschenauer, and Ginestet.

The region produces dry red wines and sweet and dry whites. By tradition the vineyards and their buildings are generally referred to as "châteaux," irrespective of whether the building is a genuine château or a domestic farmhouse of modest proportions. The traditional Bordeaux wine bottle has shoulders. The red wines

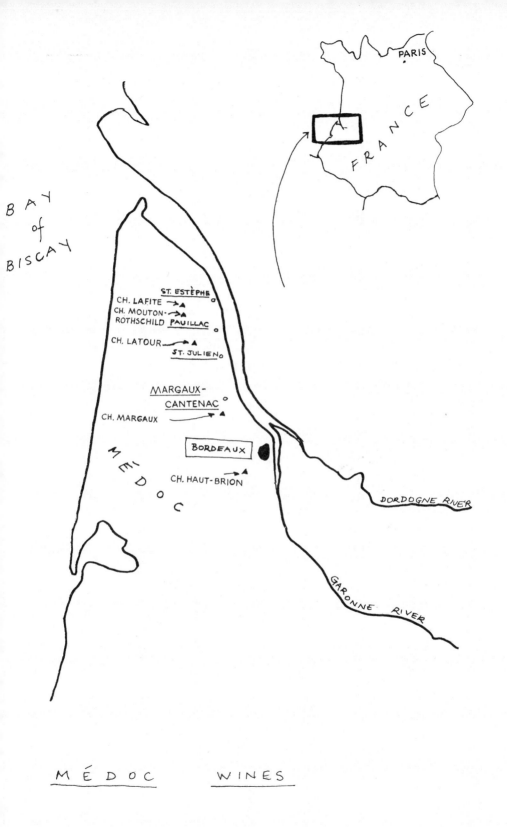

MÉDOC WINES

are put into green bottles and the white, into white. In 1855 the Bordeaux wine trade carried out a classification of the major vineyards of the Médoc region in response to a request for representation at a Paris exhibition. This famous classification, now extremely creaky, is an important part of wine lore and was followed in later years by other Bordeaux areas. So it is that now we have a classification for the wines from Sauternes, Graves, and so on. But more of this later.

Although there are nearly twenty discernible areas within the Bordeaux wine region, the major areas are Médoc, Sauternes, Graves, St. Emilion, and Pomerol.

MÉDOC This area produces dry red wines, including some of the greatest in the world. They are made from a blend of grapes, with the Cabernet Sauvignon predominating. Second in importance is the Cabernet Franc grape and to this is added a smaller quantity of Merlot. One or two other minor additions are sometimes made, but they are of little significance. The best of the Médoc wines exhibit the distinctiveness of Cabernet grapes and in this lies their greatness. They are resilient grapes and display their characteristics under a wide range of conditions in different parts of the world. Wines made from Cabernet grapes contain a great deal of tannin and take a long time to mature. Cabernet tannin also ensures longevity—clarets are among the most enduring wines made anywhere in the world. It is not unknown for them to retain their qualities for over a hundred years. The tannin, which is largely responsible for their slowness to mature and their longevity, can, however, be excessive. In these cases the pleasantly mouth-drying qualities of the wine turn harsh and can cause one to pucker.

Can one describe the qualities of a great claret? In the first place it has a richness of color and a subtle and satisfying aroma. It is firm but it mellows in time into a round and soft wine. The balance between deep fruitiness and acidity is maintained. The flavor is deep and fruity while retaining its essential dryness; it persists in the mouth, often for many hours at a stretch. The pleasing yet subtle aroma of claret successfully defies capture by words. It is often likened to the smell of blackcurrants—this is perhaps the most common description. Others discern a smell of cedarwood, others violets, and so on. The aroma is there and, once detected, most people find it comparatively easy to recognize even though they find it hard to label in words. Like Burgundy wines, clarets are without any question whatever at their best when accompanied by food. Both wines swell in the presence of food but can be unattractive taken on their own.

Some knowledge of the classification systems operating in the Médoc and elsewhere in Bordeaux is necessary when one reaches the stage of drinking these wines with regularity. The degrees of classification can be introduced by reference to a label of one of the greatest of all wines, Château Latour.

CHÂTEAU LATOUR [vineyard]

1961 [year of harvest]

Mise en bouteille au château

[château-bottled, authenticity]

Pauillac [commune in Médoc]

Appellation Controlée

(state-controlled mark of authenticity)

All five pieces of information will be shown on the label and the first three will also appear on the cork. A good deal of sound-quality wine is bottled in the cellars of merchants and shippers. This fact (cellar-bottling) will be signified on the label of the bottle. The year of harvest can be of considerable importance in Bordeaux and some general advice on the subject is provided on page 152. The A.C. mark is, of course, the state-controlled guarantee of authenticity that the wine has met the strict standards laid down by law and is from the area described on the label.

In the 1855 classification the major Médoc vineyards were placed in five categories; the full list is given below. In view of the astronomic prices asked for the class I wines, they are included simply for the sake of completeness. They now cost anything from twelve to sixty dollars per bottle and become more expensive each month. They are wines for buying and selling, rarely for drinking.

Fortunately, some of the wines in categories II–V can be had at reasonable prices and as you deserve a crack at a few at least, some are proposed in the Tasting Practices. Supplementing the classified wines are hundreds of lesser wines, many of sound quality. These are marketed under their château name or under the name of their commune, e.g., Château Martinens, 1966, Cantenac (commune), *Appellation Controlée*. In the absence of previous experience of a particular wine, the A.C. mark is your best guide.

1855 CLASSIFICATION OF MÉDOC WINES
(*All have the prefix "Château"*)

CLASS I

Lafite	Pauillac Commune
Latour	Pauillac
Margaux	Margaux
Haut-Brion	Pessac, Graves
Mouton-Rothschild	Pauillac

CLASS II

Rausan-Segla	Margaux
Rauzan-Gassies	Margaux
Léoville-Las-Cases	St. Julien
Léoville-Poyferre	St. Julien
Léoville-Barton	St. Julien
Durfort-Vivens	Margaux
Gruaud-Larose	St. Julien
Lascombes	Margaux
Brane-Cantenac	Cantenac
Pichon-Longueville	Pauillac
Pichon-Longueville (Lalande)	Pauillac
Ducru-Beaucaillou	St. Julien
Cos-d'Estournel	St. Estephe
Montrose	St. Estephe

CLASS III

Giscours	Labarde-Margaux
Kirwan	Cantenac
d'Issan	Cantenac
Lagrange	St. Julien
Langoa	St. Julien

Malescot-Saint-Exupéry	Margaux
Cantenac-Brown	Cantenac
Palmer	Cantenac
La Lagune	Ludon
Desmirail (Defunct)	Margaux
Calon-Segur	St. Estephe
Ferriere	Margaux
Marquis-d'Alesme-Becker	Margaux
Boyd-Cantenac	Cantenac

CLASS IV

Prieure-Lichine	Cantenac
Saint-Pierre	St. Julien
Branaire-Ducru	St. Julien
Talbot	St. Julien
Duhart-Milon	Pauillac
Pouget	Cantenac
Latour-Carnet	St. Laurent
Lafon-Rochet	St. Estephe
Beychevelle	St. Julien
Marquis-de-Terme	Margaux

CLASS V

Pontet-Canet	Pauillac
Batailley	Pauillac
Grand-Puy-Lacoste	Pauillac
Grand-Puy-Ducasse	Pauillac
Haut-Batailley	Pauillac
Lynch-Bages	Pauillac
Lynch-Moussas	Pauillac
Dauzac	Labarde
Mouton-Baron Philippe	Pauillac
de Terre	Arsac
Haut-Bages-Libéral	Pauillac
Pedesclaux	Pauillac
Belgrave	St. Laurent
Camensac	St. Laurent
Cos Labory	St. Estephe
Clerc-Milon-Mondon	Pauillac
Croizet-Bages	Pauillac
Cantemerle	Macau

Allowance is also made for those wines which fail to achieve greatness and for the products from the outstanding vineyards which for one reason or another (e.g., a poor harvest) fail to meet the standards required of them. Leaving aside the five classes provided for the outstanding growths, there are seven main categories into which the wine may be placed. If it is a lesser wine or a sound wine but of dubious origin, it may simply be described as "Bordeaux Rouge." If it is a wine of lesser quality but authentic, it may receive the description of "Bordeaux A.C." Wines of this type may, if they are of a sufficiently high alcoholic level, graduate to the next category, which is Bordeaux Supérieur A.C. The next jump up is to have the area name, that is, Médoc A.C. The next step up the scale is a commune name, such as St. Julien A.C. Then we go up to *artisan* and finally among these secondary wines to *cru bourgeois*. And, for the moment, that is enough of that. It is time to taste.

Tasting Practice No. 47

A MÉDOC MEAL   Why not try a royal introduction to Bordeaux? Choose the best red wine from the Médoc that you can manage and taste it in the best of circumstances—that is, with a meal. If you can, buy a classified growth produced in a good year, either bottled at the château or by a reliable firm. The list on pages 128–29 gives the choice open to you, and for drinking now, you will be safe with almost any of the classified growths from the vintages of 1953, 1955, 1959, 1961, 1962, 1966, or 1967. If you are not in a position to obtain a classified growth, try to find one of the better *cru bourgeois* wines such as château Angludet, Beauregard, Greysac, Ruat, Roland, Phelan-Segur, Liversan, Medrac, Monpelou, Lanessan, Lafon, Gloria, Dillon, Bellevue, Beau-Site, Chasse-Spleen, Haut Marbuzet, Citran, Duplessis, Verdignan.

After being transported, classic reds need a few days to recover, so rest the bottle in an upright position for a while before opening day. Allow the wine to reach room temperature gradually and then decant approximately one hour before use. All this is less bother than it sounds and you will soon do it automatically with fine red wines. It is worth the extra thought and particularly so in present times when fine bottles can be opened only on special occasions.

The wines should combine beautifully with most meats, from poultry to beef. Remember to save enough wine for drinking with some cheese after the main course. You can calculate on needing one bottle for three or four people at a meal.

When pouring, do not fill the glass. One-third of a glass is sufficient to release the aroma and is not too much to prevent you from gently swirling the wine in your glass.

The wine should have a clean and lively appearance with a light- to medium-red color. Unless you have been awfully unlucky, the aroma should be intense, clear, and adorable. Blackcurrants? Violets? Cedarwood? The wine should be smooth, full-bodied, and leave your mouth feeling dry. The flavor, probably full and fruity, should linger on for some time after swallowing each mouthful.

The weaknesses sometimes encountered are those of weak flavor, short-lived taste, and harshness. Compare your responses on the Tasting Chart to those of your companions.

If you were unlucky with the wine, please do not forego further attempts. In view of the potential goal, it is worth persisting. If you were unlucky with the cook, exercise courtesy.

THE FIVE COMMUNES Within Médoc five communes are of central importance. As you travel north from the city of Bordeaux you find, first, Cantenac, then Margaux, St. Julien, Pauillac, and St. Estephe. Although it is difficult to make generalizations about the quality of wines produced in each of these five communes, they do seem to have some distinctive attributes. The wines from Margaux, for example, are rightly renowned for the beauty of their aroma, their softness and smoothness, but the adjoining commune of Cantenac can scarcely be distinguished from its dominant neighbor. St. Julien wines are especially famous for their fruitiness, while Pauillac yields wines which are particularly firm and fleshy. The most northerly of the five, St. Estephe, gives wines with a good deal of tannin in them and as a result they are slow-maturing, big, full-bodied wines.

The prize of the Cantenac and Margaux communes is Château Margaux itself. Incidentally, be careful not to confuse a commune wine called simply "Margaux" with the superb class I wines of Château Margaux. Come to think of it, in view of their respective prices, there is absolutely no possibility of confusion—at least not in a wine shop. As mentioned above, these wines are noted for their superb aroma. Unfortunately some of the lessser château wines are too delicate. Their lovely aroma belies a weakness in flavor, which can be on the superficial side. However, when the aroma and flavor *are* in balance, then you are in for an experience. Apart from the great Château Margaux itself, superb wines are made at Château Lascombes, Cantenac-Brown, Palmer, Rausan-Segla. All of these are indubitably wines for the great occasion.

Next we come to the commune of St. Julien. The wines from this area maintain a consistently high quality and the commune wine is understandably popular. There are five class II vineyards, two class III, and four class IV plots. The best of St. Julien wines, emanating from these eleven vineyards, are deep red in color and characterized by their fruity flavor. The finest are the quintessence of claret. For example, in that excellent vintage of 1961, Château Ducru-Beaucaillou produced a beautifully balanced claret which had everything—a lively, deep-red color matched by an aroma of black currants, and a deep, lingering fruity flavor. This château has, for the past fifteen years at least, produced bottle after bottle of superb wine. St. Julien also boasts the three Léoville vineyards—Las Cases, Poyferre, and Barton. Poyferre is not as successful as the other two, which, like Ducru, turn out consistently fine wines years after year and in some vintages turn out superstars. I have a special memory store for the 1959 Las Cases, which had a heavenly bouquet and a flavor to match. Having no 1959 bottles left is a sadness. Other treasures in this commune include Château Gruaud-Larose and Château Talbot, both owned by Cordiers and both turning out splendid wines whose popularity is understandable. Like the other champions of St. Julien, these wines have a fine color, lovely aroma, and deeply satisfying fruity flavor. Château Lagrange is not quite as consistent as some of the other vineyards in this commune but the 1961 wines had remarkable depth.

The commune of Pauillac contains no fewer than three giants—Château Lafite, Château Latour, and Château Mouton-Rothschild. It is difficult to generalize about the commune wine and in any event most of the Pauillac grapes are used to produce château wines. As there are so many classed growths here, each with its distinctive qualities, broad features of the area are difficult to discern. It can safely be said however that Pauillac products are full-bodied, powerful wines with a deep flavor. In wine parlance they are fleshy wines. For many connoisseurs Château Lafite is the prince of Bordeaux reds, or more grandly, the entire world. The wines have a deep and lingering flavor, balanced by smoothness and a fragrant aroma. The wines from Latour, with the stubby defense tower that has become its famous insignia, are slow-maturing, powerful wines which are among the best in all years and better than most in off-vintages. Mouton-Rothschild also produces powerful wines marked by an amazing smoothness and prolonged aftertaste. The château contains an interesting museum of wine, open to visitors by arrangement. Like the other two Pauillac châteaus mentioned, Mouton has an aroma reminiscent of cedarwood.

Perhaps it is inevitable in a commune which contains three such giants, but for my part the other vineyards in Pauillac are something of an anticlimax. The two Pichon vineyards have enthusiastic followers, but although I have greatly enjoyed some of their bottles, nonetheless I feel that they have not maintained a consistently high standard. Among the other sites, Lynch-Bages and Pontet-Canet are both extremely popular, with good reason. Reliably good, they sometimes scale the peaks. Incidentally, the commune of Pauillac is in some respects the wine capital of Médoc and contains the headquarters of the local Order of Wine-Producers and the Maison du Vin.

The most northerly of the five communes, St. Estephe, has fewer classed vineyards—only five. Opinions about the wines from this area differ considerably. For some they are the best of the

Médoc—unmistakable, powerful, and splendidly dry. Others complain about their coarseness, lack of reliability, and excessive sediment. I enjoy their power and zest and am quite willing to put up with occasional disappointments in return for those superb bottles which are successful.

Another important attraction of this commune is the presence of a plentiful supply of nonclassed vineyards of superior quality, the *cru bourgeois* wines. They include Meyney, Phelan-Segur, Pomys, Morin, and Le Roc. The St. Estephe wines are slow to mature; apart from the class I growths, they should be the last of the Médocs to be drunk.

The three most prominent vineyards of St. Estephe are the Châteaux Calon-Segur, Montrose, and Cos d'Estournel. I have had fine drinking from each of them at different times intermingled with a few disappointments here and there. Some of the successful bottles have been memorable and, curiously enough, St. Estephe wines sometimes show better than other Médoc products in years which are generally considered to be poor vintages. The labels on Château Cos d'Estournel depict the château buildings, which are ornamented with curious pagoda-like turrets appended by one-time owners who had interests in the China trade. The label of Château Calon-Segur displays a heart, signifying the prized place this vineyard had among the possessions of Monsieur Segur, a former owner.

What are the weaknesses in Médoc wines? Well, for a start they are products of nature and in unfortunate climatic conditions unsatisfactory wines emerge. Their faults include a lack of flavor, absence of aroma, harshness, and excessive tannin. But against this one has to place their fruitiness, depth of flavor, and lingering aftertaste.

Please remember that Médoc wines are slow to mature and, if drunk before their development is completed, they can be not merely disappointing but positively unpleasant. The immature young wines are harsh and slightly on the bitter side. Unfortunately there is no single guide to the number of years which they require in order to mature; this varies with vineyard and from year to year. Broadly speaking, however, you will be fairly safe if you assume that, excepting St. Estephe wines, the superior grades require a longer time to reach maturity (from eight to twenty years). The lesser wines, commune and *cru artisan* types, can generally be drunk within four to eight years of bottling.

In general, the wines require longer to mature as one moves farther north, with the products of St. Estephe taking up to four years longer than those of St. Julien and Margaux, other things being equal. These general guidelines are subject to the variations of vintage qualities. In some years the emergent wines are soft in youth and mature relatively quickly, while in other seasons the young wines are extremely hard and require many years to lose their roughness. Lastly, the speed of maturing is influenced by the conditions under which the wines are stored. If they are maintained at the ideal, cold temperature and protected from the light, then they mature slowly. If stored at temperatures above the ideal, the maturing process is accelerated.

Young clarets need time to knit together. The fleshiness of the wine, the aroma, and fruity acidity have not bound—like an out-of-focus image seen through the viewfinder of a camera. As you adjust the range, the blurs are resolved and the image sharpens into focus. So with increasing age young clarets lose their edges and the wine's qualities come into balance—aroma, body, and flavor.

Tasting Practice No. 48

VERTICAL MÉDOCS   The wines of the Médoc can be approached in a way similar to those of Burgundy, either vertically or horizontally, or both. Once again the advantage of starting with a vertical tasting is that it allows you to become familiar with the most prominent characteristics of a single area. Then, having absorbed this first encounter, you can use it as a basis for later comparisons.

Select one of the five major communes of the Médoc for your Tasting Practice, e.g., Pauillac or St. Julien. Try to obtain a château-bottled wine from a sound harvest (classed growth), a bottle of commune wine with the A.C. guarantee, and, for purposes of comparison, a simple Bordeaux Rouge.

Open the commune wine and the château wine at least one hour before use and decant them. The Bordeaux Rouge bottle can be opened and decanted a mere fifteen minutes before you require it. Carry out a tasting of each wine on its own and then accompanied by a mild cheese and a light snack. Complete the Tasting Charts on each of the wines without consultation. Compare your assessments with those of your companions and then carry out a second tasting.

You will very likely find that the classed-growth wine is more appealing on all counts—a deeper, more lively color, fuller aroma, and deeper flavor. The commune wine will probably have similar characteristics, but in a lower key. Both of these bottles should contain a dry, well-flavored product. The Bordeaux Rouge bottle may or may not resemble the wines in the first two examples, depending on your good fortune.

The faults may include a weakness of flavor, traces of harshness, and a faint aroma. The Bordeaux Rouge may be a harsh wine on the heavy side. You may also detect a fair amount of sugar in it.

If in the course of this Tasting Practice you have been fortunate in your choice of the single-vineyard wine, you will need no urging to repeat the vertical exercise on three bottles from another Médoc commune.

Tasting Practice No. 49

HORIZONTAL REDS   This Tasting Practice introduces you to the similarities and differences found among the five great communes. With good fortune, you should be able to detect the underlying greatness common to all these areas and to notice at the same time the subtle variations among them. Choose one bottle from each of three communes for this tasting. Depending on the state of your pocket, obtain three A.C. commune wines or three single-vineyard (château) wines from a sound vintage. As in the previous tasting, you should be quite safe with any of the wines from 1952, 1953, 1955, 1957, 1959, 1960, 1961, 1962, 1964, 1966, 1967, 1969, or 1970. If you are able to afford single-vineyard wines, some interesting combinations include Léoville-Barton (St. Julien) coupled with Château Montrose (St. Estephe) and Château Lascombes (Margaux), or Château Gruaud-Larose (St. Julien) combined with Château Palmer (Cantenac) and Calon-Segur (St. Estephe). Another lovely trio could be based on Château Pontet-Canet (Pauillac) compared with Château Talbot (St. Julien) and Château Cantenac-Brown (Cantenac).

Decant the wines and leave them for at least one hour before use. Taste each of them carefully and in turn, making sure to pay adequate attention to the aroma before tasting the wine. Then carry out a second tasting accompanied by a mild cheese and then once again, accompanied by a snack. Complete Tasting Charts on each of the wines without consultation and then discuss your assessments with your companions before completing your second tastings.

The wines should all have a deep, rich color and a full, fruity aroma. They should be characterized by firmness and a smooth texture. They should all be deep-flavored and have a lasting aftertaste. They will be characterized by their unmistakable dryness.

The discernible differences will, of course, depend on the choices you have made. Broadly speaking, however, the Julien wines are particularly fruity, the Pauillac ones are full-bodied and powerful, the Margaux and Cantenac wines have a superb soft aroma and a delicate flavor, while those from St. Estephe are particularly dry, deeply flavored, and slightly on the coarse side.

Tasting Practice No. 50

THE PROCESS OF AGING In no other region of the world is the process of wine maturation quite so intriguing. Their hidden depths and their slow development over the years are in fact among the most interesting aspects of Médoc wines. Not only is the final product a smooth and rounded drink, but the unpredictability of the maturation process adds to the excitement of tasting these wines.

The simplest and most direct way to learn about the qualities of immature and mature Médoc wines is to carry out a comparative tasting. For this purpose obtain three bottles of wine produced at the same vineyard in different years, e.g., Château Talbot of 1955, 1959, and 1964. By preparing, decanting, and tasting these three examples on the same occasion you should be able to discern the differences and from these differences deduce something about the process of aging.

Decant your three wines at least an hour before starting the tasting. Carefully examine the color of each, then take a number of concentrated inhalations of the aroma, and finally carry out your tasting. After trying each of the wines unaccompanied, repeat the tasting with some mild cheese and then again with a snack, or preferably with a full meal.

Complete separate Tasting Charts on each of the wines without consultation. You will undoubtedly have a good deal to discuss when you compare your assessments. Thereafter, complete your second tasting.

In regard to color, you are likely to find that the oldest wine is the palest of the three examples and the youngest has the deepest red color. Depending on the age of each of your examples and also on the specific vineyards concerned, you may find that the oldest wine has a slightly brownish perimeter while the youngest wine may have a slightly purple tinge around the edges. You may also find that the aroma of the youngest wine does not have quite the same concentration as that of the two older examples. As to flavor, this again will depend on the exact ages and vineyards concerned, but if you have chosen wines of a high quality, it is probable that the older bottles will have a more penetrating flavor and more prolonged aftertaste.

Tasting Practice No. 51

BORDEAUX AND BURGUNDY   Now we come to one of those great comparisons, Bordeaux and Burgundy. Despite its foolishness, some people develop an exclusive taste for either Burgundy or Bordeaux wines. Yet each region produces its masterpieces and each region produces wines appropriate for particular occasions. The idea that you have to choose between Burgundy and Bordeaux is an unnecessary, self-imposed restriction which should be avoided. None of this means, however, that comparisons between these two great red wines are not fascinating —they are and have been to many people for many years.

For this Tasting Practice I suggest that you select the Burgundy red you most enjoyed in your Tasting Practices and match it with the most enjoyable claret you've encountered so far. For maximum pleasure you should select wines of comparable status and from successful vintages in each region. So, for example, you could choose a 1966 Burgundy commune wine to compare with a 1962 Bordeaux commune wine. Or at a more ambitious (and expensive) level, you might compare a single vineyard Burgundy from the 1964 vintage (e.g., Chambertin Clos de Beze) with a bottle of Château Léoville-Barton 1961. Another delightful possibility is a comparison between Le Musigny 1961, and Château Palmer 1953 or 1955. One could go on, literally for a lifetime.

Prepare the wines carefully by allowing them to stand in an upright position for at least twenty-four hours before use, at room temperature. Decant the wines at least one hour before use. Pay particular attention to the colors of the wines and inhale the aroma repeatedly. Then try tasting them and remember to concentrate. Try each of the wines unaccompanied, then with cheese and once more, with a snack. Complete separate Tasting Charts on each of the wines without consultation. I am sure that you will have a great deal to discuss before carrying out your second tastings.

The Burgundy will have a deeper color than the claret and a different and perhaps more concentrated aroma. The claret may reveal its characteristic aroma of blackcurrants. In regard to flavor, both examples should have considerable depth and prolonged aftertaste. They will very likely differ in the quality of dryness, with the claret being the drier of the two. Although both wines will almost certainly be smooth, the Burgundy may be just a bit more velvety as well as having a greater fullness of body. The claret may appear to be more austere.

CHAPTER TWELVE

Bordeaux—Graves, Pomerol, and St. Emilion

The wide distribution of the white, mostly dry, wines from the Graves region has tended to overshadow the excellent red wines from this area. The comparative obscurity of the red wines can be traced to the fact that on their labels and elsewhere their origin is given in terms of the local commune (e.g., Léognan) rather than the region—Graves. The white wines, however, are customarily described on the label as coming from Graves. Many of the best châteaux produce both red and white wine, which is convenient and also provides the basis for interesting explorations of their common characteristics. To anticipate a little, the white wines are predominantly dry but in the southernmost portion of the region bordering on the sweet-wine region of Sauternes, the Graves products have a touch of sweetness. The whites reach maturity quickly and are best consumed within a few years of bottling as they are short-lived. The red wines are strong, full-flavored, and can be exceedingly dry. They mature slowly and are long-lived. Like the Médoc reds, they are austere wines.

The grape varieties and the methods of wine production in the Médoc and in Graves are similar. Variations in the quality of the soil make a considerable difference to the final product and as Graves is particularly gravelly, its wines are even more dry than most of those in the Médoc—certainly more so than those of

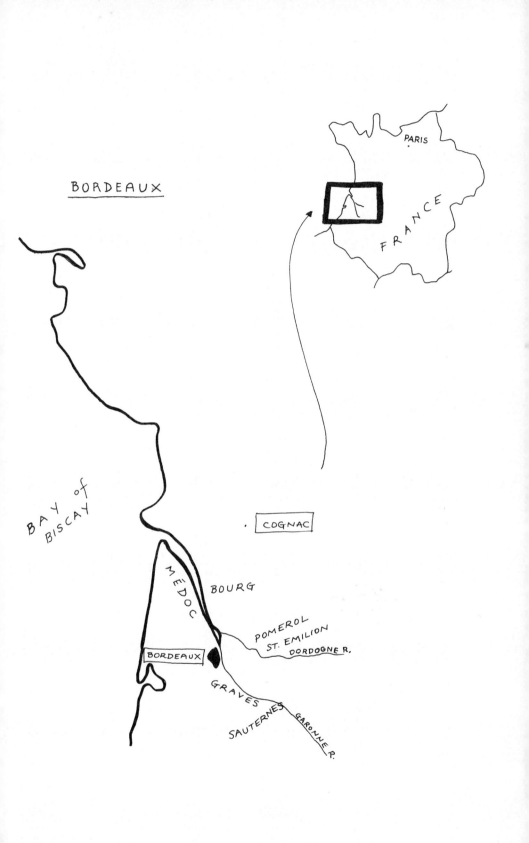

BORDEAUX

BAY of BISCAY

FRANCE

PARIS

· COGNAC

MÉDOC

BOURG

POMEROL
ST. EMILION
DORDOGNE R.

BORDEAUX

GRAVES

SAUTERNES

GARONNE R.

the northern Médoc group. They also have an earthy quality not always evident in Médoc wines. The differences between Graves and Médoc reds were aptly crystalized in a phrase quoted by Hugh Johnson in his admirable book, *Wine:* "The Médoc is to Graves as a glossy print is to the matte version of the same photograph." The Graves reds differ from that other important group of Bordeaux reds, Pomerol and St. Emilion, in a number of ways but perhaps the most important are these—the St. Emilion and Pomerol types are richer, fatter, and smoother.

The superior Graves wines, both red and white, were officially classified in the 1950s and underwent a minor revision in 1960. The official list is as follows:

CLASSIFIED GRAVES VINEYARDS

Léognan Commune:
Château Carbonnieux (*red and white*)
Château Malartic-Lagravière (*red and white*)
Château Olivier (*red and white*)
Château de Fieuzal (*red*)
Château Haut-Bailly (*red*)
Domaine de Chevalier (*red and white*)

Pessac Commune:
Château Haut-Brion (*red and white*)
Château La Mission-Haut-Brion (*red*)
Château Pape-Clement (*red*)

Martillac Commune:
Château Smith-Haut-Lafitte (*red and white*)
Château La Tour-Martillac (*white*)

Talence Commune:
Château La Tour-Haut-Brion (*white*)
Château Laville-Haut-Brion (*white*)

Villenave Commune:
Château Couhins (*white*)

Cadaujac Commune:
Château Bouscaut (*red and white*)

The leading vineyard of Graves is the famous Château Haut-Brion, at one time the property of Talleyrand and now owned by the former diplomat, Clarence Dillon. This attractive château and its vineyard are virtually in a suburb of the city of Bordeaux. The greatness of its red wines was recognized in 1855 and received the accolade of classification in Class I, along with Châteaux Latour, Margaux, and Lafite. Its red is a vigorous, long-lasting, and earthy wine with an attractive aroma. The white wine, developed in this century and marketed as Château Haut-Brion Blanc, has become one of the leading white wines of Bordeaux. Across the way from Château Haut-Brion is Château La Mission-Haut-Brion, of religious origins and now managed by Henri Woltner. The vineyard produces red wines of a differing character from Haut-Brion but superb of their kind and marked by an intensely fruity taste. Fine red wines are also produced at Château Haut-Bailly, Domaine de Chevalier, Château Bouscaut, and Château Pape-Clement. Château Olivier and Château Smith-Haut-Lafitte, both owned by the firm of Eschenauer, produce attractive red wines and vigorous, fresh white wines.

As mentioned earlier, the white wines from this area are labeled as coming from the region of Graves. Generic wines from this region are labeled "Graves" or "Graves Supérieur." The latter has a higher alcohol content. A.C. regulations are in operation in this region and the designation appears on the labels of all wines that meet A.C. standards. More white than red wine is produced and most of it is dry or very dry. The white wines are at their best when taken cold and with food, especially fish dishes.

These white wines provide one of the most interesting demonstrations of the important part that the vineyard plays in determining the properties of the final product. In both the northern and southern sections of Graves, the grape varieties used are the same—Semillon, Sauvignon, and small amounts of Muscadelle. Nevertheless, the northerly wines are considerably drier than the southerly ones. An even more emphatic difference exists between the dry white wines of northern and central Graves and the extremely sweet whites from Sauternes, the region on the southern border of Graves. The grape varieties used in Sauternes are the same as those used in Graves itself.

Tasting Practice No. 52

GRAVES WHITES   The important contribution made by the vine-yard soil can be illustrated by selecting a typical Graves white and a characteristic sweet Sauternes. Attempt to obtain single-vineyard wines from one of the châteaux given in the classified list shown on page 142 and compare it with a Sauternes bottle chosen from the list on page 155. As the Graves wines have a shorter life than those from Sauternes, be sure to use a bottle which is not more than five years of age and preferably younger than that. The Sauternes wines have a longer span and any single-vineyard example from the vintages of 1955, 1957, 1959, 1961, 1962, 1964, 1966, 1967, 1969, 1970, or 1971 will do. This practice can also be used to examine the differences between a generic or commune Graves and a single-vineyard example. In selecting a commune wine, attempt to find one which is of a recent vintage and insist on the A.C. label.

Chill all of the wines for at least an hour before opening. Taste each of them unaccompanied and then with a plain cracker. For the purposes of experimentation, attempt a third tasting accompanied by cheese, and a fourth accompanied by a snack containing fish. Complete separate Tasting Charts on each of the wines without consultation, and pay particular attention to the wine-food combination. Discuss your assessments and then carry out a second tasting.

The difference between the Graves and Sauternes wines should be obvious, the former dry and austere and the latter fat and sweet. They will probably differ in color as well, with the Sauternes showing a deeper yellow. You may well find that the Sauternes has a prolonged aftertaste. In regard to the wine-food combinations, note the effect of combining the sweet wines with fish; they can clash rather noisily. The same sweet wine accompanied by a light dessert or nonacidic fruit is a more comfortable fit. The Graves wine will probably be happiest with the fish snacks. Although they should share the same general characteristics, the single-vineyard and commune examples from Graves will probably differ in quality. Many of the commune wines are satisfactory, but they can suffer from the excessive use of sulfur or a lack of body. The thin examples sometimes come dangerously close to being on the sour side. The successful ones, however, provide a clean and refreshing drink at a reasonable price.

Tasting Practice No. 53

RED AND WHITE VINEYARDS   It is uncommon to find red and white wines produced in the same vineyard, but the combination can be found in the regions of Burgundy and Graves. The best example of this form of double success is unfortunately an expensive one—Château Haut-Brion (Red) and Blanc. Other examples that are available at more accessible prices include the vineyards of Bouscaut, Olivier, Carbonnieux, Domaine de Chevalier, and Château Smith-Haut-Lafitte. Your second two bottles should be a white and a red wine from the same commune but different vineyards. Remember also that the white wines should be drunk within a very few years of bottling whereas the reds require many bottle years to complete their development. Hence your red wine should be at least six years of age and preferably ten years if possible. Possible combinations are Château Olivier white of 1969 and red of 1962; or Château Bouscaut of 1970 (white) and 1962 (red). If you are unable to obtain a red and a white from the same vineyard, try a combination such as Château Haut-Bailly (red) and a white from Olivier or Couhins.

The white wine should be chilled for an hour or so before use and allowed to recover for a few minutes after uncorking. The red wine should be decanted approximately an hour before use. Taste each of the wines on their own and then accompanied by a plain cracker, a mild cheese, and a snack of meat or fish. Complete separate Tasting Charts on each of the wines without consultation, then discuss your assessments, and carry out your second tastings.

The most obvious similarity of red and white Graves wines is the quality of dryness. The red wines generally have more body than their white counterparts and a more persistent after-taste. As in the previous Tasting Practice, the wine-food combinations should prove interesting. On the whole, the red wines clash with fish dishes and the white wines combine well with them.

ST. EMILION AND POMEROL   St. Emilion is a hilltop town overlooking the Dordogne valley, some forty miles to the east of the city of Bordeaux. It is one of the most attractive of the wine towns and its narrow streets are ideal for loitering. Among the more interesting sights is an antique church which was carved out of the soft rock. It is a small area, less than two square miles, but it contains more than 150 châteaux all cultivating intensely.

The predominant grape used in St. Emilion is Merlot and the chief Médoc grapes (Cabernet) have a supplementary role. The wines are soft, rich, and smooth—a reflection of the comparatively rich soil and the prolific Merlot grapes. They are of an early ripening type, which can be an advantage, but this is offset by the fact that they are more fragile than the Cabernet varieties.

The St. Emilion wines are dark red with plenty of body and a full, rich flavor. They are marked by fruitiness, softness, and a warm flavor. They reach maturity within three to fifteen years of bottling and decline earlier than Médoc wines.

It is often said, with some point, that the St. Emilion wines can be described as lying midway between the Médoc wines and those of Burgundy. In my opinion, however, it is more enlightening to make a direct comparison between St. Emilion and Médoc. They have a less obvious aroma and are heavier and darker than most Médocs. They are also softer, richer, and more robust. For their part, the Médoc wines have more tannin, greater concentration, and a drier flavor. They are slower to mature than the St. Emilion wines and decline at a slower pace.

In 1953 the major vineyards of the St. Emilion area were given official classification. Two wines, those from Château Ausone and Château Cheval Blanc, were given the title of "super grand first class." Immediately below them there are nine vineyards classified as plain ordinary "grand first class." Then there are over sixty grouped into the "grand class." In the list below I have shown all of the "grand first class" vineyards and a selection of plain "grand class" sites, chosen predominantly on the basis of personal experience.

ST. EMILION
1955 Official Classification
(All names prefixed by "Château" unless otherwise stated)

PREMIER GRAND CLASS

Ausone
Beausejour-Duffau-Lagarosse
Beausejour-Fagouet
Belair
Canon
Cheval Blanc
Figeac
Clos Fourtet
Gaffelière-Naudes
Magdelaine
Pavie
Trottevieille

GRAND CLASS *(a selection)*

Bellevue	Fonplegade
Bergat	Fonroque
Cadet-Bon	Franc-Mayne
Cadet-Piolat	Grand-Corbin
Canon-la-Gaffelière	Grand-Mayne
Cap de Mourlin	Grand-Pontet
Chapelle Madeleine	Clos des Jacobins
Chatelet	Jean Faure
Chauvin	La Carte
Corbin (Giraud)	de Clotte
Corbin-Michotte	Larmande
Croque-Michotte	Laroze

St. Emilion (*continued*)

La Tour-Figeac	Ripeau
La Tour-du-Pin-Figeac	Clos St. Martin
Clos la Madeleine	Sansonnet
Le Couvent	Soutard
Mauvezin	Trimoulet
Moulin-du-Cadet	Trois-Moulins
Pavie-Decesse	Troplong-Mondot
Pavie-Macquin	Villemaurine
Pavillon-Cadet	

Of the two top-graded wines, Cheval Blanc is the more highly regarded. If market value were the sole criterion of a great wine, then Cheval Blanc is certainly one of them for its price is comparable to prices of the five great Médoc wines. I have found Cheval Blanc reliably and consistently superb while on occasions Ausone is a disappointing drink. The châteaux of Belair and La Gaffelière are almost always successful and occasionally supremely successful. In fact, the same can be said of most of the St. Emilion wines which fall into the "grand class." They can be relied upon to have a rich, full flavor, softness, and to transmit a feeling of deep fruitiness. The unsuccessful bottles rarely have even a trace of unpleasantness in them; rather, they suffer from the absence of emphasis—dull wines tending to flabbiness. I must admit that I would find it exceedingly difficult to distinguish between the wines of the "grand class" as opposed to those of the "grand first class," with the possible exception of Cheval Blanc itself.

The combination of soft quality and rich flavor is a good basis for popularity and when one adds the absence of harshness or rough edges, you have the makings of a wine with wide appeal. St. Emilions are worth considering if you are planning to have guests whose wine tastes are unknown to you. Although you may not strike a chord, most people will find the wines completely agreeable. Many people prefer St. Emilion wines to Médoc or Burgundy reds.

Tasting Practice No. 54

RICH, SOFT ST. EMILION   This Tasting Practice serves as an introduction to a large group of consistently satisfying full red wines which occasionally reach great peaks. As they are, like all Bordeaux reds, essentially wines to be drunk with food, it may be best on this occasion to combine the Tasting Practice with more serious eating. If, however, you prefer to confine the Tasting Practice to sniffs, sips, and snacks, then please do so. Select two bottles of classified wines of a good vintage from the list given. You should be quite safe in selecting wines from 1959, 1961, 1962, 1964, 1966, 1967, 1969, 1970, or 1971. They are wines which need decanting, so be sure to prepare them at least an hour before use. Carry out the usual unaccompanied tasting before combining the wine with cheese and then with a meat snack. If you plan to taste these wines, as recommended, during the course of a meal, then you will find that they combine best with meat dishes ranging from poultry to beef. Keep enough wine in reserve to drink with cheese, as the combination can be tremendous.

Complete separate Tasting Charts for each of the wines, first without consultation and then again after you have discussed your initial assessments.

With a fortunate selection you should be drinking soft, rich dark-red wines with a warm and fruity flavor. At their best they are full of body and extremely smooth; the aftertaste should persist for some time.

If you have been unlucky, about the worst that can happen is disappointment. The wines may be dull and/or flabby, have little or no aroma, and a transient aftertaste. If after tasting the wines you find this paragraph inexplicable, I have achieved my aim.

POMEROL   Pomerol is a small area adjacent to St. Emilion and its wines are similarly smooth and rich. They bear a close resemblance to some of the St. Emilion wines, most particularly those on the border between the two areas, such as Cheval Blanc. It is an area even smaller than St. Emilion but equally intensively cultivated. The soil is more gravelly and less rich than that of the greater part of the St. Emilion area. Consequently, the St. Emilion wines on its eastern border (i.e., those farthest from Pomerol soil) are more dissimilar than the border châteaux already mentioned. The wines are reasonably quick to mature and are best drunk within six to fourteen years of bottling. They can, however, last for a longer time, particularly the products of the greatest vineyards. Just as it is inevitable to compare the wines of St. Emilion with those of the Médoc, so it is unavoidable to examine Pomerol wines with those of St. Emilion itself. Although they share many character-istics, such as smooth richness and deep flavor, the Pomerols tend to be somewhat fatter (i.e., contain more glycerine) and to have a clearer aroma than their neighbors. The Pomerols differ from the Médocs in their softness, relative absence of dryness, shorter aftertaste, and less intense aroma. The wines are more gentle than those of the Médoc.

The multitude of small vineyards in Pomerol seem to invite categorization. It is universally recognized that the wines of Château Petrus are the most outstanding, and indeed on a par with, if not superior to, the greats of Médoc itself. There are a number of unofficial classifications and from these I have selected a dozen or so wines which in my experience maintain a high and consistent quality.

Château Beauregard	Château Certan-Giraud	Château Gazin
Château La Croix	Château Lagrange	Château Lafleur
Château Nenin	Château Petit-Village	Château Rouget
Château Trotanoy	Vieux-Château-Certan	Château Petrus

Tasting Practice No. 55

FOUR SUPERB REDS For this Tasting Practice compare four superb red wines, one each from the districts of Pomerol, St. Emilion, Médoc, and Burgundy. For the last two areas, select two half-bottles from previous tastings which were particu-larly successful for you. Then add to them one half-bottle from each of the St. Emilion and Pomerol lists of classified wines. Try to get wines from sound vintages in order to obtain the most from this particularly grand occasion.

Decant all of the wines at least one hour before use and taste them unaccompanied and then with cheese and a snack. Complete Tasting Charts on each of the wines without discussion and then once more, after carrying out your second tasting.

————————

The Pomerol and St. Emilion wines may in certain respects lie midway between the Médoc and the Burgundy—they may display the darker color and fullness of body coupled with a rich smoothness that typify fine Burgundy. On the other hand, their resemblance to the Médoc wines can be seen in the comparative absence of sweetness, their aroma, and the firmness contributed by the tannin.

In recognition of the fact that you have examples from four of the greatest red-wine-producing areas of the world, you may care to devote a great deal of attention and concentration to this tasting. It would be disappointing if you did not find in at least one of these examples a wine capable of driving you to lyricism.

Perhaps this is the moment to admit my personal preference for red wines, an admission which may by this time be redundant. While there are many delightful white wines, full of fruit or delicacy or fragrance or all of these things, they can by their nature never contain the zip which elevates red wines to a superior plane. Unlike the reds, white wines are not fortified by a long period in contact with the skins, stalks, seeds, and flesh of the grapes. They have a simpler constitution and as a result, less complexity of flavor or subtlety. Lastly, and this is significant, the white wines lack the robustness and body of the reds.

SOME SMALLER BORDEAUX WINES In addition to the major wines already described, Bordeaux produces large quantities of lesser but perfectly serviceable red and white wines. Among the reds, those from Fronsac and Bourg are the most noteworthy. The Fronsac wines are similar in character to those of St. Emilion but of lower quality. Their reasonable price makes them good candidates for everyday drinking. The Bourg wines are coarser, but fully flavored. For those people, predominantly men in my experience, who prefer gutsy wines, Bourg products may be on target. The slight draw-back to their strong flavor and their robust constitution is a tendency to harshness, with rough edges that become plain im-mediately after swallowing the wine.

Among the white wines those from Entre-Deux-Mers, between the Garonne and Dordogne rivers, are readily available everyday white wines of a medium-dry type. They are undistinguished but welcome, inexpensive thirst quenchers.

VINTAGES   The importance of climatic conditions in Bordeaux coupled with the fact that the most outstanding wines are slow to mature makes some knowledge of the successful vintages of recent times compulsory. In the most successful years the wines are well balanced, aromatic, and well flavored. In fair years all of these attributes are affected and the wines are on the weak side although still satisfactory. In poor or bad years the vintage may be a complete write-off or suitable only for the production of carafe wines.

CHAPTER THIRTEEN

Sweet White Bordeaux

The wine producers of the Sauternes region, some miles south of the city of Bordeaux, produce superb sweet white wines. Regrettably the reputation of the wines, especially that of Sauternes itself, has been harmed by the widespread distribution of sickly sweet imitations, some strongly reminiscent of cough syrup. One or two nasty experiences can produce lifelong abstinence. If nothing else, I hope that the Tasting Practices in this chapter will help to dispel the belief that sweet Bordeaux wines are cloying. If you are a lover of sweet wines, Sauternes is a treasure house. Even if you prefer dry white wines, a tasting of fine quality Sauternes is decidedly worthwhile. At the least you will be impressed by their concentrated aroma, smoothness, and depth of flavor. They are so far superior to ordinary sweet wines that, when one meets them for the first time, it can be a startling experience.

The Russians had a passion for the wines of Sauternes, and there are many stirring stories about the lengths to which they would go in order to ensure a steady supply. In 1859, Grand Duke Constantine of Russia paid a record sum of rubles for 240 cases of Château d'Yquem wine and reputedly dispatched an armed guard to convey it safely from Bordeaux to St. Petersburg.

In order to produce sweet wine, it is necessary to reduce the proportion of water in the grapes and concentrate the sugar. This is achieved by allowing the grapes to dry in the sun (some of the

water content evaporates) or, as is more common in producing
the great wines, by leaving the grapes on the vines until they turn
overripe. They are attacked by a fungus the name of which trans-
lates from the French as "noble rot" (*pourriture noble,* or in the
German, *Edelfaule*). The fungus cracks the grape skins and ab-
sorbs some of the water content, thereby increasing the proportion of sugar. The shriveled grapes are then turned into a concentrated, luscious sweet wine.

This method of wine-making, used in Germany and Austria
as well as France, involves greater risks by virtue of the delay in
collecting the harvest. It also requires far more labor as the pickers
have to select only those grapes which are overripe, and neces-
sitates numerous sweeps of the vineyards. The whole process of
harvesting can take up to two months to complete. Moreover, as
the water content in the grapes is reduced, the overall yield in
wine is small. For these reasons, the wines prepared in this difficult
and trying manner are on the expensive side—but it should be
noted that the French examples, with the exception of one vineyard, are considerably less expensive than the great German sweet
wines.

Within the region of Sauternes there are five wine-producing
communes of importance: Barsac, Preignac, Bommes, Fargues, and
Sauternes itself. The commune of Barsac was given the right to use
its own A.C. designation—hence the quality wines from this area
can be described as originating from the communes of Barsac or
Sauternes. The remaining three communes do not have their own
designation and are marketed under the label of Sauternes. In the
great classification completed in 1855, one vineyard—Château
d'Yquem—was awarded the title of "first great growth." Eleven
vineyards were classified as "first growths" and the twelve others
were classed as "second growths." Among them, these classified
vineyards produce one-quarter of the total sweet-wine output of
Sauternes. If the wine from a particular vintage or particular vineyard fails to meet the minimum requirements laid down by the
state board, then that parcel of wine can be downgraded or de-
classified. The wine produced by the minor vineyards and estates
is sold as Sauternes A.C. or plain Sauternes. Among the better

vineyards are the quaintly named Cru Junka and Château de Clotte, not to mention the ubiquitous Bel-Air. The wines are usually the product of a blending of three grape varieties, namely, Semillon, Sauvignon Blanc, and Muscadelle. Although the proportions vary from vineyard to vineyard the predominant ratio is in the order of six parts Semillon to three parts Sauvignon to one part Muscadelle. The Semillon (a corruption of St. Emilion?) produces full, smooth wines, while the Sauvignon is relied upon to provide the necessary fruity acidity, without which the wines would lack balance. The full list of classified vineyards of Sauternes and Barsac follows:

CLASSIFIED VINEYARDS OF SAUTERNES REGION
(1855 Classification)
(*Commune names in parentheses*)

PREMIER GRAND CRU
Château d'Yquem (Sauternes)

PREMIER CRUS

Château La Tour-Blanche
(Bommes)

Château Coutet (Barsac)

Château Lafaurie-Peyraguey
(Bommes)

Château Climens (Barsac)

Clos Haut-Peyraguey
(Bommes)

Château Guiraud (Sauternes)

Château de Rayne-Vigneau
(Bommes)

Château Rieussec (Fargues)

Château de Suduiraut
(Preignac)

Château Rabaud-Promis
(Bommes)
Château Rabaud-Sigalas
(Bommes)

DEUXIÈMES CRUS

Château Myrat (Barsac)
Château Doisy-Daene (Barsac)
Château Doisy-Vedrines
(Barsac)
Château d'Arche (Sauternes)
Château Filhot (Sauternes)
Château Boustet (Barsac)

Château Nairac (Barsac)
Château Caillou (Barsac)
Château Suau (Barsac)

Château de Malle (Preignac)
Château Romer (Fargues)
Château Lamothe (Sauternes)

The sweet wine from the legendary Château d'Yquem (pronounced "ee-kem") is the undisputed prize of French output. Since 1855 it has been recognized as a wine which is literally "in a class of its own." It has an intensity of smell and depth of flavor which are unique. For many the aroma reminds them of honey and in this and in other Sauternes wines one may detect a taste of almonds. The sweetness is soft and rich without being in the least cloying. The high alcohol content and fullness of the wine ensure that a single glassful is satisfying and the taste lingers on the palate for hours. It is yellow in youth, turns a heavy golden color in maturity, and then browns in old age. The wine adheres to the side of the glass and subsides slowly and heavily as a result of its high glycerine content. Yquem and the others of its type are best drunk on their own and preferably after a meal as one might enjoy a liqueur. (This is not a universal opinion; there are many who enjoy Sauternes with their meals.) Like all the Sauternes, Château d'Yquem should be chilled. Most people prefer to drink it sparingly—and not only because of its price.

The château and its vineyards have been owned by the Lur Saluces family for nearly 200 years. The turreted buildings, superbly kept vines, and traditional wooden wine-making equipment have helped to make Château d'Yquem one of the most frequently visited sites in Bordeaux. Visits are easy to arrange (see Chapter Twenty).

The exceptional vineyards in the Sauternes, including such prominent names as Château Guiraud, Château Filhot, and Château Rieussec, all sell at prices well below Château d'Yquem and are therefore especially good value. These wines easily last for more than ten years in the bottle and some can survive for as long as fifty years. After opening, the wines can be kept corked in the refrigerator for up to four days. Château Guiraud can produce extraordinarily fine wines, but sometimes they have a tendency to be a little on the heavy side. My personal recollection of this wine is colored by a wine-tasting which took place a few years ago. It had been organized for a community which ordinarily drank comparatively little wine, but during the tasting, exhibit number 33 had to be continually replenished. It was, of course,

Château Guiraud and proved to be so popular that twice as many bottles of this wine were drunk as its nearest competitor, a pleasing Beaujolais.

The neighboring commune of Barsac produces wines whose fame is exceeded only by that of Château d'Yquem itself. The vineyards of Château Climens and Château Coutet are especially well known and with good reason—their wines are always superior and sometimes superb. Barsac wines are a shade less heavy and less sweet than many of the products from the Sauternes commune. They are also inclined to be more delicate and perhaps less obvious than Sauternes wines. Two of the eleven first growths are Barsac wines and seven of the twelve second growths. For quietly sipping during a long, relaxed evening they can scarcely be bettered.

The great misfortune of these superb wines is that for many people they seem to blend with relatively few foods and as a result they are underused and undervalued. They do combine well with desserts, but nowadays fewer and fewer people eat desserts except at formal meals. The wines also combine satisfactorily with non-acidic fruits. For my taste, however, they are at their best sipped as one would an after-dinner liqueur. With the decline in demand for their wine, it would be understandable if the *vignerons* of Sauternes dreamily yearn for a return of the Romanoffs.

Tasting Practice No. 56

TRUE SAUTERNES The major aim of all three tastings in this region is to acquaint you with the remarkable qualities of true Sauternes. In addition, it is worthwhile making comparisons between the communes of this region and finally pitting a French pair against a German pair.

In preparing and carrying out these three tastings, remember that high-quality sweet wines of this type will last for several days after opening if you are careful to replace the cork and keep them chilled. This is important to bear in mind because you may well find that not all of the wine obtained for the tasting will be used.

For the first Tasting Practice go up the scale—from the common Sauternes bottle which does not carry an A.C. guar-

antee to a Sauternes regional wine which has the A.C. guarantee on the label, then to a single-vineyard wine. For this
last selection obtain one from the list of classified vineyards
on page 155. If you are fortunate enough to be able to afford
a bottle of Château d'Yquem, include it. Otherwise, you will find
that one of the first- or second-growth wines can be obtained
at a comparatively reasonable price. In either event, when you
make your purchase make sure that the wine does not have a
brownish tinge (this indicates aging). Lastly, in order to emphasize the sweetness of these wines, select a sound bottle of
dry white wine from the neighboring region of Graves. Try
to obtain a single-vineyard wine from a recent vintage, or, failing that, one which has an A.C. label and is not more than five
years old.

Chill all of the wines for at least an hour before use and give
them a minute or two to recover after uncorking them. Taste
each wine in turn, paying particular attention to the aroma,
which can be one of the most compelling features of these wines.
Then taste each one accompanied by a nonacidic fruit or a nonacidic dessert. Complete separate Tasting Charts on each wine
without consulting your companions. Then compare your experiences and carry out a second tasting as usual.

The single-vineyard Sauternes should show the best features
of these wines—a clear golden color, rich, penetrating aroma,
and a deep, sweet, smooth flavor. The aftertaste should be prolonged and full. As you go down the scale from the single-vineyard wine to the regional wine and finally the nonguaranteed
bottle, these qualities may fade. If you have been unlucky in
your choice of these minor wines, you may find some unpleasant
qualities. They may be cloying, heavy, sulfurous, metallic,
brown, or musty. The Graves wine should be characteristically
dry and will serve to emphasize the sweetness of the Sauternes
bottles.

Tasting Practice No. 57

SAUTERNES AND BARSAC Select a regional example of Sauternes
and one from Barsac, making sure that both bottles have the

A.C. guarantee on their labels. Then add two single-vineyard wines, one from Barsac and one from Sauternes, using the list of classified growths as your guide. Try to ensure that both of these bottles are from the same vintage and preferably between four and ten years old.

As in the previous tasting, chill the bottles for an hour before use and allow them a minute or two to recover after uncorking them. Taste each wine on its own and then accompanied by a light dessert or nonacidic fruit. Complete Tasting Charts on each of the wines, discuss your assessments, and then carry out a second tasting.

The differences between the Sauternes and Barsac wines, which should be clearest in the single-vineyard wines, may include the following: The Sauternes may be more yellow and more clinging on the side of the glass. Differences in aroma may be slight. The two wines may differ in body, with the Barsac being the lighter of the two. In regard to flavor, the Sauternes may be deeper and it is almost certainly going to be sweeter. Both wines will in all probability be smooth and fully flavored. It is unlikely that they will differ much in duration of aftertaste.

Tasting Practice No. 58

FRENCH AND GERMAN   You are now in a position to indulge in a time-honored tasting comparison. Discussions of the relative merits of French and German sweet white wines have continued for more than a century both in print and verbally. The debate rarely becomes heated and it cannot, of course, by its very nature, be resolved. It should not be thought, however, that the impossibility of a resolution detracts from the pleasures of the exercise. Before you undertake the great comparison, it might be fun to predict among the members of your group which of the two varieties each will prefer.

For the French representatives, choose two single-vineyard wines from one of the sound vintages mentioned earlier. If in your previous Tasting Practices you have encountered a Sauternes which gave you particular pleasure, then enter it as at least one of the competitors. If in the course of the previous Tasting Practices you came across *two* Sauternes which pleased you, then enter both of them. For the German representatives you might consider relying on your previously completed Tasting Charts from Chapters Four, Five, and Six. If these charts are no longer available, try to rely on your memory of one or more German sweet wines which appealed to you. You may also find it helpful to refer back to these chapters before embarking on this present tasting. My own choice would be a fine example from the Rheingau and another from the Mosel region. In your selections choose wines classified as *Auslese* or *Beerenauslese* or, better yet, *Trockenbeerenauslese.*

Chill the wines for approximately an hour before opening and remember to allow a few minutes for the wines to recover after uncorking them. Prepare the table, glasses, and snack plates with due ceremony.

Pour not more than a third of a glassful of each example, swirl it gently in the glass, and take several deep inhalations with your nose close to the rim of the glass. Repeat this a few times, allowing yourself rest pauses between inhalations. As the aroma of these wines is one of their most appealing attributes, do not be in too much of a hurry to pass on to the tasting stage. When you do finally start tasting, try it unaccompanied by any distracting food. Then when you feel that you have begun to appreciate each wine's qualities, try tasting accompanied by a plain cracker and/or nonacidic fruit or a mild dessert. Complete separate Tasting Charts on each wine without consultation. Then discuss your assessments with your companions and carry out your second tasting. Thereafter, sit back and enjoy the remainder of the wine while taking care not to be led into a state of impaired consciousness by their sweetly concealed high alcohol level.

The French examples will probably have more yellow in them. They may also have a heavy appearance, that is, they will cling to the glass more obviously. Depending on your particular choices, the aroma from the German wines may be characteristic of the Riesling discussed in Chapter Six, or of the spicy Traminer (Chapter Seven). The French examples should display a penetrating honeyish aroma. In the tasting, the French examples will be heavier in body, but all four examples should be smooth and easy to drink. The French examples may be richer and sweeter and followed by a more enduring aftertaste. The delicacy of the Mosel example may be in the same relation to the Rheingau wine as the Barsac is to the Sauternes. Assuming that you have a liking for sweet wines and that you have been fortunate in your selections, this Tasting Practice may be an occasion to remember.

CHAPTER FOURTEEN

Diversions

Discussions of wine and formal tastings occasionally lapse into solemnity. As an antidote I suggest that you examine the curious possibilities contained in the names of wines and vineyards, particularly those of the Bordeaux area. It requires self-discipline to maintain a solemn air in discussing the qualities of wines from, say, the vineyard of Cru Junka in the Sauternes or Château de Clotte (St. Emilion). Wines from a minor vineyard in Bas Médoc called Château La Gore might provide a fitting accompaniment to rare steak. From the same area you can get wines which carry the vineyard label of Cru de Bert, which might cause some perplexity if you asked for it in a wineshop—particularly if you run the first two words together. You may be tempted to order a bottle of Château de Bastard (Sauternes area), but can you present it to someone as a gift? You'd be better off to buy the comfortable-sounding Sauternes called Cru Camelong.

Famous proprietors include Talleyrand, who at one time owned Château Haut-Brion, now the property of former diplomat Clarence Dillon. Talleyrand's adversary at the Congress of Vienna, Metternich, owned the splendid Rheingau vineyard of Schloss Johannisberg, which remains in his family to this day. Charlemagne owned substantial vineyards in Burgundy, one of which retains his name, Corton-Charlemagne. Montesquieu owned a magnificent château in the area of Graves which is still maintained in fine condition. This Château de La Brede produces a small amount of dry white wine, but it is difficult to come by except in the region itself. Also in this region is the vineyard named after Pope Clement and bearing his name—Château Pape-Clement. It was planted by the Bishop of Bordeaux, who initiated the vineyard before he left for Avignon as Pope Clement. It is a full, dry red wine of high quality. In St. Emilion, the vineyard of the Roman poet Ausonius bears his name, Château Ausone. With Cheval Blanc, Ausone is the leading vineyard of this area.

For many centuries European viticulture was a major occupation of religious orders. Among the more famous vineyards which still carry religious names are Clos Vougeot, an outstanding Burgundian vineyard planted by the Cistercian order of monks and enclosed by a tall and extensive wall. The same order was responsible for a similar walled vineyard in the Rheingau area where wines are still produced, under the name of Steinberg. Pope Clement has already been mentioned and near Avignon he left his mark with the wine known as Châteauneuf du Pape, a strong and long-lasting red wine. Near the enclosure of Vougeot in Burgundy, an order of nuns established their own vineyard, which goes by the name of Clos de Tart. The vineyards no longer have any religious connection but continue to produce fine Burgundy reds. In Italy large numbers of wines have religious names and connections. One of the most striking is the medium-sweet to medium-dry white wine produced near Vesuvius, called Lacrima Christi. The curious-sounding name of Est! Est! Est! describes a white wine from an area near Rome which derived its label from an incident in the twelfth century when a German bishop instructed his servant to precede him on his travels and mark those places which served good wine by chalking up the sign *"Est!"*— "It is"—a sort of primitive Guide Michelin for wines. The servant appears to have been elevated by the white wines from near Lake Bolsena and marked his approval by the words which now describe the wine—"Est! Est! Est!"

If you wish to organize a tasting of religious wines, consider this combination: Start off with a bottle of Steinberg from the

Rheingau, closely followed by some Pape-Clement, and conclude all with a bottle from Clos Vougeot. You might also care to try a tasting consisting of "animal wines": Start with a bottle of Schwarze Katze ("Black Cat"—a light white wine from Mosel), followed by the strong and not refined red wine from Hungary which goes by the name of Bull's Blood, and finish it off with some Tiger's Milk, a sweet white wine from Yugoslavia.

A medical evening? Will Asprino, a dry white wine from Naples, help? If not, try some Montonico, a dessert wine from southern Italy. Twice daily, by glass or teaspoonful. Either or both of these whites might be necessary after overindulging in the Calabrian red called Primitivo. These lesser Italian wines are virtually unobtainable outside their local regions; otherwise it might be entertaining to pair the sweet Sardinian wine called Monica with sophisticated Gloria, a superior French château wine. Split Grk is a light white Yugoslavian wine produced near the town of Split—quite true!

For the record only, you may be interested to know that the Chinese produce a considerable variety of wines, predominantly but not exclusively for medicinal purposes. Some of the more extravagant examples include snake wine, which *does* contain some of that reptile. Usually the presence of the reptile can only be detected from the description on the label or by playing on a flute, but in some bottles parts of the snake are left to float in the wine. In the case of lizard wine, these smaller reptiles are frequently displayed floating in the contents of the bottle. On the only occasion when I tasted one of the Chinese herbal (but non-reptilian) wines I found it to be fortified by alcohol and closer to a bottle of spirits than to grape wine. I understand, however, that wine fermented from grape juice is produced in China.

Visitors to Greece will find that they have a large selection of red and white wines, both dry and sweet. But you should be forewarned that most of the Greek wines contain resin, which was originally put in as a preservative but finally became an accepted and desirable part of the flavor of home-consumed wines in Greece. For people unaccustomed to these wines with *retsina,* it comes close to being repellent. If you do visit Greece, you might be tempted to have a go at it.

Perhaps it is inevitable that in an area as replete with vineyards as Bordeaux, there should be duplication of names—much as Britain is crammed with pubs by the name of "The Red Lion," "The Green Man," "The King's Arms," and the like. So it is that in Bordeaux I have been able to find no fewer than thirteen vineyards which go by the name of Bel-Air. They are found in the following areas of Bordeaux:

Loupiac	Cerons	Pomerol (two)
Preignac	Graves (three)	St. Emilion (three)
St. Estephe	St. Croix-du-Mont	

As to Château Bellevue, I was able to track down no fewer than fifteen vineyards which bear this name or a slight variation on it.

Finally, you might wish on one occasion to organize a tasting for Ladies' Night. If you do, you might consider choosing the wines from Clos de Tart (Burgundy red, founded by nuns), Château Montrose (owned by Madame Charmolue), or from her neighbor, Madame Audoy, who owns Château Cos Labory—both in the commune of St. Estephe in the Médoc. Two sweet white wines from Sauternes owned by women are Château Broustet (Madame Fourney) and Château Filhot (owned by the sister of the Marquis who possesses Château d'Yquem). If you add Château Gloria, it will be for its name alone—it is owned by Monsieur Martin and produces dry reds. The champagne trade has a strong feminine influence and widows have been particulary prominent. You might care to cap your evening by indulging in a bottle of chilled Veuve Cliquot.

CHAPTER FIFTEEN

Italian Wines

Italy and France between them produce nearly half of the world's wine. With some exceptions, Italian growers knowingly sacrifice quality for quantity. Only a small proportion of their wines fall into the category of "fine wines."

Italians consume most of their own wine. It is as much a part of the daily diet as bread and is treated with as little ceremony. For example, most red wines are taken with liberal dashes of water —a sensible mixture if you are drinking coarse, robust reds.

The vines are seen everywhere, but rarely in the imposing isolation of German or French fields. They are mixed in with vegetable crops, olive trees, orchards, and arbors. Most aspects of Italian viticulture, from the disarray in the fields to the confusion of the 700 and more wine titles, are in a state of happy anarchy. The wines are described by place name, grape variety (well over one hundred of these!), or invented names. Since most of them are of interest only to travelers in Italy, this chapter is confined to a discussion of a selected group of superior Italian wines.

Most of the superior wines are produced in the northern, more temperate regions of the country—Lombardy, Piedmont, Tuscany, and Veneto. They tend to be dry wines of robust constitution. Farther south the major wines are sweet dessert types. Although the introduction of wine laws in 1963 helped to reduce the chaos, the rules and controls cover only a small amount of the total production. Nevertheless, bottles displaying labels with the word *"Denominazioni di Origine Controllata"* (D.O.C.) are guaranteed to be authentic as to origin and to have met the standards prescribed by the National Board of Control. Although they are a far better bet than bottles without the D.O.C. sign, the fundamental unpredictability of Italian wines has not changed substantially. Variations in quality, especially in wines outside of D.O.C. control, are extremely wide. The best products are fully flavored, gutsy wines and the worst are harsh, bitter, and unpleasant. Few Italian wines emit a significant aroma and numbers of them leave a not unpleasant bitter aftertaste. But in a country with such a lavish supply of natural and created beauty, the unpredictability of its wines can be excused.

Chianti

The fame and popularity of Chianti has tended to overshadow all other Italian wines. As white Chianti is insignificant both in quality and in quantity, for present purposes "Chianti" will be taken to mean the warm red wines produced in the large designated area between Florence and Siena. They are blended from a mixture of four grape varieties: Sangiovese (roughly three-quarters of the whole), Canaiolo (roughly one-fifth of the total), and small quantities of Malvesia and Trebbiano. A great deal of wine is produced in this extensive area and most of it derives from large estates. Like their German counterparts, the remnants of the Italian aristocracy devote a good deal of their attention to cultivation of vineyards and in this Tuscany area they are almost as common as in the Rheingau.

There are two main types of Chianti, young and old. The former are customarily marketed in their characteristic wicker-blanketed bottles while the mature Chiantis are usually sold in bottles with shoulders, as in Bordeaux. These older wines are referred to as *"reserva* wines." Here as in other parts of Italy this indicates that the wine is at least three, four, or five years of age depending on the descriptive system used in the particular area

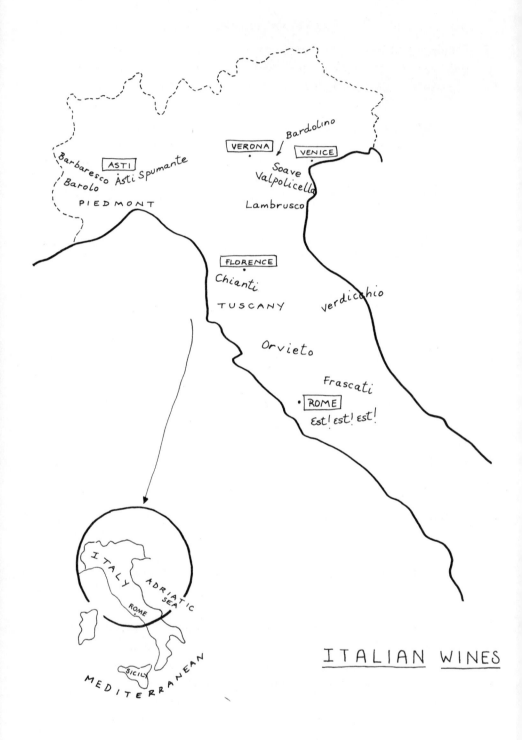

ITALIAN WINES

concerned. Within the delimited area of Chianti there are further divisions, the most important of which is the Chianti Classico area. These wines, which are generally of the mature and superior type, can be identified by the black cockerel shown on the label. They have to reach a minimum alcohol level of twelve percent. In addition to this most prominent of all subdivisions, there are eight other, smaller areas worth mentioning. Each of them is preceded by the title "Chianti": Raetini, Empolesi, d'Elsa, Fiorentini, Pisane, Senesi, Pistoiese, and Rufina (to be distinguished from the commercial firm of Ruffino).

True Chiantis are among the few Italian wines which emit a discernible aroma, of a flowery nature and sometimes likened to violets, although this is not an experience I can corroborate. They are strong and fully flavored wines of deep-red color. Many of the younger wines have a prickly, refreshing quality and can even be drunk on their own. The mature bottles are undoubtedly at their best when accompanying food—they are particularly enjoyable with flavored cheeses. For my tastes, the younger wine in the wicker basket, which incidentally goes by the name of *fiasco* (flask), is best appreciated at the lunch table. The *fiasco* invites one to have a swig at the bottle, but it looks a great deal easier to do than turns out to be the case. It is a trick you might prefer to attempt when wearing overalls or your neighbor's jacket. As with all the other young wines referred to earlier in this book, the Chianti youngsters tend to lose their most attractive and refreshing qualities after some years. Hence it is desirable to select bottles with recent dates on the labels. The awkward *fiasco* shapes preclude long-term storage, as wine bottles should be stored horizontally—in order to keep the corks wet and hence avoid shrinkage.

Tasting Practice No. 59

YOUNG AND MATURE CHIANTIS   As an introduction to this most popular of all Italian wines, start with an examination of the similarities and differences between young and old wines. Depending on the number of people involved, obtain one or two examples of both young and mature Chiantis. The mature bottle could well be a Chianti Classico, and make quite sure that you have one at least five years of age. As to vintages, although these are by no means as important as they are in Germany and France, particularly good years were 1957, 1962, 1964, 1967, and 1968. Treat the Classico wine in much the same way as a claret. That is, allow it to stand in an undisturbed upright position at room temperature for several hours before decanting it. Allow it to breathe for at least an hour in the decanter before use. The younger Chianti in the wicker-covered bottle will survive less meticulous treatment, but it is as well to give it an undisturbed period and also to decant it roughly thirty minutes before use. Taste each of the examples in turn and complete Tasting Charts on them. After tasting each of the wines unaccompanied, notice the considerable changes that occur when they are accompanied by cheese and other foods (meat snacks are good here). Compare your Tasting Charts and then carry out the second tasting after your discussion.

———————

You will quite probably observe differences in the color of the young and old wines. The older wine is likely to be a deeper red. It is also likely to be smoother, fuller in flavor, and to linger in aftertaste. The younger wines will probably be a brighter but paler red color. You might notice a prickle in the younger wines, which are also likely to be lighter in body and more tempting to gulp than to sip. While the older wine may emit a flowery, fruity smell, you might not pick up much aroma from the young Chianti. Both types are likely to be warm, fruity, and dry to the taste.

If you have been unlucky in your selections, you may find harshness or traces of bitterness. All but the most exceptional examples of Chianti lack the subtlety of classic French reds.

The Italian wine which in my opinion comes closest to the quality of the classic French reds is Barolo, which is made in Piedmont from the Nebbiolo grape. It is a heavy red wine which needs bottle age in order to mature. This strong and deep wine should be accompanied by meat dishes in order to display its exceptionally fine qualities. It has an intense flavor and leaves a pungent aftertaste. Dry, robust, and slow-maturing, it should not be drunk sooner than six years after bottling. Its intensity of flavor is combined with a smoothness that is unmatched in other Italian red wines. If you drink it too young or are unlucky in your choice, it may be excessively hard or display an unpleasant harshness.

Barbaresco is a lighter version of Barolo, made from the same Nebbiolo grape. Like its more alcoholic neighbor, it is a dry, smooth, and deep-red wine to accompany a serious meal.

A third Italian red wine is Bardolino, an even lighter and less alcoholic wine. It is light red in color, dry and fresh. Unfortunate examples have a touch of bitterness in them, but their most common shortcoming is a weakness of flavor.

Another comparatively light, dry red wine is the well-known Valpolicella. At its best this is a fruity and fragrant wine, but far too often it is dull and almost flavorless. It can also contain an unpleasant harshness.

Lambrusco is an attractively scented, semisparkling pale-red wine. It is fresh and fizzy and exhibits a short-lived frothiness when poured. These qualities combined with its raspberry flavor bring to mind, or should I say to tongue, fizzy raspberry-flavored soft drinks.

Before getting down to your next Tasting Practice, you will need to be familiar with a few Italian words which regularly appear on wine labels. *Amabile* and *abboccato* both mean "sweetish"; *dolce* means "rich and sweet"; while *secco* means "dry." *Bianco* means "white"; *rosso* is "red"; *rosato* is "pink" (i.e., rosé). *Spumante* means "sparkling" and is commonly encountered. Asti Spumante, produced in Piedmont, is a rich, raisiny, sweet, sparkling white wine which quickly elevates one's spirits and is always successful at times of celebration.

Tasting Practice No. 60

ITALIAN REDS   For this Tasting Practice I suggest that you use a mature Barolo, a lighter red wine such as Bardolino or Valpolicella, and to round things off, a bottle of frothy Lambrusco.

In the case of the lighter red wines it is as well to select bottles bearing a recent date.

The Barolo needs to be treated like a serious French red and given an undisturbed period at room temperature before decanting. The lighter red wines, Bardolino or Valpolicella, do not require decanting. Unusually for a red wine, Lambrusco benefits from being chilled for approximately half an hour before drinking. Because of its fizziness, the makers of this wine have to insert larger corks and these sometimes give a good deal of trouble when you try to extract them.

Try each of the wines on its own, then accompanied by cheese. The Lambrusco will not do too well with meat snacks and may respond best with a dessert. The heavier red wines, particularly Barolo, will shine when accompanied by meat snacks and cheese. Complete Tasting Charts on each of the wines without consultation. After discussing your assessments, carry out the second tasting as usual.

––––––––

The Barolo should have a dignified, deep color and accompanying smoothness. It should be full-bodied and expand your satisfaction when accompanied by cheese or meat. The flavor should be intense and prolonged. In the case of the lighter red wine, the flavor will be more shallow but you may experience a compensating freshness. It will probably be lighter in color than the Barolo. The scented, light, and fizzy raspberry flavor of the Lambrusco should be in marked contrast to the heavy dignity of the Barolo.

It is unlikely that the Barolo will share the weakness common to the lighter wines of a weak flavor. If you have been unlucky, you are far more likely to taste a harsh but strong flavor. The lighter wines may suffer from this weakness of flavor or traces of bitterness.

Italian Whites

Italian whites provide a larger range of choice than do Italian red wines. In vineyards near Verona, they produce a straw-colored dry, light, fresh wine called Soave. At its best, this wine has an attractive aroma and a flavor sometimes likened to ground almonds.

It often has a slightly bitter aftertaste which is by no means un-pleasant. The weaknesses sometimes encountered are excessive acidity or sulfur, or dullness.

Frascati is a pale-yellow, dry wine produced in a town near Rome. At its best it is crisp, easy to drink, and refreshing. It is, however, deceptively high in alcohol and can make you unex-pectedly tipsy. I regret to say that I have frequently found Frascati too hard and this drawback is not compensated for by a clear or attractive flavor. Unfortunate examples are also on the acidic side.

Verdicchio from the Marches region is a well-balanced, light, dry white wine. It has a delicate aroma and a pleasant, fresh quality. Its drawback is an uncomfortably bitter aftertaste. Orvieto comes from a hill town near Florence. Unlike most of the other better-known Italian white wines, it is semisweet. This is achieved by the addition of sweet, dried grapes. Orvieto also yields a fuller flavor than is customary in Italian white wines. When successful, it is a soft and attractive wine with a honey nose and discernible flavor, finishing with a bittersweet farewell. The unsuccessful bottles are uninteresting but rarely unpleasant.

Tasting Practice No. 61

ITALIAN WHITES   This Tasting Practice serves to introduce you to a range of whites. Select a bottle each of Soave, Verdicchio, Frascati, and Orvieto wines. Chill each of them for thirty to sixty minutes before use and remember to allow each of them a few minutes to recover after extracting the cork.

Try each of them unaccompanied and then again with cheese and fish snacks. Complete separate Tasting Charts on each of the wines, discuss your assessments, and then carry out the second tasting.

It may be difficult to distinguish between the Frascati, Verdic-chio, and Soave on the basis of their appearance—they will all be pale yellow in color. I expect that you will find that all three improve when accompanied by fish snacks—these wines are not particularly pleasant to sip on their own.

Orvieto is a little unusual and sometimes resembles a fortified wine, the aroma recalling a vermouth apéritif. The honeyish smell is challenged by a competing bitterness. It is a full wine with high glycerine content that gives it a glass-clinging quality. It will keep for days if corked and cooled. Although it goes with fish, it is better with desserts. A useful wine for mystery tastings, but it can be too bitter or too bland.

You may find that the Frascati, Verdicchio, and Soave are marred by acidity, hardness, or a slightly bitter aftertaste. Another shortcoming of many of these wines is a weakness of flavor.

❧⬧❧

CHAPTER SIXTEEN

Some Wines of Central Europe

A considerable amount of wine is produced in Central Europe, with Austria, Hungary, and Yugoslavia making the most important contributions. In the main the wines are light, popular whites that bear a general resemblance to those produced in Germany. The Central European wines are less distinctive and less emphatic than German wines and this is reflected in their relatively inexpensive price. They are ideally suited for everyday drinking. Their sound quality makes them a far better value than many of the everyday whites produced in Western Europe. You could do a lot worse than stock a supply of these Central European wines—use them readily and without ceremony. They are particularly enjoyable in summertime.

In all three countries mentioned the usual practice is to describe the wine in terms of area and grape variety. The area generally precedes the grape description, e.g., Lutomer Riesling, Lutomer Sylvaner, Balatoni (sometimes given as "Badasconyi") Furmint, Balatoni Riesling. A full range of white wines from dry to lush sweet is available but the red wines are rather limited in scope and quantity.

The Austrian vineyards are situated in Burgenland, Lower Austria, and the region of Vienna. They specialize in light white wines which resemble those of Germany—in fact, the choice of grapes, style of cultivation, and methods of wine production are all similar to German viticulture. The wines of these two countries are not, however, identical, and the comparison of Austrian and German wines is a pleasant undertaking.

I concede there are no adequate Austrian competitors for the greatest products from the Rheingau and Mosel regions. Nevertheless, the refreshing, clean, and tasty whites of Austria can be fully satisfying and their classified wines are sometimes exceptionally fine. The Austrian wines are among the few bargains still available in the wine trade. They are reliable wines, rarely disappointing, and their main shortcoming is a lack of flavor.

The most commonly used grape varieties are Riesling, Sylvaner, Traminer (especially popular in Alsace), and the Veltliner, which is far more common in Austria than in Western Europe. The vineyards are usually kept in splendid shape and the wine is produced under the most hygienic and advanced conditions. In addition to the attractions of the wine regions themselves, Austria, of course, is a traveler's delight.

The popular names in Austrian exports are Krems (on the labels this would be Kremser), Rust(er), Loiben(er), Klosterneuberg (wine museum as well), and Gumpoldskirchner.

Hungary has large and ancient vineyards which produce mainly white wines. In addition to the common grapes such as Riesling, Sylvaner, Traminer, and Veltliner, the Hungarians also use their own varieties—e.g., Kadarka (red) and Furmint (whites). The best known of the red wines is undoubtedly Bull's Blood, while Tokay (Tokaj) is their famous sweet white dessert wine (the dry Tokay is of less interest).

Sweet Tokay is a golden brown, robust, and long-lived wine that is prepared with varying degrees of sweetness, ranging from three to six *puttonis*. These degrees of sweetness (*puttonis*) are produced by adding three to six containers (*putts*) of concentrated sweet, overripe grapes to each hectoliter of wine. The end product is extremely popular in Eastern Europe. It has a far smaller following in Western Europe and seldom seems to provoke the joyous surprise so often observed in those introduced to a fine bottle of German white wine.

The ordinary whites, sweet and dry, are fresh, tasty wines and have gained deserved popularity as moderately priced, reliable wines. The differences between the Hungarian Riesling, Sylvaner, and Furmint types are interesting and might repay your attention if you take to the Hungarian style of wine.

Bull's Blood (also known as Egri Bikaver) is a firm, full red wine which makes a pleasing accompaniment to rich and spicy Hungarian meat dishes such as goulash. At wine tastings, in the absence of accompanying food, it can be underrated. If that is how you first meet it, then avoid reaching a conclusion until you have drunk it during the course of a full meal. Its striking name derives from the defense of Eger, the town of the wine region, by Hungarian troops against the invading Turks. The wine, so they say, was the source of their bravery—the blood of the bull.

Yugoslavia produces a good deal of popular light white wine which resembles the lesser products of Austria and Germany. Named by grape and region, they are usually fresh and refreshing. Best regarded as quaffing wines, they are particularly useful for summer drinking. In addition to the whites produced by the familiar Riesling, Sylvaner, and Traminer grapes, the local variety *ranina* produces a sweet white wine. The brand name is Tiger's Milk.

Tasting Practice No. 62

CENTRAL EUROPEAN RIESLINGS The present Tasting Practice combines an introduction to Central European wines with a comparative German bottle. In selecting wines from Central Europe, remember that light white wines are at their best when fresh, so attempt to obtain wines with a recent vintage date on their labels.

Acquire one bottle each of a Yugoslavian Riesling (described simply as either Yugoslavian Riesling or Lutomer Riesling), a Hungarian Riesling, Austrian Riesling, and a German Riesling from the Rheingau district. Obtain the German Riesling from the 1971 vintage if possible.

Chill all of the wines thirty to sixty minutes before use and remember to allow them a minute or two to recover after you remove the corks. Taste each wine on its own and then accompanied by a light snack and a mild cheese. Complete separate Tasting Charts on each wine without consultation. Then discuss your assessments and carry out a second tasting.

You should discern important general similarities in all four wines. Ideally they will all be appetizing, fresh wines with a satisfactory balance between fruitiness and acidity. In color they will probably be a pale yellow and the aroma should be flowery, with the German example having the most penetrating aroma of the four. They should all be soft and smooth and make pleasant drinking.

The faults commonly found in these wines are a lack of flavor, lack of depth, and lack of aroma. They rarely contain harsh or off-putting qualities.

Tasting Practice No. 63

SWEET CENTRAL EUROPEAN WHITES   Select a Tokay sweet wine, preferably with four or more *puttonis*. Add to this a bottle of Yugoslavian Tiger's Milk and any Austrian bottle of late-harvested wine, i.e., *Spätlese, Auslese,* or *Beerenauslese.*

In carrying out this examination you would do well to remember that sweet wines generally have a higher alcohol level than dry wines, despite their deceptive smoothness. The high alcohol level allows you to store them for some days after opening them. If you remember to recork them and keep them in a refrigerator, they should last for from two to six days.

A problem in tastings involving sweet white wines is that of selecting suitable accompanying foods. If you prefer to take your sweet white wines accompanied by desserts, then the problem is one you have already met. If, on the other hand, you prefer to drink these wines unaccompanied by food, there is no problem. For the present Tasting Practice I suggest you prepare such suitable accompaniments as crackers, desserts (especially those with sponge-cake bases), and nonacidic fruit. Chill the wines for at least an hour before use and remember to give them a few minutes to recover after you uncork them.

The wines should be yellow and, in the case of the Tokay, may even have a brownish-yellow aspect. All three wines should have a clear and penetrating aroma, but the Tokay is likely to be different in quality. Where the other two have the by-now recognizably sweet and flowery smell encountered in German sweet wines, the Tokay will probably be a new experience. It is strong and penetrating and, for me, reminiscent of a fortified wine—not unlike a sweet sherry. In taste the Austrian wine should resemble superior German products while the Tiger's Milk may be a little on the flabby side. The Tokay leaves a prolonged aftertaste, which may be missing in the Yugoslavian wine and present to a lesser degree in the Austrian example.

The possible faults in the Yugoslavian and Austrian wines are the familiar ones of insufficient flavor or depth. In the Tokay, unsuccessful bottles sometimes have a slightly unpleasant bite.

CHAPTER SEVENTEEN

California Wines

In the 1870s Europe's vineyards were decimated by a parasitic disease. The louse called phylloxera was killing off the vines at a frightening pace and none of the multitude of attempted remedies was able to halt the spreading devastation. Finally a solution was found—and only just in time. It was discovered that the vines could be saved by grafting them onto the naturally resistant roots of the vine native to the East Coast of the United States. This timely remedy saved the European wine industry—to the gratitude of generations of drinkers on both sides of the Atlantic. Fifty years later the Eastern seaboard came to the rescue of California vineyards when they in turn were threatened with destruction—by the Volstead louse. With the approval of the public, a louse-resistant remedy called FDR, a native of New York State, was introduced in 1933 and the vineyards were able to survive and then flourish.

At present the United States is experiencing an amazing wine boom. Production of wines is climbing steeply and the consumption of both domestic and European wines has doubled in the last four years. It has been estimated that in 1972 over two billion dollars was spent on wine.

It is generally agreed that the better-quality North American wines are produced in California (responsible for most U.S. wine), so this discussion is confined to bottles from the West Coast. Like

Europe, California produces substantially more everyday wine than quality wine. In both continents the bulk of the wine is mass-produced, sold, and drunk young and unceremoniously. As indicated earlier in this book, it is not my view that mass-produced wines should be dismissed without appreciating the important part that they play—or should play—in our eating habits. A diet of fine-quality wines would pall. Access to large quantities of well-made, inexpensive wine provides a foundation for superior cooking as well as pleasant accompaniments to modest meals.

In California a small amount of fine wine is produced in vineyards where quantity is willingly sacrificed for quality. The awkward and smaller-yield vines (e.g., Chardonnay) are cultivated in preference to the prolific types, but the extra care and smaller yields inevitably lead to higher prices. Some U.S. bottles now reach prices which approximate those of fine European wines. The quantity wines, produced almost exclusively by the big companies, are considerably cheaper than their European competitors and good value for the money.

A unique feature of the North American wine industry is the broad range of grapes used and wines produced. Most wineries seem to find it essential to offer a wide variety of wines—reds, whites, and rosés. The many selections on their wine lists suggest an ice-cream parlor offering its range of flavors. Super-companies such as Gallo (responsible for nearly half of California's wine production) make and market an exceedingly wide range of wines. Their Modesto winery has the appearance of a vast oil refinery (perhaps refineries *should* be transformed into wineries!).

Mass production, coupled with an overambitious range of wines, leads to excessive uniformity. An astringent French wine producer has observed that Californian wines resemble Coca-Cola. Amusing, but quite unfair. California can and does yield some fine wines whose quality matches that of superior, but not supreme, European bottles. The new trend is for the smaller producers to resist the temptation to provide an enormous range of flavors. Instead, they are increasingly concentrating on a limited number of wines produced from a single grape variety (producing wines which are called "varietals"). Here one thinks of fine, full-bodied white wines produced exclusively from Pinot Chardonnay grapes (e.g., the products of Hanzell, Heitz, Freemark, etc.). In the reds one can point to the Cabernet Sauvignon wines of Souverain, Oakville, Beaulieu, Krug (no relation), among others.

Although it seems to me that the proliferation of large numbers of wine types is conceivably a commercial error, some marketing practices seem to me to be highly desirable. Two examples are the full and informative labels provided on most bottles and the provision of "sampler baskets" by wine merchants. This sale of samplers should be adopted by European wine merchants; it enables you to purchase at one go six or twelve types of wine from the same region or the same grape variety. After sampling them, you are in a position to reach a rational choice when making your large order. The practice could be extended, e.g., a basket of wines suitable for Durac's Tasting Practices Nos. X, Y, and Z, etc.

On the agricultural side, the production of single-grape-variety wines might be further encouraged, steps might be taken to ensure the survival of a sufficient number of the smaller vineyards, and attempts could be made to encourage the production of wines which take longer to mature before being ready for the market. This applies particularly to wines made from the Cabernet grapes, which *do* improve with age—they soften and acquire deeper flavor. It is also a good idea to place the date of production on all wine bottles, even those which are not expected to improve with age. The advantage of this information is that it enables one to select bottles containing young and fresh wines—both desirable qualities in rosé, white, and some red wines.

California produces more than three-quarters of American wine. Of this total approximately half are dessert wines or sparkling wines. The most successful wines are to be found in the table-wine group and most of these have their origin in the northern coastal counties. The particularly important counties and valleys are those of Napa, Sonoma, Santa Clara, Santa Cruz, Monterey, San Benito, and Livermore. A curious feature of Californian wine growing is the large number of grapes cultivated. They include the Cabernet, Zinfandel, Gamay, Pinot, Grenache, Mission, Barbera, Syrah, and Grignolino (among others) for red wines. For whites, the grapes grown include Semillon, Chardonnay, Pinot, Chenin, Sauvignon, two types of Riesling, Traminer, and Sylvaner (among others). There is no question but that from the point of view of wine quality better results would be obtained if the producers specialized in the grape varieties found to be most responsive on their soil rather than compete in attempts to offer an overextended range of wines.

The consistent, predictable weather means that annual fluctuations in the wine crops are slight. Hence the importance attaching to different vintages in some of the European wine areas does not apply. In this respect and in some others, Californian wines resemble Italian varieties rather than French.

All of the important early attempts at producing wine in the west of America were made by missionary orders. They were then followed by individual entrepreneurs, most of them immigrants from wine regions of Europe. At the end of the last century the Californian wine industry received a vital boost from the massive influx of European immigrants. Naturally, those from wine-producing areas such as Piedmont and Bordeaux, Burgundy and Tuscany turned their minds to the possibilities inherent in the California soil. The growth of Californian vineyards over the next few decades was largely the result of their efforts and their lineage is easily traced in most of the prominent vineyards of today. Many of these have a spectacular history despite their comparative youth. Among the Italian-Americans who have made a notable contribution to California wines are Sebastiani, Martini, Parducci, and Foppiano. Contributors of German origin include Schram, Beringer, Kornell, Becker, and Wente. French contributors include Vignes, Latour, Beaulieu, Thee (Almadén), and Masson.

Wine production was suppressed for nearly fifteen years following the introduction of prohibition. The reprieve, in 1933, came at an unfortunate time from an economic point of view and although the roots for later expansion were established in this time, the great leap forward had to wait until the postwar years. One of the most attractive aspects of the modern California wine scene is the substantial and increasing part played by people who have turned to wine production from other occupations, sometimes at

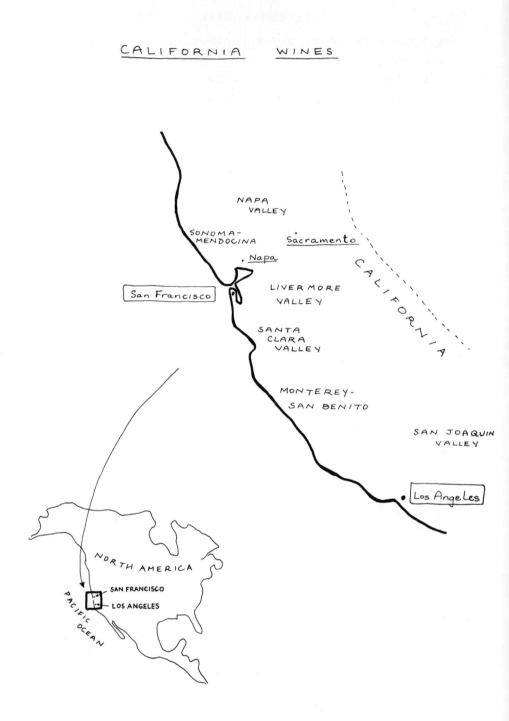

CALIFORNIA   WINES

NAPA VALLEY

SONOMA-MENDOCINA

Sacramento

Napa

San Francisco

LIVERMORE VALLEY

SANTA CLARA VALLEY

CALIFORNIA

MONTEREY-SAN BENITO

SAN JOAQUIN VALLEY

Los Angeles

NORTH AMERICA

SAN FRANCISCO

LOS ANGELES

PACIFIC OCEAN

considerable expense, driven by an overwhelming desire to produce grapes and wines in which they can take pride. For the successful converts to wine making it is a dream come true—especially in the peaceful parts of the Napa valley.

Of the five wine regions in California the most important for the production of quality table wines is the north coast, i.e., the region to the north and south of San Francisco Bay. Although most wineries appear to be obliged to produce a comprehensive range of red, white, and rosé wines, it is generally agreed that the most successful white wines are produced in the Livermore valley and the outstanding reds come from the Napa valley and from Sonoma. They are made from the Cabernet Sauvignon grapes, which thrive there. The producers of the best reds are concentrated in a comparatively small area and include the firms of Krug, Martini, Heitz, Freemark, Beringer, Sebastiani, and Mondavi. Consistently sound everyday wines are produced in large quantities by the Italian Swiss Colony, the Christian Brothers, and one or two other large producers. The dominant grape in this area is the Zinfandel, which produces attractive, light red wines; almost all wine producers in California make a Zinfandel red. Another prominent red grape is the Pinot Noir, which bears a remote resemblance to its relative in Burgundy. In my opinion this is one of the less successful transplantations. The California wine resembles Italian reds more closely than its Burgundy ancestors. The French Gamay grape, which produces the fruity, light Beaujolais wines, is also cultivated in California, where it yields attractive light wines that do not much resemble their European ancestors. Taken on their own, they make an attractive lunchtime drink. The Grenache is a prolific grape and widely grown for the production of the rosé wines which are so successful in this part of the world. A number of Italian grape varieties are also cultivated, but none of them produces wines of exceptional quality.

The soil of the Livermore valley is gravelly and well suited to the production of white wines. The two most successful white-wine grapes cultivated in California and particularly in the Livermore area are the Pinot Chardonnay and the Sauvignon Blanc. In the best California vineyards the white wines produced from these grapes are full-bodied, well flavored, and deep. The best products are a match for the superior wines of Burgundy and Bordeaux, but cannot compete with the supreme products from those areas. The (white) Riesling grape is also fairly popular in California, but to my taste is less successful. The wines do not achieve that astonishing balance between sweetness and acidity that is so striking an achievement of German Rieslings. Neither do they attain the depth of flavor and aftertaste which mark the German product. Nevertheless, the best California Rieslings make pleasant summertime drinking, despite the fact that their alcohol level is generally higher than that found in the European Rieslings. The other European white-wine grapes have not been notably successful in California. Although Sylvaner and Traminer grapes are cultivated and wines produced from them, they seldom give rise to exceptional products. Two of the most successful white-wine producers in the Livermore valley area are the Concannon and Wente vineyards. Concannon produces a fine Sauvignon wine and a passable Chablis. They also make a pleasantly dry rosé from the Zinfandel grape. The Wente white wines have a large following and with good cause. Their Pinot Chardonnay wines are especially successful and they also have dry wines made from Sauvignon Blanc and Semillon grapes, separately and in combination. The blended wine, which has a touch of Muscadel as well, is an attractive sweet wine marketed as Château Wente. Their Riesling wine is not based on the German grape of that name and is in any event one of their less successful bottles. At the Villa Armando vineyard the good-quality white wines are marketed under their generic names, for the most part. The White Burgundy and Chablis wines are among the most successful.

Much of California everyday wine is of a sound quality, but too large a proportion is bland and uninteresting. There is also a tendency, it seems to me, to produce wines which are too sweet and hence flabby. The rosés are among the most successful everyday products.

Two paths are open in approaching the tasting of California wines. You can either compare California types with each other (grape varieties against grape varieties, or regions against regions, etc.) or you can compare California wines with European types. It is interesting that this tasting choice mirrors a long-standing conflict in the California wine industry itself. Almost since the early beginnings of wine cultivation producers have been trying to decide whether it is preferable to make distinctly California wines based on a single grape variety or to attempt to produce wines which bear some resemblance, however remote, to a well-known European type of wine. The latter wines, called "generics" in the California area, can be misleading to drinkers accustomed to European conventions. The example which floored me on first meeting was Pink Chablis. To return to the question of tasting, however, my preference is for an examination of California wines as California products, followed by a look at the degree of similarity between them and some European examples.

California rosé wines are of sound quality, marked by flavor and a welcome freshness. On the whole they are sweeter than their European rivals, but there is not a great deal to choose between them.

Tasting Practice No. 64

CALIFORNIA REDS   A far more interesting group of wines is the California reds. They range from the lighter types made from the Zinfandel grape to the fuller-bodied and heavier wines made from Cabernet grapes. For this first Tasting Practice I suggest that you make a comparison between a bottle of Cabernet Sauvignon, a bottle of Zinfandel, and a bottle of Pinot St. George. For the Cabernet attempt to obtain a bottle from one of the better vineyards such as Oakville, Freemark, Souverain, Sebastiani, Martini, Beaulieu, or Krug. Good Zinfandel is produced by Oakville, Ridge, and Souverain among others. For the Pinot St. George or Pinot Noir you might try Beaulieu, Mondavi, Sebastiani, or Martini.

The wines are at their best when accompanied by food, but the Zinfandel, it should be remembered, is a lighter wine and would do better with a snack than a dinner. For a fair test, decant all the wines and allow them to breathe for at least an hour before using them. They are at their best at room tem-

perature. Try tasting them on their own and then accompanied
by a snack. Complete separate Tasting Charts on each of the
three wines without consultation. After discussing with your
companions the outcome of your first assessments, carry out a
second tasting.

The Cabernet is likely to be a heavier wine than the other
two. None of the three may have a particularly strong aroma,
but the Zinfandel may come out best on this score—it often has
the bouquet of raspberries. The Cabernet will probably be a
darker red color than the other two, the Pinot usually has a
ruby color, while the Zinfandel is pale red. Of the three the
Cabernet is likely to be the driest and have the fullest body.
The Pinot generally has a medium-dry taste and medium body.
Both the Cabernet and the Zinfandel have a reliably pleasant
flavor, but the Pinot can be less reliable on this score. Of the
three only the Cabernet is likely to have a protracted aftertaste.

Tasting Practice No. 65

CALIFORNIA WHITES   If you have never devoted much attention
to California whites, then you may be in for a pleasant surprise.
The Chardonnay grape wines, when at their most successful,
are particularly fine. For the purpose of this introduction to
California whites select *two* bottles made from the Chardonnay
grape and compare them with each other and with a third bottle
derived from the (white) Riesling grape. As with the European
white wines, these California products are at their best when
chilled. Leave the bottles in the refrigerator for an hour or so
before use; remember also to allow the bottles a few minutes
to recover after removing the corks. Good examples of Pinot
Chardonnay wines come from the vineyards of Freemark,
Hanzell, Heitz, Wente, and Parducci. Pleasant Riesling wines
are obtainable from Ridge, Freemark, and Souverain. These
wines are at their best accompanying fish dishes or lightly
flavored poultry dishes. For the purpose of the wine tasting I
suggest that you supply light snacks. Try tasting each of the
wines on their own and then accompanied by snacks. After
completing your first assessments without consultation, discuss

the outcome with your companions and then carry out the
second tasting.

You may well find that the Chardonnay bottles have greater
depth and fullness of body. Although they generally have only
the slightest of aromas, their taste lingers for a while after drinking. At their best they are fresh, dry, and particularly satisfying wines. The Riesling example is likely to be of pale color,
light in body, and mild in flavor. They rarely have a pronounced aroma or aftertaste but are welcome wines for quaffing,
particularly in summer.

Weaknesses include an absence of flavor, blandness, and/or
too faint (or nonexistent) aroma.

CALIFORNIA REDS VS. FRENCH REDS Comparisons between these
two groups of wines are of considerable and lasting interest providing that they are approached in a constructive rather than in a
fault-finding fashion. You should attempt to avoid the opposing
sins of overrating or underrating the home-grown product. The
comparison will be all the more fruitful if, instead of attempting
to grade them in terms of superiority and inferiority, you pay attention to those characteristics of the grape which come through
in the California soil and those characteristics which have been lost
in transportation across the Atlantic or are muted by the California
soil or climate. In general, California reds have a higher level of
alcohol and a lower acidic level than the European varieties. Moreover, the superior California reds are without exception based on
single grape varieties. The supreme French reds include major
groups which are the product of blendings of different grape varieties. Take claret. These wines at their best are superb and, in
the opinion of many, unmatched. They are not, however, the
product of a single grape variety. Although the Cabernet Sauvignon
grape is the major constituent of the Médoc leading wines, it is
supplemented by Cabernet Franc and Merlot grapes plus, in some
mixtures, a small amount of the Malbec grape. The superior California red wines, although they too are based on the Cabernet
Sauvignon grape, are free of blending varieties. For these reasons,

a comparison between a sound claret and a fine Californian Cabernet Sauvignon wine is of considerable interest.

Tasting Practice No. 66

If you have a special fondness for claret, choose two bottles of claret and two California Cabernets for examination. If, however, you would prefer a broader spectrum, include a reasonable Beaujolais to compare with a California Zinfandel —both light and fruity, refreshing wines. Choose your claret and California Cabernet bottles from previous successes—see earlier Tasting Charts.

Allow all four bottles of wine to rest in an upright position at room temperature for a little while before decanting them. Leave them in their decanters for thirty to sixty minutes before pouring them. These are wines which are at their best when accompanied by food, so provide an ample supply of snacks and some cheeses.

Taste each wine in turn, alone and then accompanied by food. Complete separate Tasting Charts on each of the wines without consultation. After discussing your initial assessments, carry out the second tastings and then amend your Tasting Charts or use new ones if too many revisions are deemed to be necessary.

In the comparison between the claret and the Cabernet wines you are likely to find that the French example has a more penetrating and pronounced aroma. It is also likely to contain more acidity, have a more prolonged aftertaste and greater astringency. The California example is likely to be comparably dry and warm but contain less acidity and a higher level of alcohol. Both of the lighter wines are likely to have a pleasant fruity aroma; the California Zinfandel may be reminiscent of raspberries, while the Beaujolais recalls strawberries. They should both have a good clear, bright color and pleasant flavor. Both examples should be light in body but neither of them can be expected to have a particularly prolonged aftertaste.

The weaknesses are lack of flavor and/or aroma. The claret may contain traces of harshness or be too astringent, while the

Californian Cabernet may suffer from flabbiness as a result of inadequate acidity. The light wines may be too bland.

Tasting Practice No. 67

CALIFORNIAN WHITES VS. EUROPEAN WHITES A major point of interest lies in examining the similarities and strengths of the Chardonnay grape as grown on two continents—reflected, of course, in the end product, the wine itself. As mentioned earlier, this grape is one of the best of the European transplants and provides some of California's most successful bottles. After completing a broad introduction to the two groups of wines, I suggest that you take time to look at the similarities and differences between the German Riesling wines and the (white) Riesling products of California.

Select the bottle of California Chardonnay from Tasting Practice No. 65 which received your superior rating and examine it against a Burgundy white which you approved in earlier tastings. On the Riesling side carry out the same principle of selection, i.e., take a German Riesling which met with your approval and compare it with an American (white) Riesling of your choice.

As with all white wines, chill these before use. Although the Chardonnay wines are certainly at their best when accompanied by foods, the Rieslings can be enjoyed on their own or with food. For the purposes of the present tasting it is both more interesting and more practical to take each of the wines alone and then accompanied by food.

Taste each of the wines unaccompanied and then with some snacks. Complete separate Tasting Charts on each of the wines before you consult with your companions. After discussing your initial assessments, carry out the usual second tasting and revise your judgments if necessary.

You are likely to find some similarities in the two Chardonnay wines. With any luck, you will have the pleasure of tasting white wines which combine fullness of body with a freshness of approach and a dryness of flavor. Only a few Chardonnay wines exude a strong aroma, but in both cases the aroma (weak or clear) will be refreshing in quality. As with all wines, the balance between sugar and acidity should be correct for the wine to be enjoyable. Compare the extent to which the two examples of Chardonnay achieve this. In the case of the Rieslings, you are likely to find greater differences than are present in the Chardonnay examples. The European Rieslings will probably have a darker-yellow color than the California wine, more pronounced flavor, and almost certainly a stronger, fresh, and flowery aroma. It is likely that the German wine will have a more prolonged aftertaste than the Californian example. The U.S. Riesling may well be stronger than the German (i.e., higher in alcohol) and possibly drier. This will depend on your specific choice of German wine; they range from dry to deeply sweet, whereas the California Rieslings are predominantly dry wines.

The weaknesses are inadequate flavor, occasional unpleasant traces, or thinness approaching a watery quality.

CHAPTER EIGHTEEN

Wine and Food

Most wines bloom when combined with food. Allowing for individual differences in taste and eating habits, a number of successful combinations have been developed over the years and are worth bearing in mind. Among such memorable combinations are roast beef and full, rich red Burgundy, sole in butter sauce accompanied by cool yellow-white Burgundy, Chianti Classico and full, creamy cheeses, lobster and cool Chablis, stuffed roast turkey with a mature, soft claret, and peach tart and cream accompanied by a rich yellow Sauternes. Some notoriously poor combinations include delicate fish with strong reds and red meats with sweet white wines.

These blends and clashes are among the most interesting aspects of wine drinking. Here, perhaps more than in any other part of wine lore, there are entertaining opportunities for self-exploration and discovery.

Before giving an account of some of the more prominent blends and clashes, a short digression is in order on the subject of tastes and their variations. As mentioned earlier, physiologists have classified taste sensations into four primary types. They are salty, sour, sweet, and bitter. Because of our anatomical limitations substances have to be transformed into solutions before we are capable of tasting them. It should be borne in mind, however, that the perception of taste is never an isolated experience. Taste is influenced by smell, vision, the texture of the substance, and its temperature. Another powerful influence on our sensations of taste is that of suggestion, largely through the medium of other people. If in a group of ten people whose opinions we value we are told that a mediocre wine has superb qualities, it requires considerable maturity not to be influenced by that common false opinion.

Anatomically and physiologically the closest association exists between taste and smell. In most instances they coexist peacefully and indeed supplement each other. It should not be thought, however, that there is an absolute correspondence between the two senses. I pointed out earlier in this book that an odorless wine can have a discernible and pleasant flavor. Similarly, the aroma of a wine may be far greater and more attractive than its attendant flavor in the mouth.

The influence of temperature on taste perceptions is, of course, obvious and a matter of common knowledge. In the case of wine drinking, temperature plays a major part. As we have seen, most white wines benefit from being drunk chilled whereas most red wines suffer from this treatment. Contrariwise, tepid white wines can be abominable. Taste sensations are also influenced, albeit to a lesser extent, by vision. One has only to observe the effect of an unusual-looking food on the appetite of a small child to have the point demonstrated spectacularly. I suspect that the taste of wine is not much influenced by its appearance, except in the most extreme cases where a beautiful-looking wine might seem to have its taste improved thereby and a muddy-looking concoction might be underestimated.

FUSION   When two or more solutions are mixed in the mouth, a fusion takes place. The various tastes may be entirely submerged and unrecognizable as distinct entities, or they may retain their own qualities to a noticeable extent. Broadly speaking, substances which have a weak taste fuse more easily than those which have intense qualities. Moreover, sweet, sour, and salty substances fuse well—providing, of course, that they are not above moderate intensity. Bitter tastes do not mix well at all. They not only survive a mixture with any of the other tastes, but also persist far longer than the other three categories of taste sensation. Although it is possible to rescue a wine with too sour a flavor by the addition of sugar, there is little that can be done for a wine that is bitter.

In the approach to food wines, fusion is of primary importance. Which wines enhance which types of food? Which foods suppress wine? Which wines will survive even strongly flavored food? Although there are a few general guidelines, and these will be mentioned presently, most of our information about successful and unsuccessful combinations is derived from the experiences of other wine drinkers. As to general guides, wines which have a powerful flavor are more capable of surviving in the presence of strongly flavored foods, whereas the milder wines such as those from the Mosel area will submerge without trace. On the whole, those foods which are mildly flavored are the best choice for wine drinkers—so curried dishes are hardly ever accompanied by wine. Mild foods, such as many of the cheeses available nowadays, can provide a harmonious accompaniment to a wide range of wines. A saying in the wine trade is that one should "buy on apple and sell on cheese"—cheese tends to flatter the wines and apples expose their weaknesses. If one took that piece of advice too literally, however, it could lead to bankruptcy, but taken as a sensible reminder from time to time, it is useful.

As pointed out in an earlier chapter, our powers of taste and smell are easily fatigued if they are subjected to the same aroma or substance repeatedly over a short space of time. Hence a drink that might taste sweet or even sour at the first sip frequently seems neutral by the end of the glass. This is because of the power of rapid adaptation which our senses of taste and smell exhibit. Furthermore, wines which have a weak flavor adapt more rapidly than those which are more powerful.

There are two ways in which we can counteract this tendency to adapt rapidly—and, incidentally, rapid adaptation in the drinking of wine means that one's enjoyment and appreciation are diminished. Our sensitivity to taste and smell will return given a rest period in which to recover. We can further the recovery of our sensitivities by rinsing the mouth with a liquid other than wine. A quick rinse with water is often quite satisfactory. In fact, when it comes down to it, the best and quickest way to recover taste sensitivity is by interposing a different sensation to the one that is causing taste fatigue. In plain language, if you are eating a large steak, you will derive greater pleasure from it if, after every few mouthfuls or so, you have a drink of wine. This is the most important secondary value of food wines. Their first value is, of course, their intrinsic merit and the second is the part they play in helping one's palate to retain its sensitivity throughout the entire course of a meal. The way in which wine helps one's palate to recover is best illustrated in the consumption of fatty foods. For example, a roast duck accompanied by a sound red Burgundy is decidedly more satisfying, not least of all because the wine helps to cut through the duck fat. In the absence of an appropriate wine, one's palate tires quickly and most of one's enjoyment of the dish is completed by the time you have had your fourth mouthful. The accompanying wine, by helping to restore taste sensitivity, improves and prolongs appreciation of the food.

One has also to remember that the taste of a particular substance is greatly influenced by the taste of the substance immediately preceding it. So a plum will taste sour if eaten after a sugary sweet, but will be moderately sweet if eaten after sucking a lemon. In practical terms this means that the taste of the wine is influenced not only by the food with which it is drunk but also by the foods and/or drinks which preceded it. For this reason wines are best drunk in the order light to heavy, rather than the other way around. A light wine which succeeds a heavy one will almost certainly be diminished by its large predecessor. In a similar way, sweet wines will have a marked influence on light dry wines if they are taken at a later stage in the same meal. Because light wines cast less of a forward shadow, it is preferable to drink them before the sweet varieties.

Food and wine can be taken alone or in combination. In all there are four possibilities. One can drink the wine on its own— and this is the preferred style of drinking where delicate wines such as those from the Mosel are concerned. Then there are those foods which do best without accompanying wines. Here one thinks of such heavily flavored foods as curries or other highly spiced dishes. There are practically no wines that can live with curried dishes and the food will in any case suffer from the acidic content of the wines.

Then there are wines which make excellent appetizers, i.e., they should be drunk *before* eating. Here one thinks of fortified wines such as sherry, which is a great stimulant of appetite, or a light and tart white wine such as Sancerre. At the other end of the meal there are those wines which seem to be a natural curtain for a meal. Port comes to mind as the best example of a terminating drink, but many of the sweet dessert wines (such as Sauternes or sweet Hock) are excellent in this role. Finally we come to those foods and wines which combine well with each other.

WINE-FOOD FUSIONS   Over the years people have discovered wines which combine well with hors d'oeuvres, soups, fish dishes, meats both red and white, cheeses, and desserts. Soups appear to do best on their own, but in those few instances where they are elevated by wine, it is usually one of the fortified types, most notably sherry —either with the soup or more frequently in it.

Fish dishes combine well with dry or medium-dry white wines such as Graves, Burgundy, Alsatian, Loire, some Hocks, and Mosel. A suitable combination, in which the fish neither overwhelms nor is overwhelmed by the wine, should improve both food and drink. The taste of fish is enhanced by the delicacy of the smell and taste of the wine, which also cleanses the palate and thereby ensures a greater appreciation of the food. The fish in its turn should help the wine to fill out and reveal more of its facets. One of the most successful of all fish-wine combinations is the fusion of shellfish and bone-dry wines such as Chablis or Sancerre. The crisp clarity and beauty of true Chablis complements the fleshy saltiness of shellfish in a remarkable manner. As the demand for Chablis exceeds the meager quantities produced, some sound alternatives worth considering include Muscadet, Sancerre, Pouilly-Fuissé, Frascati, and Soave.

Seldom successful are such combinations as fish and red wine, and fish and sweet wine, for example, a Sauternes. The first combination usually results in the wine's tasting sour and the second can be cloying and incongruous.

Poultry dishes are complemented by light red wines from Beaujolais, clarets, and Loire wines such as Bourgueil. They also combine agreeably with medium-dry whites including Hock, Mosel, Vouvray, and Frascati. Most people find sweet white wines to be too cloying for chicken. Pork and veal dishes usually do best with dry or medium-dry white wines. The wines proposed for poultry dishes can be applied equally well here.

Game, red meat, and meat dishes prepared with heavy sauces are enhanced by full-bodied red wines. Burgundy can be a superb accompaniment. Hermitage from the Rhone and the Italian Chiantis and Barolo are at their best with these dishes and provide fullness and flavor.

Lamb, mutton, and similar meat dishes are agreeably accompanied by red wines such as claret, Beaujolais, or Bourgueil. Some people opt for fuller wines such as Burgundy or Chianti, and these variations in preference can be used to advantage in constructing group-tasting experiences. The different views which inevitably emerge serve to emphasize the individuality of taste preferences and thereby display the futility of propounding universal rules of wine tasting. All too often people are intimidated by the written or spoken injunctions of veterans and professionals, which can inhibit the expression of genuine opinions. Worst of all, it discourages the exploration of wine. Try to avoid an overready acceptance of guidance, and above all test out as many recommendations as you can, including those in this book which may escape the net of self-instruction. In addition, the search for new qualities of wine and new food and wine combinations can be entertaining and rewarding.

Although most cheeses enhance the taste and even the texture of wine, powerful and highly flavored cheeses tend to overpower delicate wines. For example, the soft and subtle flavors of a Mosel are lost in the salty ripeness of Stilton cheese. On the other hand, claret and Cheddar usually mingle well. Chianti Classico is a very good cheese wine and can be enjoyed with everything from mild to strongly flavored cheeses. In general, mild and medium cheeses provide the best companionship for wine.

Sweet wines such as Barsac, Sauternes, and the rich German variety clash with many kinds of food but can be exquisite with fruits, nuts, or desserts. In many parts of France they are combined satisfactorily with pâté, but I must admit that this mixture has not appealed to me. The heavy sweet wines, despite their unquestioned quality, are underused and underrated mainly because they combine with so few foods. The lighter sweet wines such as the late-harvest Hocks and Mosels are a joy on their own but also combine well with desserts, mild cheeses, and snacks.

Are there any wines which make satisfactory drinking throughout a meal? Well, in the opinion of some people, champagne is the ideal accompaniment for drinking throughout several courses. Others claim that the soft, dry German white wines do the job better, while yet others make the surprising claim that sweet white Sauternes are suitable for drinking throughout a meal. If I had to choose from the various alternatives, my vote would go for dry white German wines or well-flavored rosé wines. Incidentally, Hocks and rosés are a pretty safe bet when you are asked to select a wine for drinking during a restaurant meal where members of the company have ordered a variety of conflicting dishes (conflicting in the sense of the choice of an appropriate accompanying wine). Although it is the exceptional rosé wine which makes a clear, positive contribution to any meal, they are extremely useful because of their adaptability. For summertime drinking they are frequently the best choice for complementing light meals in hot weather. They also make an ideal picnic wine.

Superior-quality wines have the disadvantage that their finer attributes are easily smothered or distorted by certain types of food. Eggs, spices, vinegary salad dressings, various sauces, curried foods, lemons, and chocolates among others may blunt the wine. Smoking (and tobacco smoke) blur the aroma and taste of fine wines and should be postponed if possible. Coffee makes wine taste sour.

Tasting Practice No. 68

FOOD AND WINE COMBINATIONS To approach the subject in general, obtain three wines—a medium-dry white wine, a full red wine, and a sweet white wine—and drink each of them with each of four courses in a protracted meal. The purpose of trying each of the three wines with each course is to demonstrate the fusions and clashes which occur.

For the dry or medium-dry white wine I suggest that you select one from Graves, Burgundy, Loire, or the Rheingau. For the full red wine, try a Barolo or Chianti Classico or a French bottle from Bordeaux or Burgundy. The sweet white wine is best chosen from Sauternes or Barsac. This Tasting Practice is rather demanding of wine glasses as you will need three glasses for each member of the company. Ideally the meal should contain four courses: a fish dish, a meat dish, a cheese, and a dessert. Incidentally, most wine drinkers find that cheese is best appreciated if it is eaten after the main course but *before* dessert. In this way it is possible to drink the remains of the full-bodied red wine with the complementing cheese rather than with the clashing dessert. The dessert, usually sweet, coming at the end of the meal, is ideally placed for accompaniment by a sweet white wine.

This Tasting Practice is merely the outline for any number of similar practices based on the same principles but incorporating different selections of wine and different combinations of food. Three variations form the subject of the next few Tasting Practices.

Tasting Practice No. 69

FOOD AND SWEET WHITE WINES As a variation on the main Tasting Practice try drinking a sweet white wine throughout all the courses of another ambitious meal. Because of its emphatic qualities, I suggest that you select a sweet white wine from the Sauternes region.

Chill the wine for approximately an hour before opening and remember to make arrangements for keeping it at a cold temperature throughout the meal (an old-fashioned bucket of ice will do admirably or you can resort to frequent trips to and from the refrigerator).

You will probably find that the wine clashes with most of the fish and meat dishes, but that it combines superbly well with dessert. The exceptions to this last combination include acidic desserts and those strongly flavored by liquor. Sauternes combine well with a very limited range of cheeses, but remember that many people regard the wine as a suitable accompaniment to pâté.

Tasting Practice No. 70

FOOD AND DRY WHITE WINES For this variation on the basic Tasting Practice concerning food and wine you have a wide choice of bottles open to you—from Graves, Burgundy, Sancerre, Chablis, Frascati, or Soave, or one of the dry German wines. As in the previous Tasting Practice, remember to chill the wine for at least an hour before use and make arrangements to maintain its cold temperature throughout the meal.

You may well find that the wine combines well with hors d'oeuvres and particularly well with fish dishes. It is unlikely to fuse well with meat dishes, but may do well with mild cheeses. It will probably clash with most desserts, particularly those of the sweet variety.

Tasting Practice No. 71

FOOD AND DRY RED WINES In the opinion of many people, myself included, wine and food provide a peak of enjoyment when a happy fusion between food and a quality red is arranged. For the purpose of this tasting try to obtain an attractive bottle of claret from a good year or a comparable red Burgundy. Remember to leave the bottle standing in an upright position for at least twenty-four hours before use, at room temperature.

Decant the wine at least an hour before use.

You may well find that the wine combines moderately well with some hors d'oeuvres, clashes badly with fish, and reaches a climax of satisfaction with meat dishes. These wines combine with most cheeses in an extremely satisfying way, but once again there is a clash when they meet up with desserts, especially those of the sweet variety.

CHAPTER NINETEEN

Mystery Tastings

Attempting to guess the identity of wines is a popular parlor game, or should I say dining-room game. Although the additional excitement is appealing, some people find the whole business loathsome. Public failures in the mystery-wine game can easily ruin an entire evening. On the other hand, the successes are extremely rewarding and keep one going from mystery to mystery. If you have failures, and, of course, you will, try to console yourself with the thought that even the most skilled connoisseurs fail embarrassingly often.

In this chapter I aim to assist you in approaching the mystery game. First off, if you want to make life a little uncomfortable for wine buffs, arrange a catch tasting by pouring one half of a selected bottle into one decanter and the remaining half of the bottle into another decanter. Then ask the buff to identify which regions the two wines come from and to remark on their similarities and differences. Because of their intermediate qualities, the red wines from the St. Emilion area are particularly suitable for this catch tasting.

For more serious blind tastings, remember that you are more likely to score successes if you approach the matter in a systematic manner. Except in those instances where you instantly recognize a familiar friend, the mystery game is best approached by the systematic exclusion of prominent possibilities. Rule number one is to avoid rushing into a decision. Observe, sniff, and taste repeatedly—even at the risk of provoking some impatience—until you feel reasonably confident of having excluded the main alternatives.

One way of approaching this process of exclusion is to follow the outline of the Tasting Charts, with some additions. The four attributes to which you will need to pay most attention are appearance, aroma, taste, and aftertaste.

The color is, of course, the most important aspect of the wine's appearance. For example, a pale-red wine may indicate that it is from a thin vintage, or from a region which uses the Gamay grape, or that it is an aging claret. The appearance of purplish tinges around the perimeter will indicate a young wine, whereas brownish traces indicate an aging wine. Hence, a combination of pale-red color and brownish tinges supports the idea that it may be an aging claret. On the other hand, the appearance of purple traces in a palish-red wine will help you to exclude most of the Bordeaux types. In the case of white wines, a pale color generally indicates a wine which is on the dryish side and a deeper-yellow color usually signifies a sweeter wine. If the deeply yellow white wine has a heavy appearance, such as clinging to the sides of the glass, this may be an indication that it is a Sauternes. If the yellowish wine has brown traces in it, you will have to include the possibility that it is an aging sweet wine, possibly from the Bordeaux region. And so on.

Next we turn to the aroma of the wine. Here one is guided to a large extent by experience. Many of the fine-quality wines have quite distinctive aromas which one will learn first to recognize and then recall, only by repeated meetings. If the aroma is distinctive and familiar, it is an important but not necessarily definitive pointer toward its true identity. If the aroma is unfamiliar, you will have to go through the process of exclusion in a more systematic way. Is it a full or slight aroma? Is is sweet or dry? Penetrating or superficial? The answers to each of these questions, some drawn from the Tasting Charts, will help you to exclude certain possibilities and at the same time to make others more prominent. To take one example: If the pale-red color and apparent weight of the wine lead one to include Beaujolais as one of the possible answers, then the aroma should help to confirm or deny this possibility. A dry aroma reminiscent of blackcurrants will lead one to doubt the possibility of the wine's coming from Beaujolais. Along similar lines, a full and penetrating aroma will almost certainly lead one to exclude the possibility that the red wine is from Italy.

When it comes to the taste qualities of the wine, the Tasting Chart can be used as a helpful guide. Ask each of five questions here: Is the body of the wine light, medium, or heavy? Is it a soft, firm, or harsh wine? Is there a balance between acidity and fatness? Is it a pleasant, light, and/or full-flavored wine? Is the flavor familiar? Does the wine have a rough, mild, or smooth finish? The answers to these questions should help a great deal to identify the wine. In your first few attempts to pinpoint the identity of some wines, I strongly advise using the Tasting Charts as an aid.

Lastly, there is the aftertaste of the wine. Except in those cases where the aftertaste is plainly unpleasant, such as that of a bitter wine, the duration of the aftertaste is generally a rough index of the quality of the wine. The more protracted the farewell, the deeper the flavor and the better the quality. The type of after-taste can also be a useful indicator of the type of wine—for example, in the case of Orvieto, that unusual white wine from Italy, the aftertaste is a mingling of sweet and bitter. This in itself might be the final clue in making the correct identification.

MYSTERY TASTING PRACTICES These can be organized around different themes which can be examined separately or, more comfortably, in combination. For example, you can arrange a Mystery Tasting around a wine's origin or age. On the whole it is preferable to combine a problem such as age with an esti-mate of the country or region of origin. You might present three red wines (blind, in decanters) and ask the entrants to estimate first the age of the wine and second the area in which it was made. Some excellent subjects for Mystery Tastings in which this sort of comparison is made are the following: Bordeaux reds versus Burgundy reds, young clarets versus old clarets, Rhone reds versus Italian Chiantis, French dry whites (e.g., Graves or Chablis) versus dry whites from Germany, Graves or Chablis versus Soave/Frascati, Vouvray versus Orvieto, Barolo versus Pomerol, Sauternes versus German late pickings, French versus Portuguese rosés, Austrian versus German Rieslings, Beaujolais versus Valpolicella.

Another Mystery Tasting, mentioned in an earlier chapter, which affords some amusement is that in which the tasters are blindfolded and asked to guess the color of each of three different wines—red, white, and rosé. If you are on the receiving end of this particular mystery, your best guides to a successful identification are the weight of the wine, its aroma, flavor, and depth of aftertaste. Best of luck.

CHAPTER TWENTY

Wine Travel

Wine travel serves the admirable end of combining an interest in the outer world with a healthy concern for the inner man. Who could possibly fault a journey around the cultural wealth of Italy (with an informed curiosity about the local grape products)? Or a fortnight devoted to our musical heritage (and the local grape products) in Austria? The Loire valley is soaked in history and architecture (and wine). The Mosel valley is calm and beautiful (and *wet*). These are some of the choices open to you.

Wine travel can be approached in a variety of ways. One can make a trip or tour specifically to visit vineyards and wine regions or simply to taste the local products. More commonly, a growing interest in wine will simply add to one's ordinary pleasures when traveling, especially in Western and Central Europe.

If you plan a holiday dominated by wine, then the large number of European wine festivals may determine your itinerary. Or you may prefer to go on a personal or conducted tour of the vineyards in a particular region. On these visits you will have an opportunity to observe the methods of vine cultivation and wine production; moreover, all major wine-producing areas provide tasting facilities. These include conventional tasting stations, permanent exhibitions in the wine centers, and even more commonly the provision of roadside tasting kiosks. In the major European wine areas the best motor route to follow is marked by signposts indicating the *"Routes du Vin"* and the relevant maps can be obtained locally. All of the important wine regions have local wine councils and offices (a list of the more important ones is provided at the end of this chapter). There are a number of wine museums of considerable interest (listed at the end of the chapter). For those of you who might want to participate in a wine harvest, two suggestions are given in the information appended to this chapter. You will also be given some advice about how to buy a vineyard. Finally, it may come as something of a surprise to learn that London and New York are interesting wine cities despite their distance from the areas of production. The attractions include regular wine auctions.

LONDON   In spite of its comparatively small overall annual consumption (320,000,000 bottles), Great Britain has an efficient and well-informed wine trade. Its connections with the vineyards of Europe have been established over centuries. In former days the trade catered predominantly to the wealthy and kept them supplied mainly with first-growth clarets, ports, and Hocks. Although the service now reaches a wider range of people and the demand for everyday wines is on the increase, the inflation of prices for fine wines threatens to close the historic circle. It is an interesting reflection, however, that in many parts of Great Britain one is offered a wider choice of wines than in France.

The famous wine auctions are an entertaining and useful feature of the London and New York scene. Two firms dominate the action, and of these Christie's has a larger share of the wine trade than their rival, Sotheby's. Both firms deal mainly in artistic treasures and many millions of pounds pass through their rooms each year. In 1971 Sotheby's had a gross turnover of 43 million pounds (approximately 100 million dollars) and Christie's a turnover of 25 million pounds (roughly 63 million dollars). The wine auctions are a small but interesting part of this considerable trade.

The auctions provide an opportunity for buyers to obtain rare survivals of old vintages and a wide range of younger wines from all over the world. They also enable the merchants to bolster diminishing stocks. For the sellers it provides a channel for moving selected parcels. For both sellers and buyers, in and out of the rooms, the prices recorded at the auctions function as an important guide to market trends. So, for example, if a merchant wishes to assess the drift of prices of 1964 claret, he might send a few parcels to Christie's to test if the water is warm.

The sales at Christie's take place weekly for a large part of the year and are conducted in one of the sale rooms of their imposing premises at 8 King Street, St. James's, London SW1. Walking past walls hung with superb paintings, sitting in a room surrounded by antique furniture, watching people coolly pay astronomical prices for bottles of old wine can be an unsettling experience. Fortunately it is relieved by the courtesy of the staff and the friendly good humor of the auctioneer. The wines are sold in lots of a dozen bottles or six magnums, in most instances. The whole process of buying is made simple and, if your bid is successful, one of the attendants brings around a slip on which you state your name and address. Payment is requested within one or two weeks of the sale and delivery is arranged through Christie's or their agents. Catalogues for the sales can be had on application to Christie's and payment of the subscription fee. You can also purchase from them the lists of prices recorded at each sale. Presale tastings are arranged weekly and the time and place are given in the sale catalogue and in *The Times.*

Although Christie's dominates the wine auctions, the firm of Sotheby's has its triumphs. For example, in 1972 they assisted in the sale of wines donated by the French firm of Nicolas as a contribution to the "Save Venice" charity. The highest price paid at this remarkable sale was 4,661 pounds for a jeroboam of Château Mouton-Rothschild, 1870. A (Bordeaux) jeroboam contains roughly five bottles of wine and someone calculated that the price paid for this large container worked out at 111 pounds per glass, or roughly 275 dollars. On another remarkable occasion the price of 2,850 pounds was paid for a jeroboam of 1929 Château Mouton-Rothschild. A bottle of 1846 Château Lafite fetched the price of 5,000 dollars two years ago. A list of the prices paid for fine wines at Sotheby's and Christie's sales in recent years can be had from the firms on application. The address of Sotheby's wine department is 34 New Bond Street, London W1. Their sales take place less frequently, roughly once a month.

TOURING   As mentioned earlier, all of the important wine-producing areas provide route maps, tasting facilities, and advice. In France, as in Germany, the local wine growers' council usually provides a central office of information. A list of these is provided on pages 214–15. It is advisable when planning a trip to one of these wine regions, or to one of the festivals described, to write to the relevant wine council before making final plans. Naturally the precise dates of festivals and other occasions vary from year to year, and for this reason it is necessary to complete your inquiries with the local wine council before making your travel arrangements.

There are so many inviting possibilities that only a few can be mentioned here. I think that the most interesting visits are those to the Mosel valley, the Loire valley, Piedmont and Tuscany, Austria, the Rhine, Burgundy, and Bordeaux. All of these can be enjoyed as motoring holidays or more simply arranged through one of the travel agencies that specialize in this sort of trip.

For the motorist, a wine drive from Bonn to Coblenz, Wiesbaden, Mainz, Worms, Strasbourg, Colmar, Dijon, Mâcon, and Lyons would combine scenic beauty, history, and some of the finest vineyards in the world. The Loire valley trip makes a splendid holiday and so does the trip around Burgenland in Austria, going from Gussing to Eisenberg—a lovely and hilly route. Of course, the Rhine and Mosel trips can be carried out along those majestic waterways. The boat journeys up and down the Mosel and Rhine rivers take the best part of one day and are well worth contemplating. In the Mosel area Trier is a particularly attractive and interesting old town as well as being the local wine center. Four times yearly the local wine seminar provides two- or four-day courses—but at least a rudimentary knowledge of German is necessary. General information about touring in these areas can be obtained from the German Tourist Office at 61 Conduit Street, London W1, or German National Tourist Office, 630 Fifth Ave., New York 10020.

To give you some idea as to how one of these trips might be enjoyed, here are some suggestions for a Burgundy one. You can arrange to visit the museum at Clos Vougeot, the museum at Ige near Mâcon, the ancient Hospice of Beaune, and as many of the legendary vineyards as you have time to take in. For wine tasting, you would do well to visit the Maison du Vin at Mâcon and the tasting stations at Chagny, Mercurey, Buxy, Lugny, Solutre, Vinzelles, and Vire among others. Moving slightly south, you can go from tasting station to tasting station in Beaujolais, which is particularly well provided with this civilized facility. Among others, there are tasting stations at Chenas, Julienas, St. Amour, Chiroubles, Beujeu, Perreon, Pommiers, Romaneche, Morgon, and St. Lager.

In Bordeaux, begin with a visit to the Maison du Vin, in the center of the city. From here it is possible to arrange visits to vineyards, tastings, and a trip to the wine museum in Château Mouton-Rothschild. At each of the main commune villages in the Médoc, Pomerol, Graves, and St. Emilion, there are local wine offices and opportunities to taste the products. The wine routes are clearly marked in all the major districts of Bordeaux.

In the Loire you will find the local wine councils to be as helpful as in other areas, and tasting stations are available at the following places, among others: Lire, Montjean, Brissac, Gennes, Rochefort, Beaulieu, St. Lambert, Pigny, Distre, Chace, St. Hilaire, Parnay, Saumur, Chinon, Vouvray, and Montlouis.

In Germany most of the wine villages have tasting bureaus or offices for tourism that can direct you to local vineyards and opportunities to taste the wines. These German wine villages are particularly keen on festivals and there is a healthy rash of them, particularly in late summer.

MUSEUMS   There are interesting wine museums in Italy, Germany, France, and Austria. The most prominent of these are as follows:

Germany:
>   Kloster Eberbach (Rheingau)
>   Rudesheim (Rheingau)
>   Oppenheim (Town Hall), Rheinhessen

France:
>   Ige, near Mâcon (Burgundy)
>   Château Mouton-Rothschild (Bordeaux)
>   Clos Vougeot (Burgundy)
>   Hospice de Beaune (Beaune, Burgundy)
>   Musée du Vin de Champagne, 13 avenue de Champagne,
>   Epernay

Italy:
>   Enoteca Italica Permanente, Siena
>   Martini Museum, Pessione, Turin
>   Nizza Monferrato, Asti, Piedmont

Austria:
>   Klosterneuberg, near Vienna

WINE FESTIVALS   Wine festivals usually last for two to six days. Almost all of them provide ample opportunities to taste the local products either in tasting booths or in large halls. The custom is for the taster to pay a small fee which enables him to taste several wines from a particular producer or small area. Most of the festivals take place in the late summer, but it is possible with careful planning to go from festival to festival for six of the twelve months of the year. The most important of the French wine festivals takes place in Burgundy—the famous "three glorious days" are held late in November in the town of Beaune and immediate environs, to coincide with the celebrated annual wine auction. In May the French National Wine Festival takes place in Mâcon and you are provided with an opportunity to taste hundreds of different wines, inexpensively.

Because of the variations in dates from year to year, I strongly advise you to check the date of particular festivals with the French national organization called Sopexa, or "Food from France," or the relevant wine council (see pages 214–15 for addresses). The same advice, of course, applies to all other festivals no matter where. Once again, the relevant addresses are provided on page 215.

The practice of celebrating the harvest or some other wine occasion is, thankfully, widespread. In Greece the wine festival takes place in the last two weeks of July at Daphne, near Athens. In Cyprus it takes place at Limassol in September. In Austria the festival is in Burgenland in late August. In Spain it takes place in early September at Jerez (near Cádiz). There is another one in Spain, in mid-September at Logrono.

Most German wine-producing villages have a festival at some time during the year—usually in the latter part of October. Among the larger occasions are the following: Rheinhessen—Bingen in September. In the Mosel valley they take place in July at Zell, Winningen in early September, and Bernkastel in mid-September. In the Rheingau region the main festivals take place in Mittelheim in June and Eltville in July. The Baden region has three large festivals—Batzenberg in early May, Wiesloch in late August, and Kirchhofen in September. In the Rheinpfalz a large festival takes place in May in the town of Deidesheim. It should be emphasized that this is a summary list of some of the major festivals; dozens of smaller ones are not mentioned but information about them can be obtained by writing to the local wine councils (see pages 214–15).

The major Italian wine festivals take place in early October in the towns of Siena, Verona, Asti, and Florence. Full details can be supplied by the local tourist boards (pages 214–15).

In France the large wine festivals run from May to December; many of the minor festivals are not noted here. In May there is the large festival at Mâcon already referred to, and another, smaller one, in St. Emilion. In June there are festivals in Beaune, St. Emilion, and Pomerol. In July the Alsatian wines are on show at Ribeauville and again in August at Colmar (major exhibition) and Dambach. In early September there are festivals on the Loire in the city of Tours, in Burgundy at Dijon, in the Jura region at Arbois, and at St. Emilion in Bordeaux. In late September the Soave region has a festival at Champlitte, Alsace celebrates at Itterswiller, the Loire at Chinon, and Burgundy at Chablis. In early October the Alsace region has two festivals, one at Barr and one at Mollsheim. Late October is a busy time with festivals at Languedoc (at

Herault), at Fronsac in Bordeaux, Ponte Chrétien (Loire valley), and at Romaneche in Beaujolais. Early November sees two festivals in Beaujolais, one at Fleurie and the other at Villefranche. Late November sees the most famous of all, the Burgundy festival, which coincides with the Beaune wine auction. December is a lean month with only Tours in the Loire and Lacenas in Beaujolais having festivals to offer.

Purchase of land in Italy or France can be extremely complicated and you will need the services of a local solicitor and estate agent. In London the firm of Knight, Frank and Rutley act as agents for some vineyard vendors in France and Italy, and if they are able to meet your needs, they will complete all of the legal and other arrangements on your behalf. For example, they recently sold a substantial vineyard in a minor region of Bordeaux for 534,000 pounds, to include a ten-room house. If this sort of idea must remain for you, as it must for me, a pipe dream, try consoling yourself with a well-chosen claret.

Some Useful Addresses

FRENCH WINE BUREAUX
(*Vineyard visits, general and touring information, festival dates, etc.*)

SOPEXA (National Bureau), 63 rue de Naples, Paris 8e.
Food from France (Festivals and General), 14 Berkeley Street, London. W1 *and* 1350 Avenue of the Americas, New York 10019.
Bordeaux Maison du Vin, 1 cours du 30 Juillet, Bordeaux.
Alsace Comité des Vins, 8 place de Lattre de Tossigny, 68-Colmar.
Champagne Comité des Vins, 5 rue Henri Martin, 51-Epernay.
Arbois Comité des Vins, Fruitiers Vinicole, 39-Arbois.
Société des Vins du Jura, Maison de l'Agriculture, 39 Lons Le Saunier.
Armagnac Bureau, 39 rue Gaubil, 81-Gaillac.
Jurancon Cooperative de GAN, 5 place de la République, 64-Pau.
Jurancon Syndicat, Maison du Paysan, 72 rue Castelnau, 64-Pau.
Cognac Bureau, 3 rue Georges Briand, 16-Cognac.
Conseil des Vins Anjou Saumur, 2 boulevard Foch, 49-Angers.
Comité des Vins Touraine, 12 rue Berthelot, 37-Tours.
Comité des Vins de Sancerre, Mairie, 18-Sancerre.
Conseil des Vins de Corbiers, 55 avenue Clemenceau, 11-Lezignan Corbières.

Comité des Vins de Rhone, 41 cours Jean Jaures, 84-Avignon.

Comité des Vins de Provence, 3 avenue de la Gare, 83 les Arcs sur Argens.

Beaujolais Union des Vins, 24 boulevard Vermorel, 69-Ville Franche.

Comité des Vins la Côte d'Or (Burgundy), Petite Place Carnot, 21-Beaune.

Comité des Vins de Bourgogne (Burgundy), 3 bis rue Gambetta, 71-Mâcon.

ITALIAN WINE INFORMATION
(Provided by local and national tourist offices)

London Office—ENIT, 201 Regent Street, London W1.

New York Office—ENIT, 630 Fifth Avenue, New York 10020.

Siena—EPT (Ente Provinciale Turismo), Via di Città 5, Siena, Tuscany.

Florence—EPT, Via Manzoni 16, Firenze.

Asti—EPT, Piazza Alfieri 34, Asti, Piedmont.

GERMAN WINE INFORMATION

German National Tourist Office (particularly helpful), 61 Conduit Street, London W1.

German National Tourist Office, 630 Fifth Ave., New York 10020.

Trier Tourist Office—D55-Trier, An der Porta Nigra, Postf 38 30.

Mosel and Rhein Boat and Other Trips—Clarksons, Clarkson House, Sun Street, London EC2.

AUCTIONS

Sotheby's Wine Dept., 34/35 New Bond Street, London W1.

Christie's Wine Dept., 8 King Street, St. James, London SW1.

Heublein Inc., Munson Road, Farmington, Connecticut. Write for information; Attention Mr. B. Y. Dunn.

Glossary of Wines and Grapes[*]

Ahr: one of eleven regions designated for Grm. quality wines.
Aloxe-Corton: full reds, Côte d'Or, Bgn.
Alsace: one of five main wine regions (Fr.), mainly light whites.
Anjou (Rosé): generic name for rosés, Angers (Loire).
Arche, Ch. d': quality sweet white, Sauternes (Bx.).
Asti: sparkling whites, Piedmont town (It.).
Auslese: fine whites from selected quality grapes (Grm.).
Ausone, Ch.: outstanding reds, St. Emilion (Bx.).
Ayler Kupp: fine white Mosel Riesling.

Bad Kreuznacher: quality whites, Nahe (Grm.).
Baden: one of eleven regions designated for Grm. quality wines.
Balatoni Furmint/Riesling: fresh whites, Lake Balaton (Hungary).
Bandol: light red, white, and rosé (Provence).
Barbera grapes: produce full reds (Piedmont, It.).
Barbaresco: fine soft reds, Nebbiolo grapes (Piedmont).
Bardolino: fresh light reds, Garda (It.).
Baret, Ch.: dry white, Graves (Bx.).
Barolo: outstanding It. reds, slow-maturing and long-lived (Piedmont).
Barsac: sweet whites (Bx.).
Batailley, Ch.: class 5 claret, Pauillac (Bx.).
Batard Montrachet: full whites (Bgn.) See *Montrachet.*
Beaujolais: popular fruity light reds, Gamay grapes (S. Bgn.).
Beaujolais l'année: fresh young Bj. red, taken chilled.
Beaune: Bgn. wine town; fine reds and outstanding whites (Côte de . . .).

[*] The following abbreviations are used: Bgn.: Burgundy; Bj.: Beaujolais; Bx.: Bordeaux; Ch.: Château; Fr.: France; Grm.: Germany; It.: Italy.

Beauregard, Ch.: fine red St. Emilion (Bx.).
Beausejour, Ch.: fine red Pomerol (Bx.).
Beerenauslese: rich sweet whites, overripe grapes (Grm.).
Bel-Air, Ch.: fine red St. Emilion (Bx.); many lesser wines of same name.
Belgrave, Ch.: class 5 claret, St. Laurent (Bx.).
Bellet: rosé and some whites, near Nice.
Bellevue, Ch.: fine red St. Emilion (Bx.); many lesser carry same name.
Bereich: wine district (Grm.).
Bergat, Ch.: St. Emilion red (Bx.).
Bernkasteler Riesling: generic for light white Mosels.
Beychevelle, Ch.: class 4 claret, St. Julien (Bx.).
Binger: light whites, Rheinhessen (Grm.).
Blaye (Côte de): medium reds (Bx.).
Bonnes Mares: fine reds, Morey St. Denis (Bgn.).
Bonnezeaux: sweet whites, Anjou (Loire).
Bourg (Côte de): medium reds (Bx.).
Bourgueil: fruity light reds (Loire).
Bourgneuf, Ch.: fine red, Pomerol (Bx.).
Boyd-Cantenac, Ch.: class 3 claret, Cantenac (Bx.).
Branaire-Ducru, Ch.: class 4 claret, St. Julien (Bx.).
Brane-Cantenac, Ch.: class 2 claret, Cantenac (Bx.).
Brauneburger: fine whites, Mosel.
Brouilly: fruity light reds, Bj. commune.
Bull's Blood: robust reds, Eger (Hungary).
Buzbag: full reds, Turkey.

Cabernet Franc: variant of Sauvignon grape (Bx.); for blending (Bx.) or plain (Loire).
Cabernet Sauvignon: major Bx. red-wine grape; slow-maturing.
Calon-Segur, Ch.: class 3 claret, St. Estephe (Bx.).
Camensac, Ch.: class 5 claret, St. Laurent.
Canaiolo: red Chianti grape (It.).
Canon, Ch.: fine red St. Emilion (Bx.).
Canon-la-Gaffelière, Ch.: fine red St. Emilion (Bx.).
Cantemerle, Ch.: class 5 claret, Macau.
Cantenac-Brown, Ch.: class 3 claret, Cantenac (Bx.).
Canteval: medium red. Brand name, Nicolas.
Carbonnieux, Ch.: fine dry whites, Graves (Bx.).
Casal Garcia: popular fresh white (Portugal).
Certan, Ch. (Vieux and *Giraud):* fine red Pomerols (Bx.).
Chablis: dry whites, Bgn. Much imitated.
Chalon: sound reds and whites (S. Bgn.) (Côte de . . .).
Chambertin: great full red, Bgn.
Chambertin, Clos de Beze: neighboring fine vineyard.
Chambolle-Musigny: full reds, Bgn. commune.
Chardonnay grapes: produce full, fruity whites, especially Bgn., Chablis, champagne.

Chassagne-Montrachet: full whites, Bgn. See *Montrachet.*
Chassepre: branded dry white, Nicolas.
Châteauneuf du Pape: robust reds, some white (Rhone).
Chenas: light reds, Bj. commune.
Chenin Blanc grapes: produce fresh whites, especially in the Loire.
Cheval Blanc, Ch.: outstanding St. Emilion red.
Chevalier Montrachet: full whites, Bgn. See *Montrachet.*
Chianti: robust reds and slight whites, Tuscany.
Chianti Classico: finer reds, limited region (Florence).
Chinon: fruity light reds, Loire.
Chiroubles: light reds, Bj. commune.
Claret (Clairet): red Bx. wine.
Clerc Milon, Ch.: class 5 claret, Pauillac.
Climens, Ch.: superb sweet white, Barsac (Bx.).
Clos de la Roche: fine red. Bgn. vineyard, Morey St. Denis.
Clos de Tart: outstanding red, Bgn. vineyard, Morey St. Denis.
Clos de Vougeot: fine reds, fragmented vineyard (Bgn.).
Clos St. Denis: fine reds, Morey St. Denis (Bgn.).
Corton: superb smooth red, Aloxe Corton (Bgn.).
Corton-Charlemagne: exceptional white, Aloxe Corton (Bgn.).
Cos d'Estournel, Ch.: class 2 claret, St. Estephe (Bx.).
Cos Labory, Ch.: class 5 claret, St. Estephe.
Côte de Beaune: fine reds, outstanding whites (Bgn.).
Côte d'Or: superb reds (Bgn.).
Côte Rotie: strong reds (Rhone).
Couhins, Ch.: dry white, Graves (Bx.).
Coutet, Ch.: superb sweet white, Barsac (Bx.).
Croizet-Bages, Ch.: class 5 claret, Pauillac.

Dauzac, Ch.: class 5 claret, Labarde.
Deidesheimer: fine whites, mainly Riesling grapes, Pfalz (Grm.).
Desmirail, Ch.: class 3 claret, now defunct.
Doisy-Daene, Ch.: fine sweet white, Barsac (Bx.).
Domaine de Chevalier: outstanding reds and whites, Graves (Bx.).
Ducru-Beaucaillou, Ch.: class 2 claret, St. Julien.
Duhart-Milon, Ch.: class 4 claret, Margaux.
Durbacher: quality whites, Baden (Grm.).
Durfort-Vivens, Ch.: class 2 claret, Margaux (Bx.).
Dursteiner: fine whites, Wachau (Austria).

Edelzwicker: wine blended from superior grapes (Alsace).
Egri: robust reds, including Bull's Blood (Hungary).
Eiswein: Literally, "ice wine"; rare rich wines from frozen grapes (Grm.).
Entre-Deux-Mers, Entre-Deux-Rives: medium whites (Bx.).
Erbacher wines: classic Rheingau whites, mainly Riesling.
Erdener: classic Mosel whites, Riesling.
Evangile, Ch. l': fine soft red, Pomerol (Bx.).

Ferrière, Ch.: class 3 claret, Margaux.
Figeac, Ch.: outstanding red, St. Emilion (Bx.).
Filhot, Ch.: fine sweet white, Sauternes (Bx.).
Fixin: full reds, Bgn.
Fleurie: fresh, fruity reds, Bj. commune.
Forster: outstanding whites, Rheinpfalz (Grm.).
Fourtet, Clos: fine reds, St. Emilion (Bx.).
Franken (Franconia): one of eleven designated areas for quality wines (Grm.).
Frascati: dry, crisp whites, near Rome.
Fronsac: medium-quality dry reds (Bx.).
Furmint: outstanding Hungarian white grape, especially Tokay.

Gaffelière-Naudes, Ch.: fine reds, St. Emilion (Bx.).
Gamay grapes: produce soft, fruity reds, especially Bj.
Gattinara: full red, slow-maturing; Nebbiolo grape (Piedmont).
Gazin, Ch.: fine red, Pomerol (Bx.).
Gevrey-Chambertin: full red wines, Bgn. commune.
Gewürztraminer grapes: produce spicy whites, especially Alsace.
Giscours, Ch.: class 3 claret, Labarde (Bx.).
Goldener Oktober: brand name, blended Mosel white.
Graacher: fine Riesling whites, Mosel.
Grand-Puy-Lacoste, Ch.: class 5 claret, Pauillac (Bx.).
Graves: fine, dry reds and whites, Bx. region.
Grenache: sweet grapes producing rosés and reds, especially Rhone (Tavel) and California.
Gruaud-Larose, Ch.: class 2 claret, St. Julien (Bx.).
Guiraud, Ch.: fine sweet white, Sauternes (Bx.).
Gumpoldskirchen: medium and fine whites, Austria.

Hallgartener: fine whites, especially Riesling (Rheingau).
Hambledon: white wine, Hampshire.
Hattenheimer: classic white Rieslings, Rheingau.
Haut-Batailley, Ch.: class 5 claret, Pauillac (Bx.).
Haut-Brion, Ch.: class 1 claret, Pessac (Bx.).
Haut Médoc: medium and superb reds, Bx. region.
Hermitage: long-lived full reds, medium whites (Rhone).
Hess: one of eleven defined regions for quality wines (Grm.).
Hirondelle: brand name for red, white, and rosé, blended in Austria.
Hochheimer: fine Rieslings, Rheingau.
Hock: wines from Hochheimer; British term for Rhine-type whites.
Hospice de Beaune: site of famous annual wine auction, Bgn.

Issan, Ch. d': class 3 claret, Cantenac (Bx.).

Janos (Riesling): fresh whites, Hungary.
Julienas: fruity, light reds, Bj. commune.
Justina: brand name, sound, everyday reds, whites, and rosés (Portugal).

Kabinett: superior quality (Grm.).
Kadarka grapes: produce full reds, Hungary.
Kirwan, Ch.: class 3 claret, Cantenac (Bx.).
Kremser: fine whites, Wachau (Austria).

Lachrima Christi: light dry white, Vesuvius (It.).
La Croix, Ch.: fine red, Pomerol (Bx.).
Lafite Rothschild, Ch.: class 1 claret, Pauillac.
Lafleur, Ch.: fine red, Pomerol (Bx.).
Lafon-Rochet, Ch.: class 4 claret, St. Estephe (Bx.).
Lagrange, Ch.: class 3 claret (St. Julien) and fine red Pomerol (Bx.).
La Lagune, Ch.: class 3 claret (Ludon).
Lambrusco: fruity, light, prickly red, Emilia (It.).
La Mission-Haut-Brion, Ch.: fine dry red, Graves (Bx.).
Langoa Barton, Ch.: class 3 claret, St. Julien.
Lascombes, Ch.: class 2 claret, Margaux.
Latour, Ch.: class 1 claret, Pauillac (Bx.).
Latour, Blanche, Ch.: sweet white, Sauternes (Bx.).
Latour-Carnet, Ch.: class 4 claret, St. Laurent.
Latour Haut-Brion, Ch.: fine red, Graves (Bx.).
Layon, Côteaux du: sweet whites, Anjou (Loire).
Léoville-Barton, Ch.: class 2 claret, St. Julien (Bx.).
Léoville-Las-Cases, Ch.: class 2 claret, St. Julien.
Léoville-Poyferre, Ch.: class 2 claret, St. Julien.
Liebfraumilch: generic term, blended white soft Grm. wines.
Lion d'Or: brand name, sweet white.
Loibener: medium and fine whites, Wachau (Austria).
Loire: one of five main French wine regions, predominantly whites.
Lutomer (Riesling): light white everyday wine (Yugoslavia).
Lynch-Bages, Ch.: class 5 claret, Pauillac.
Lynch-Moussas, Ch.: class 5 claret, Pauillac.

Mâcon: good reds and whites, Bgn. district.
Magdelaine, Ch.: fine red, St. Emilion (Bx.).
Main: one of six designated *Tafelwein* (table wine) areas (Grm.).
Malbec grapes: blends with other Bx. red varieties; claret.
Malescot, Ch.: class 3 claret, Margaux.
Margaux, Ch.: class 1 claret and Bx. commune name.
Marquis-d'Alesme-Becker, Ch.: class 3 claret, Margaux.
Marquis de Terme, Ch.: class 4 claret, Margaux.
Marsanne grapes: produce whites, especially blending (Rhone).
Mateus Rosé: light, fresh, prickly, popular rosé (Portugal).
Médoc: medium and superb reds, Bx. region.
Mercurey: medium reds and whites, Bgn.
Merlot grapes: used in blending clarets.
Meursault: full-bodied whites (Bgn.).
Mittelrhein: one of eleven designated quality-wine regions (Grm.).

Monbazillac: sweet whites, Bergerac.

Monthelie: full reds, Bgn. commune.

Montrachet, Le: superb full white (Bgn.); adjoining vineyards Bâtard and Chevalier.

Montrose, Ch.: class 2 claret, St. Estephe.

Morey St. Denis: full, smooth reds, Bgn. commune.

Morgon: fruity, light reds, Bj. commune.

Mosel: light whites; one of six *Tafelwein* regions of Grm.

Moselblumchen: blended everyday Mosel whites (generic).

Mosel-Saar-Ruwer: one of eleven quality-wine regions (Grm.).

Moulin-à-Vent: full, fruity reds, Bj. commune.

Mouton-Baron Philippe, Ch.: class 5 claret, Pauillac.

Mouton-Cadet: brand name, popular blended claret.

Mouton-Rothschild, Ch.: one of five superb clarets, Pauillac.

Muller-Thurgau grapes: hybrid Riesling-Sylvaner; soft whites.

Muscadet: dry whites (Loire); also grape name.

Musigny, Le: full, smooth red; vineyard in Chambolle Musigny (Bgn.).

Nahe: one of eleven quality-wine regions (Grm.).

Nebbiolo grapes: produce It. finest reds, especially Barolo.

Neckar: one of six *Tafelwein* areas (Grm.).

Nenin, Ch.: fine red, Pomerol (Bx.).

Nicolas: brand name for popular range of everyday wines.

Niersteiner: abundant soft, light whites, Rheinhessen.

Niersteiner Domthal: blended light whites, Rhine (generic).

Nuits St. Georges: full reds, Bgn. commune.

Oberrhein Burgengau: one of six *Tafelwein* areas (Grm.).

Oberrhein Romertor: one of six *Tafelwein* areas (Grm.).

Olivier, Ch.: dry white, some medium reds, Graves (Bx.).

Oppenheimer: attractive soft whites, Rheinhessen (Grm.).

Oppenheimer Goldberg: soft white Rheinhessen wines (generic).

Oppenheimer Krotenbrunnen: soft white Rheinhessen wines (generic).

Orvieto: full whites; *secco*—dry, *abboccato*—sweet; Paglia (It.).

Palmer, Ch.: class 3 claret, Margaux (Bx.).

Palomino: white grapes used in blending sherry.

Pape-Clement, Ch.: fine, dry red, Graves (Bx.).

Pavie, Ch.: fine red, St. Emilion (Bx.).

Pedesclaux, Ch.: class 5 claret, Pauillac.

Pernand Vergelesses: full reds, Bgn. commune.

Petit-Village, Ch.: fine red, Pomerol (Bx.).

Petrus, Ch.: outstanding red, Pomerol.

Piat: brand name for French firm's wines.

Piat Beaujolais: popular branded, fruity red.

Pichon-Lalande (& Longueville), Ch.: class 2 clarets, Pauillac.

Piesporter: fine light whites, Mosel (Grm.).

Piesporter Goldtropchen (& Michelsberg): light whites, Mosel (generic).
Pinot Noir: great red Bgn. grape.
Pinot St. George grapes: produce soft, fruity red, Napa (California).
Pomerol: medium to fine soft reds, Bx. district.
Pommard: medium reds, Bgn. commune.
Pontet-Canet, Ch.: class 5 claret, Pauillac, large volume.
Pouget, Ch.: class 4 claret, Margaux.
Pouilly-Fuissé: dry white, Bgn. commune.
Pouilly-Fumé: dry white, Loire.
Prieure-Lichine, Ch.: class 4 claret, Margaux.

Qualitätswein: class 2 in tripartite German wine classification, state supervised; authenticity.
Qualitätswein mit Prädikat: highest grade in tripartite classification (see preceding entry); literally "quality wine with distinction."
Quarts de Chaume: sweet white, Anjou (Loire).

Rauenthaler: particularly fine whites, Rheingau.
Rauzan-Gassies, Ch.: class 2 claret, Margaux.
Rausan-Segla, Ch.: class 2 claret, Margaux.
Retsina: wine containing resin preservative, Greece; strictly for locals.
Rhein: one of six *Tafelwein* areas (Grm.).
Rheingau: one of eleven quality-wine regions (Grm.).
Rheinhessen: one of eleven quality-wine regions (Grm.).
Rheinpfalz: one of eleven quality-wine regions (Grm.).
Rhone: one of five major French wine regions.
Richebourg: outstanding red-wine vineyard, Vosne (Bgn.).
Riesling: supreme white-wine grape, especially in Rheingau and Mosel; U.S. term, "white Riesling."
Ripeau, Ch.: fine red, St. Emilion (Bx.).
Romanée-Conti and *La Romanée:* supreme Bgn. red wines, Vosne.
Rouget, Ch.: fine red, Pomerol (Bx.).
Roussanne: grapes for blending whites, especially Rhone.
Rudesheimer: fine whites, Rheingau; wine center.
Rulander: white-wine grape (Grm.).
Ruster: medium whites and reds, Wachau (Austria).

Sancerre: dry white, Loire.
Sangiovieto: main Chianti grape.
Santenay: quality reds, Bgn. commune.
Saumur: sweet, dry, and sparkling whites, Loire.
Sauterne: whites, not necessarily sweet (U.S. term).
Sauternes: fine sweet whites, Bx.
Sauvignon grapes: blended with semillon to produce sweet white Sauternes.
Savigny Les Beaunes: quality reds, Bgn. commune.
Scharzhofberger: fine whites, Mosel.
Schloss Bockelheimer: fine whites, Nahe (Grm.).

Schloss Johannisberg: great whites, Rheingau; Metternich property.
Schloss Vollrads: great whites, Rheingau.
Schluck: brand name popular light white (Austria).
Sciatino: brand name (Nicolas), rosé.
Sekt: sparkling wine (Grm.).
Semillon: grapes blended with Sauvignon to produce sweet Sauternes whites.
Smith-Haut-Lafitte, Ch.: dry red, Graves (Bx.).
Soave: dry white, Verona (It.).
Spätlese: rich whites from late-picked grapes (Grm.).
Spumante: sparkling wines (It.).
St. Amour: light reds, Bj. commune.
St. Croix-du-Mont: sweet white, Bx.
St. Emilion: medium and fine reds, Bx. district.
St. George, Les: fine, full red, Nuit St. Georges (Bgn.).
St. Pierre, Ch.: class 4 claret, St. Julien.
Steinberger: fine whites, Rheingau; Bismarck's choice.
Steinwein: dry whites, flagon bottles, Franconia (Grm.); generic.
Sudbahn: white-wine region (Austria).
Suduiraut, Ch.: fine sweet white, Sauternes (Bx.).
Sylvaner: prolific white-wine grape, especially Rhine and Alsace.
Syrah grapes: produce robust, enduring reds (Rhone).

Tache, La: supreme Bgn. red, Vosne Romanée.
Tafelwein: grade 3 in tripartite wine classification (Grm.); authentic.
Talbot, Ch.: class 4 claret, St. Julien.
Tavel: quality rosé, Rhone.
Terre, Ch. de: class 5 claret, Margaux.
Tiger's Milk: brand name, sweet white (Yugoslavia).
Tokay Aszu: sweet white dessert wine (Hungary).
Tokay Szamorodni: dry white (Hungary).
Traminer grapes: produce light, spicy whites, especially Alsace.
Trebbiano grapes: produce white wines, including Soave (It.).
Trockenbeerenauslese: rich, sweet whites from selected overripe fruit (Grm.).
Trollinger grapes: produce everyday reds, especially Württemberg (Grm.).
Tropiong Mondot, Ch.: quality red, St. Emilion (Bx.).
Trotanoy, Ch.: fine reds, Pomerol (Bx.).
Trottevieille, Ch.: quality red, St. Emilion (Bx.).

Unterloibener: quality whites, Wachau (Austria).
Urziger: fine whites, Mosel.

Valpolicella: fresh, light reds, Garda (It.).
Valpolicella Superiore: higher-quality fresh, light reds, Garda (It.).
Valtellino: sound reds, Nebbiolo grapes, Como (It.).
V.D.S.Q.: official French classification for second-quality wines.
Veltliner grapes: produce white wines, especially Wachau (Austria).

Verdicchio: light, dry whites (It.).

Vesuvio: light whites including Lachrima Christi, Vesuvius (It.).

Vieux Ceps: brand name, full reds (Nicolas).

Vieux-Certan, Ch.: outstanding Pomerol red, Bx.

Viktoriaberg, Hochheimer: Hock vineyard named after Queen Victoria.

Volnay: quality reds, Bgn. commune.

Vosne-Romanée: medium to superb reds, Bgn. commune.

Vouvray: quality whites; sweet, dry, and sparkling (Loire).

Wachau: Austrian white-wine region.

Wachenheimer: fine whites, Rheinpfalz (Grm.).

Wehlener: classic Riesling whites, Mosel.

Winzerverein: wine cooperative (Grm.).

Württemberg: one of eleven defined regions for quality wines (Grm.).

Wurzberger: dry whites, Franconia (Grm.).

Yquem, Ch. d': the supreme sweet white, Sauternes.

Yugoslav (Riesling): light white everyday (generic).

Zeller Schwarze Katze: brand name (Black Cat), light whites, Mosel.

Zeltinger: fine whites, Mosel.

Zierfandler grapes: produce pleasant whites, especially Gumpoldskirchen (Austria).

Zinfandel grapes: produce popular, light reds (California).

Zwicker: wines blended from common grapes (Alsace).

Index

(For wine and grape varieties, please refer also to the Glossary.)

TASTING CHART

DATE: *October 24*

NAME: *Ch. Guiraud (A.C.)*   REGION: *Sauternes*   CLASS: *2*

YEAR: *1966*   MERCHANT: *Château-Bottled (C.B.)*

SUPPLIER: _____   PRICE: _____

Cloudy		Dull		Clear, Lively	APPEARANCE
—	—	—	x		

Unpleasant	Nondescript	Clear	Pleasant	Extremely Pleasant	AROMA
—	—	—	x		

Very Sweet	Sweet	Medium Dry	Dry	Very Dry	
x	—	—	—	—	

Extremely Light	Light	Medium	Full	Heavy	BODY
—	—	—	x		

Soft		Firm		Harsh	
—	—	x			

Acid		Balanced		Flabby	
—	—	—	x		

Unpleasant	Flavorless	Light	Moderate	Full-Flavored	
—	—	—	—	x	

Rough Finish		Mild Finish		Smooth Finish	
—	—	—	—	x	

Fades Quickly	Gone within 5 secs.	Lingers up to 1 min.	Lingers 1–60 min.	Lingers + 1 hour	
—	—	x			

NOTABLE CHARACTERISTICS: *Intense aroma and full flavor.*

FOOD/OCCASIONS: *Sipping, sponge desserts, or nonacidic fruit.*

GENERAL COMMENTS: *Good example from a fine château.*